Alive
with Passion & Purpose

ALIVE WITH PASSION AND PURPOSE

Published by Plumbline Ministries
2367 W. La Palma Ave
Anaheim, CA 92801

First Edition

This book and other materials can be ordered from
Plumbline Ministries
www.PlumblineMinistries.com
714-224-0126

Printed in the United States of America
ISBN: 978-1-931640-09-1

Cover Design: Hanna Scheidegger
Interior Layout: Megan Caldecourt
Editing: Arthur Burk & Sandy Brannon
Photo: Sarah Longoria Durham

Dedication

To my mother

who taught me nursery rhymes before I was two
and bought me an unforgettable set of historical
biographies when I was seven.

She had my first poem published in the
church bulletin when I was seven,
then waited patiently all my life
for me to write something else.

Table of Contents

Forward

Incarnated truth!

That is the Plumbline war cry.

When I first met Sandy Landry, she was frustrated over a bunch of truth she had, which simply was not working in her life. It was as though she had areas of her life that were Teflon® coated and the truths that worked for others, mysteriously did not work for her.

Don't you love her already?

Now, only a very few years later, she is coaching others in how to incarnate the truths of the redemptive gifts in their own lives.

How did she make that transition?

Painfully. Tenaciously. Awkwardly some times and spectacularly at others. Alone and with help. Three steps forward and one step back. Giving up a bunch of times. Getting back in the game a few more times than she gave up.

And that is what I love about Sandy.

She was a very unspectacular person for years – an English teacher married to a local businessman in a small town. She was a gracious hostess, a happy mother, and a loyal Bible teacher at church.

Slowly her pleasant, ordinary life unraveled internally and externally, but the core foundation was solid and over time she built a new life which is very different.

Pleasant and ordinary has given way to being alive with passion and purpose.

Arthur Burk

About Sandy Landry

Sandy is a Southern woman. Her early roots were in Mississippi and Louisiana. In her adult life she graced the town of Cleburne, Texas, while also traveling far and wide for business, ministry and pleasure.

She has seen the hard edge of generational poverty, the elegance of Southern hospitality, the disruption caused by hurricanes and the excesses of the gas and oil industry.

She has seen flagrantly dysfunctional lives, dysfunction covered by a thin veneer of culture, and the beauty of people living big.

Sandy loves life as it was meant to be lived. Whether parenting her own children or teaching high school English students, she tried to help people bring the disparate parts of their lives together to unleash the treasure that was in them.

After learning about the redemptive gifts of land, she tried her hand for quite awhile on the spiritual and cultural dysfunctions of her own community.

Through all of this, she was living big, seeking, searching for the sweet spot in the game of life. While she helped many others, it eluded her.

Then she started writing this book and the Scrabble tiles seem to leap off the tray in the right order to spell a gloriously alive word.

She discovered how naturally research comes to her. She found great joy in distilling a mountain of irrelevant data into a story line where the visible was actually driven by this invisible force called the redemptive gift.

Her word smithing abilities finally found a large enough playing field to soar and dance as she captured subtle shades and nuances followed swiftly by the sublime.

Sandy is a wife, a mother, a grandmother, a friend, a teacher, a writer, a Southern lady - but more to the point, she is more gloriously alive, with passion and purpose than she has ever been before.

Introduction

This is a book for the Mercy season.

It is not a linear, detailed listing of all the characteristics of each of the redemptive gifts. Rather it is a series of portraits of the redemptive gifts in action.

We took a Biblical example of each gift, then a historical figure who walked out their gift well, and added the story of a person who severely perverted their gift. With three snapshots of each gift, you should come away with a strong sense of what the gift feels like.

And no, we did not put the stories in order of the gifts. Part of the flavor of the Mercy season is the beauty and intimacy of discovery. We invite you to read each story with your spirit. Allow the Holy Spirit to highlight the particular aspect of the beauty of God that He has expressed in each gift.

Savor it, don't study it.

And as a tiny concession to those of you who just HAVE to get it right, there is a page buried somewhere in the back of the book with the rather inelegant title "Cheat Sheet."

This book is not about figuring out what someone's gift is. It is about finding passion and purpose through living out the gift that you have.

The majesty of Christianity is that when we are doing the thing that brings us the greatest joy and fulfillment, we are simultaneously doing the greatest good for the Kingdom.

So we invite you to focus on the joy and the passion in the stories. Our prayer is that you will find levels of aliveness that you never knew before, through walking out your gift.

Arthur Burk

Alive

with Passion & Purpose

Chapter 1
They Learned to Accept His Obsession

Emma had been alternating between sitting and pacing in the tiny, claustrophobic examining room for a good two hours, on top of the one hour she had spent in the waiting room with all the other hopefuls. She thought that when she had been ushered into the inner sanctum the wait would be over. She had been depressingly wrong.

She had crossed and uncrossed her legs, and repeatedly contemplated the sad view from the window of a pitiful little patch of dead, brown grass, encircled by an industrial gray chain link fence. She read almost every article in both magazines and was now studying the planet chart on the right wall, although she usually had very little patience or interest in science. *Poor Pluto,* she thought. *I think I can identify with your sense of abandonment and rejection. O.K. Now she was talking to the solar system. This was getting really bad!*

She checked for messages on her cell phone compulsively and sent a few text messages claiming that she had been captured and was being held against her will, which bordered on the truth. *When is the doctor coming? When is the doctor coming?* She tried not to think the same thought over and over again in such a maniacally obsessive way, but she could find little else to focus her thoughts upon.

About the time she was seriously considering playing a solitary game of tic tac toe on the white paper that covered the examining table, he knocked politely on the door and entered. So this was Dr. Lyles! He was a little famous in this area; people said he was "good," and he didn't take new patients which made his regular patients say he was "really good." He had a reputation for listening and for fixing things that no one else had been able to fix.

She thought all these judgmental things, while simultaneously giving the doctor her most engaging smile.

The only reason Emma got in to see him was that her friend, Cheryl Anne, knew the doctor personally and had begged him to see Emma as a new patient. White coat, white beard, white hair, well worn cowboy boots. *Now that's a comfortable and unpretentious look,* Emma thought, although she wasn't about to forgive his tardiness so quickly just because of his attire. *Well, he doesn't look scary or arrogant and he isn't out of breath from hurrying, but just what has he been doing for the last three hour? Playing dominoes with the patient next door?* Emma wondered silently. She squirmed a little as she realized he was sizing her up too, already into study, fact finding, and quiet observation.

"How are you? Sorry about the wait."

Now that's polite, she thought. *Dr. Jonas never apologized for being late, but it is going to take a bit more than politeness to get my blood pressure back down in the normal range. Does he make Cheryl Anne wait like this? And more importantly, if he does, why didn't Cheryl Anne give me that little tidbit of info?* She thought all these judgmental things, while simultaneously giving the doctor her most engaging smile. No need to offend him too quickly even if there was a preposterous wait. She might as well try for a diagnosis; she could always yell later.

She had learned to sum her problem up in a single sentence because that was the absolute, outside limit of any doctor's concentration span.

Emma was visibly nervous. She had been to several doctors already and she was tired of telling her symptoms, tired of not getting better, and especially tired of what she felt was polite condescending or downright boredom on the part of the doctors. She had been made to feel like a whiner, a hypochondriac, and a liar, but this incredible tiredness she had been feeling for months was not going away. This is my last kick at the cat, she promised herself. *I don't want to spend the rest of my life sitting in some doctor's office all for nothing.*

She turned her attention from her emotions to the physical report. "I don't know what is wrong," Emma said. "I have been so tired lately that I don't want to do anything." She had learned to sum her problem up in a single sentence because that was the absolute, outside limit of any doctor's concentration span. She often wondered how they made it through third grade, never mind medical school, with such an unwillingness to listen.

"What kind of tired? Is it at a particular time of day, or all the time? How long have you been experiencing this tiredness?" With question after question, he pursued tiny clues, reminding her of her uncle's prize bloodhound carefully sniffing along to find the trail that could lead somewhere important. He didn't seem eager to jump to any particular conclusion. In fact, he seemed quite content to chase a rabbit or two just to be certain that they were really rabbits and not the fox himself.

Emma felt herself beginning to relax. He didn't appear like he was going to dismiss her worries. "I think it might be my thyroid," Emma ventured finally, bracing herself for the "Now who's the doctor here?" patronizing smile she got the last three times she offered her own diagnosis. No blood work had ever confirmed it, but she had family history and the symptoms. She knew that most doctors considered the results of blood work to be sacred; what the patient said they felt rarely got factored into the diagnosis.

"Well," he responded, "I like to listen to my patients because sometimes they know!"

What? Emma couldn't believe her ears. She was amazed that thus far, this was easy. She felt her anger dissipate slightly at having to wait so long, but she wasn't giving in too easily. True, he hadn't judged her, dismissed her, or reacted in an arrogant or belittling way about anything she had said, but he hadn't diagnosed her either yet or made her feel an itty bit better or done anything except ask forty questions, some of which seemed highly irrelevant to her. She remained obdurately in the "wait-and-see mode."

He asked her if she had been under stress lately, if there were family issues affecting her, and if her energy was noticeably lower during times of stress. She found herself telling him intimate things about her reaction to her mother's recent death, several issues related to stress at work, and the latest crisis with her daughter, but still she wondered how all of this related to her illness. She started to get defensive again. *Was he going to suggest that she go to some kind of counseling?*

Emma also made a mental note to not personally affect Cheryl Anne's longevity.

When she told him about her extended family's history of thyroid problems, he was visibly interested, and did not just benignly humor her the way that odious Dr. Philips had done.

Finally, Dr. Lyles appeared to be ready to share the conclusions he had reached from that jumble of data he has so meticulously collected. He tied a lot of her answers together by explaining to her Wilson's Temperature Syndrome, something she had never heard of before. "In periods of extended stress, the metabolism can slow down as a coping mechanism. Several of the situations you described would seem to qualify as significant stress. I am going to recommend a simple procedure of taking your temperature every few hours along with blood work and that should tell us what we need to know. I am also ordering a few more tests, to rule out a number of other possibilities."

Emma couldn't help but be impressed by a man who asked the right questions and got answers that no one else had discovered before. *O.K., maybe he is good. Maybe.* Emma also made a mental note to not personally affect Cheryl Anne's longevity.

"Just a minute, I need to show you something." Left alone in the room, Emma refused to gaze again at the brown grass. This time she counted her toes that were peeking at her through her sandals: still ten. She was, however, more relaxed than two hours ago.

Dr. Lyles had gone back down the hall to get an article that he had been reading recently. He looked at his cluttered desk with all of the articles earmarked, and spent a few minutes trying in vain to find one in particular, but it wasn't to be found. He knew he remembered most of it anyway, certainly as much as the patient would probably understand or remember, so he picked up another pad from the pharmaceutical rep and started back to the room where he had left Emma.

While she had at times been compassionate, mercy was not her strong suit.

Jenny, the nurse, stopped him in the hall to get authorization for some prescription requests from the pharmacy. Efficient, precise, and formidable, she was a perfect compliment to him and an essential part of his practice. If you needed Dr. Lyles, you went through Jenny first, and she was no easy mark. It was a system that they had worked out, though not officially, and he knew how badly he needed her tough demeanor to run this office. She wasn't about to see him overloaded or taken advantage of, and because she knew he was an easy touch, always landing too heavily on the side of other people's needs defining his life, she let her "tough side" shine through.

Given free rein, he would have certainly squeezed in a few last minute patients and then stayed until the wee hours of the morning. She knew how long he took per person, calculated it in real time, and guarded the appointment book with a fierce defiance of all the emergencies in the world. While she had at times been compassionate, mercy was not her strong suit, especially when someone was trying to manipulate the good doctor whom she was sworn to protect in whatever way she deemed necessary.

Something about her hinted at "ways" that made even the pathologically aggressive patient reconsider. She knew exactly how many patients he could see in a day and would often help those who were granted appointments calculate what a 4:30 appointment "really meant." No one wanted to, intentionally or inadvertently, be on Jenny's bad side. Occasionally, Dr. Lyles himself landed there with his heavy reliance on Jenny and his inability to see when she became overworked, or stressed or just needed rest. But he was the one person she seemed to forgive easily because he helped so many people.

She began to feel a bit responsible for the poor patient pacing in the room next to her.

Unbothered by the interruption, Dr. Lyles returned with the notepad and began to draw little diagrams and give careful descriptions of the thyroid gland and how it functioned. He explained that if it were beginning to malfunction, that medicine might immediately stabilize it, or it might continue to crash in increments. He would test it in three month intervals. He wrote down the names of the best medications and the dosages that might be required. He then discussed side effects, long term studies, expense, and anything else that would enable Emma to decide her course of action.

It wasn't time to decide anything yet, but when the test results arrived, he wanted her to be ready. He didn't like pushing patients or deciding for them, although he lamented that some of his patients wanted him to. Every question Emma asked, he answered thoroughly, writing down anything she might need to remember on his pad.

Emma decided to stop asking questions. She began to feel a bit responsible for the poor patient pacing in the room next to her. She thought she might have heard him groan and hit the wall with a sort of weak thud. Maybe he was merely doing calisthenics to revive the blood flow, but she didn't want the responsibility of keeping the doctor any longer. Besides, she was definitely on information overload already as she had in her sweaty hands eleven pages of scientific notes that he had written for her during their two hours together.

How many patients can he possibly see in a day if he spends this much time with each of them? Emma wondered as she scheduled her follow-up appointment and picked up her purse. She walked stiffly out the door like some sort of Frankenstein monster who had only recently been released from his chains in the basement. *Wow, sitting motionless in that little office chair has paralyzed my legs,* Emma thought as she wobbled down the hall, free at last.

The sun had long since finished its duties and the night air was Texas hot and humid. The icy coke she had left in the cup holder was melted warm brown liquid, but she drank it anyway. She didn't know which felt better, a hopeful diagnosis, or precious freedom after five hours of incarceration. She debated it and concluded that she couldn't decide. She wasn't well yet, in spite of the unusual diagnosis, and the night air and freedom did feel pretty good. *O.K. It is freedom that feels better.* She hoped he was going to help her, but she knew it was still just hope.

Ted Lyles knew that his medical practice was not ordinary. He had consciously determined that it wouldn't be, for he knew that there was no way for him to be true to himself and to his knowledge of medicine, or for that matter, true to his patients, without departing from the status quo. Seeing an unending procession of nameless faces in fifteen minute intervals, making a quick professional assessment, and scribbling undecipherable potions on a prescription pad was not the life he had determined to have when he plodded through medical school and his internship.

He had seen medicine practiced in all sorts of ways, from caring professionalism to overburdened and shameful neglect. He had seen doctors make crucial decisions when they were focused and diligent, as well as when they were tired and distracted. He despised the arrogance that sometimes crept into the hearts of those who thought they had the power over life and death or the madness that came upon some when they blithely made easy decisions about difficult problems. He was a careful man who believed that spending the time to give exact answers to the patient's questions was time well spent.

As usual, thinking "that" thought caused him to cringe.

He loved scientific knowledge; whenever he had a spare moment he scoured medical publications for the latest research, as evidenced by the piles of books and magazines in his office, on his desk at home, by the sofa, and by his bed. He had a memory for details, giving patients the percentages and the success rates of dozens of medicines instantly, drawing little graphs and charts on his pad as though he had prepared for a classroom lecture.

He liked being responsible for his patient's health; he even liked searching out cheaper medicines for patients who needed them. He liked everything connected to his office infinitely better than being responsible for the countless things at home that always needed to be done. As usual, thinking "that" thought caused him to cringe, because several looming items appeared on the radar instantly. There was the lawn to be mowed, the stack of bills on his desk, and Chad's birthday.

When is that anyway? Chad was in law school out of state, but Ted had planned to send a card personally this year. He was notorious for forgetting the kids' birthdays, and although his wife covered for him, it had become a family joke. This year he had determined to take care of it himself. His kids had never confronted him on his "neglect." They each knew it was not intentional, and how could they find fault with a man who only ignored them because he was helping many others, anyway? They coped with his preoccupation the same way their mother always had. They had all learned to accept his obsession with medicine and with his practice, and they didn't require much of him on the home front.

They didn't require much of him on the home front.

At 10:00 P.M., Dr. Lyles pulled into his own driveway. He had ushered Mrs. Emma Kane, the last patient, out at 9:30, passing the night janitor and unlocking the front door himself since his nurse had gone home. *Why had she left early?* He couldn't remember, except he knew she had told him about some family event she was having - somebody's birthday or something like that - or maybe her mother was in the hospital again. He couldn't remember which one it was, but usually she didn't leave him early.

He typically saw patients in the afternoon and evening after his hospital rounds, and this had been a typical day. As he stepped out of the cab of his truck, he noticed that the boxwoods needed trimming. *Maybe Saturday,* he thought to himself. He had always liked doing his own yard work. He enjoyed the exercise and the change of pace, and although it usually had to get pretty out of control before it moved to the top of the list, he insisted on doing it himself.

He went into his study to relax for a moment before going to bed. He sighed when he noticed the pile of bills that were stacked on the magazines, waiting for his attention. On top of the bills, there was a thank you note from Chad which his wife had opened and placed there. He read it first: "Dear Mom and Dad, thanks for the check for my birthday. It was really needed and appreciated. Love to you both. I hope to see you soon." He looked at the wall with the calendar and there it was; Chad's birthday had been two weeks ago. His wife had covered for him once again, and if Chad knew, which he probably did, he was purposefully ignoring it too.

Under the letter was his favorite journal with a new article on diabetes in children. He sat down, opened the journal, and began to read.

Chapter 2

Fulfilled, Challenged and Alive!

She glided gracefully down the long aisle, lighting her way with a small Turkish lamp. Her lone companion was her shadow, attending her as she walked the corridor of fallen soldiers. Her footsteps and the rustle of her long skirt provided welcoming, maternal sounds to those wounded soldiers still unable to sleep. This final round had become a tradition of hers, and a compulsion. She needed to check on her "children" one last time. Although she was weary from yet another demanding day, there was something about the dark, the solitude, and a soldier's occasional "Thank you, Miss Florence," when she offered a sip of water or wiped a brow, which gave her the strength needed to continue in her nightly ritual.

This four-mile pilgrimage down the corridor of wounded British soldiers had earned her the revered title, "Lady with the Lamp." The British public had come to esteem her as a romantic heroine, an angel of mercy, and while she could not think of herself in such grandiose terms she did believe with all her heart that she was finally strategically aligned with her purpose and destiny - more fulfilled, challenged, and alive than she had ever been. The time was two o'clock in the morning.

Soldiers reached out to embrace her presence as she passed, for she was a picture of the tenderness of a wife or mother as she moved among them with gentle reassurance and selfless devotion. They were aware of how she exhausted herself on their behalf, worked tirelessly for their much needed supplies, as she extended her sweet, steel grace. A particularly young soldier of only seventeen was sobbing, crying out for his mother, and Florence moved to his bed, bent down, and said, "Allow me to give you a kiss on your mother's behalf." The soldier stopped crying, fortified by her woman's touch. These men knew how fortunate they were to have the "Lady with the Lamp" watching over them in the night. What they didn't know was how hard her own battle had been to be among them and what tenacity her victory had instilled in her spirit. She gave to them sustenance from the deep well which her intense struggle had brutally dug within her.

Although she recorded it in her journal, she prudently never breathed a word of it to a human soul.

At seventeen, Florence had been sure of her call. While walking on the grounds of the elegant English estate that was her home in Hampshire, England, she heard the voice of God calling her into the field of nursing. Although she recorded it in her journal, she prudently never breathed a word of it to a human soul.

In the very same year, there was an outbreak of influenza among the servants in her home. While the rest of her family fled to avoid it, she and the cook stepped in and cared for all fifteen patients until they were well. It was a time of intense happiness and fulfillment for her, demanding that she rise at dawn and tirelessly cares for the helpless men and women who needed her assistance for everything. She bathed, fed, cleaned, and comforted with the passion of a person who had found her life's work.

Florence had to have purpose to be content, but not just any purpose would do, for there was only one that would ever satisfy the heart of Miss Florence Nightingale, one that she and no other than God had secretly agreed upon.

Her father, William, was a very intelligent man and a gifted teacher. He had educated her and her sister himself and, fortunately for them, he was quite progressive in his thinking about educating women. He taught both Florence and Parthenope, her older sister, much more than would have been deemed necessary for Victorian ladies. Her family was also part of an intellectual and socially prominent group which made it possible for her to converse with some of the brightest minds of the day. She was well aware of the progress being made in science, which thrilled her, but the one area of science to which she was most drawn was medicine. While the medical field was beginning to emerge from being primitive, it still consisted largely of bleeding, purging, opiates, and administering a toxic breed of medicines

It was the missing link in hospital care and she knew it, not just intellectually but with fierce conviction and holy zeal.

containing heavy metals. Patients often died of the treatments before they could die of the illnesses.

Florence dreamed of pursuing medicine as a career. Although she was intelligent enough to become a doctor where a few brave women were paving the way into that more socially acceptable career, she remained doggedly determined that it was nursing where she was most needed. A doctor's diagnosis, irregular visits, prescriptions, or surgery still left the patient desperately needy of a watchful eye, proper administration of medicines, a healthy diet, bandage changes, remedies for fevers, and procedures to insure cleanliness. It was the missing link in hospital care and she knew it, not just intellectually but with fierce conviction and holy zeal.

Nurses had the most awful of reputations at the time, seen by most as nothing better than morally bankrupt chambermaids. Undaunted, Florence had the audacity to think she could change that. She knew the only nurses at the time who were respected were Catholic nuns and there was a brief period when she thought of converting to Catholicism to further her ambitions, though she was far too principled to do it. She had made, however, in typical Nightingale fashion, a thorough investigation of the possibility.

She decided instead that she could tackle professional nursing and bring it up to a respectable level, creating perhaps a Protestant sisterhood of nurses. Florence was a born reformer, possessing everything she needed to meet the challenge - the call, the intelligence, the passion, and the drive. She would transform the most unseemly profession and make it an essential part of the healing process, because she was able to see beyond its present shabby state into its noble potential in a way no one else could. Florence intended to personally lead nursing from its lowly place in the dark into the glorious light. While that was her long-range dream, her immediate goal was that she be given a single opportunity to start that journey by rolling up her own sleeves.

She decided if she had the chance she would first demand cleanliness, having concluded that it was essential to recovery. Hospitals at the time were appallingly filthy, home to rats, fleas, and lice which tormented the indigent patients - and hospitals usually housed only the indigent. The middle and upper classes tended to their sick at home with the help of doctors who were hired to attend them personally. The hospital's resident vermin were carriers of disease, enemies of health, culprits Florence intended to annihilate by ridding bodies, beds, and facilities of these unwanted pests as a basic first step. She was ambitious for power, but only because she knew it would take a certain amount of power to bring about the total change she deemed necessary. She was confident enough to believe she knew exactly what needed to be done and was ready to start. She needed only her parents' blessing.

Florence's parents were well-meaning, over-protective members of the upper class in Victorian society. Their primary aspirations for both of their daughters were that they be cultured, genteel, proper, and of course married. Florence's mother, Fanny, a popular socialite, believed in "doing good deeds" and "Christian charity," but she could not approve of Florence's ambition. Fanny was largely guided by class pride and Victorian prudence, determined to maintain her daughters' reputations at all costs.

The thought of "her" Florence serving the lower classes, scrubbing their bodies, emptying their bed pans, and tending to their diseased and wasted bodies sent her into hysteria. She accused Florence of tormenting her with her ridiculous ambition and she would not budge, perhaps thinking if she held out long enough Florence would come to her senses or a suitor would arrive in time to save her.

Numerous suitors came and went and there were a few Florence seriously considered. Perhaps if one had matched her in passion and ambition, she would have married. If she believed she could have had both a successful marriage and a successful career, she most certainly would have married. There were happy times for Florence during her almost twenty-year battle to be free, times when it appeared she would embrace her privileged lot in life and marry well. She could be charming and engaging, to be sure, and in those hopeful seasons her mother breathed a sigh of relief.

Then the pendulum would swing and Florence would become so depressed by her own failure to fulfill her dreams that, to her, life was unbearable. She suffered in a place of torment, blocked from God's call, and at times making herself sick with despair. She would become so despondent that when she thought of the time she was wasting, she would sometimes take to her bed believing she was truly ill. She was tremendously frustrated and when Florence wasn't happy, neither was the family, because her mood would become dark and critical. She rebelled in her heart, if not outwardly, and she punished those around her for her misery, pulling them into the pit with her if they allowed her to.

There was no one to truly confide in for it seemed to her that female friends didn't share her unconventional thinking.

She not only had the task of convincing her parents, but she had a second formidable adversary - Victorian society itself. Prudence, decorum, and restraint were the highest virtues of the day and to one who wanted to be at the forefront of reform, those virtues were adversaries. Nursing was not a prudent notion. She in no way wanted to lose her reputation or defame her family, but giving in to the restraints placed upon her left her in her prison. She wanted desperately to be released, but there was enough Victorian lady in her to refuse to do it any other way than the "proper" path of family blessing. Her life was one of inner turmoil and conflict and she was at odds with her parents, herself, and the entire culture in which she lived.

Florence looked down on the useless society of rich English women, her mother's cohorts, who talked passionately about many things and did little or nothing about any of them. Philosophically, life was no holiday, no walk in the park to Florence. It was a divinely purposeful struggle with evil, an ongoing battle. Yet she was not much different than they, for she couldn't break free from the social restraints either, so what she thought of the idle rich, she thought also of herself. She judged herself most harshly of all because like them she too was failing to impact anything, even with all of her high ideals, passion, and keen eye to see exactly where the problems lay.

There was no one to truly confide in for it seemed to her that female friends didn't share her unconventional thinking, and she would cut off relationship with the ones who began to question her or express fear over her "chosen path." Even her own sister, Parthenope, who adored Florence, thought quite differently and couldn't support her dreams. Parthe wanted the family together, safe, and happy, and she used her influence on their mother to get her way. There were women reformers emerging both in Britain and America who were paying high prices to effect change, but she didn't know them personally, nor could she delude herself that their lives were easy.

The one thing she did enjoy that was not related to nursing was travel. If she had become inconsolable, languishing in a state of despair, occasionally her parents would permit her to travel with friends to Europe, and once to Egypt, in order to pull her up out of the pit and grab for themselves a reprieve from her misery.

If she had made herself ill with melancholy, once she was invited to travel she would become vibrant and alive. She filled little notebooks with minute details and facts and wrote home delightful letters filled with witty anecdotes. While traveling, she always had amazing physical energy, absorbing architecture and art with passion. She loved Italian opera where moody and dramatic characters paraded about on stage and expressed their passions freely, blissfully unfettered by the rules of English society.

She was in His furnace where He was tempering her mettle, the leader's mettle, before sending her out.

God's timing required that she wait and wait and wait while He shaped her and reshaped her, perfecting her design to be the mother of her profession. He knew what would be required of her in the days ahead, that she would have to understand how to reform with patience, skill, timing, and, most of all, humility. He challenged her impulsiveness, her pride, her recklessness, and forced her to wait until the time was right - when she was bendable, teachable, and grateful to be allowed to go forward.

It was demanding and difficult work, but she thrived under the pressure.

Her profession would have to understand how to lead and serve at once. While it would be yoked in the same harness with medical doctors, nurses would need to understand submission to the doctors' decisions. She was in His furnace where He was tempering her mettle, the leader's mettle, before sending her out. If Florence could have understood His plan, she might not have swallowed the poison of her own anger, an anger that would resurface years later as rage and bitterness when she remembered all the "wasted" years when she had been forced to wait.

Before her parents finally relented, she enjoyed a period of relative contentment as a teacher in the Ragged Schools, which were started for the very poor by men such as Charles Dickens. She had always loved the lowest class of people and helping them seemed to make her come alive. Coming home late in the evenings, disheveled and muddy, she was happy, since for a brief moment she had purpose and meaning. She loved the eagerness of the students: young women who worked long shifts but managed to attend her classes, eager with desire to learn to read and better themselves.

By the time she was thirty-five, she had finally won her family over with her tenacious perseverance and her stringent determination to be dissatisfied with anything else, and her father, who had at last become her champion, agreed to supply her five hundred pounds a year to live on. She had won her independence and when she was appointed Superintendent of the Institute of Sick Gentlewomen, consisting mostly of ailing governesses, she accepted the job with gratefulness.

It was demanding and difficult work, but she thrived under the pressure. She established order, routine, and cleanliness and, to everyone's surprise, some of her patients recovered and resumed their lives. Many of those who had doubted her came to admire her abilities and she earned the highest praise from workers, patients, and the Board of Supervisors. She was in her element at long last.

When the British went to the Crimea to fight Russia, she had earned enough reputation and had enough friends in high places to be called on to go. Her dear friend, Sidney Herbert, had been appointed Minister of War and begged her to lead a group of nurses to Turkey. However, even though she was considered to be an aging spinster, she still both wanted and needed her parents' approval for such a journey. Agreeably supportive at last, they gave her the respect and permission she needed, and when they finally capitulated, her mother and sister became some of the most faithful contributors to her and the war effort.

She worked harder than any of them and demanded more of herself than she ever could have from them.

Florence's search for nurses to accompany her was harder than gaining approval from her family. High-minded, dedicated Catholic nuns volunteered, as did a number of Anglican ladies with evangelism on their minds. A few nurses were willing to go, some in shameless search of a husband. She eliminated the applicants who were too pretty, too young, or "too drunk." It was a diverse and uncohesive bunch with a woman at the head who, though she could organize and direct in a calm and authoritative way, had no experience living in crowded quarters with women and really did not possess the temperament for that kind of intimacy.

Florence loved solitude which perhaps was why she found the quiet of the late night walks around the deserted halls of the hospitals so tranquilizing and useful. She had her battles cut out for her with this group of almost forty women. She would fight all of their personal agendas - their proselytizing, their flirtations, their marriages, and their occasional drunkenness - but she rarely dealt with insubordination because they respected her. She worked harder than any of them and demanded more of herself than she ever could have from them.

Her battles were not just with her nurses, for when she arrived on the front, the men were suffering more with cholera than from war injuries. One fourth of the 37,000 British soldiers were ill from the mysterious disease which was developing endemically in the warm, brackish coastal waters and thriving on the shells of the crustaceans the soldiers ate. All Florence knew, and she knew it instinctively, was that it wasn't contagious. She never had much fear of becoming ill, for she thought of herself as immune to disease, but she was ready to apply her favorite philosophy: sanitation, clean linens, and bathed soldiers in clean dress, would be more likely to recover.

The nurses who made the unprecedented journey to the front were greeted with hostility by the overburdened and exhausted doctors. Some of the hostility was undoubtedly because of the accolades from the press that said they were going to "save the day." They were initially not allowed near the wounded, but Florence had learned patience in her own struggles, and she waited until the doctors were overwhelmed with new casualties and her nurses were there with water, bandages, and the kind of efficient help they desperately needed.

She brought her sanitation reforms, as well as her keen sense of justice, to bear on the place by refusing to treat the rank and file soldiers any differently than the officers. It was customary at the time to treat officers first and with far greater diligence than enlisted men. To the consternation of some of the officers, her unwavering decision caused her to be even more idolized by the enlisted men.

For two and a half years she worked, inspired, and led by example. She sometimes spent eight hours a day on her knees soaking and removing dried bandages which had been in place for ten days while the soldiers were transported by ship to the hospitals. Beds lined a path that was four miles long, and when she arrived she said the vermin were "tame," because they ran with such freedom. Her nurses sewed mattresses, rid the men of lice, fought fleas, scrubbed floors, washed linen, established a kitchen that served reasonable, healthy meals, and put up screens to shield patients from being unnecessarily traumatized by surgery being performed in a bed next to their own. She didn't believe that it was God's will that these men suffer, and she set her heart to alleviate all of it she could. She called them "children of the spirit" and when she died some fifty-five years later, some of the "children" she served would carry her coffin to its place of rest, honoring her for her heroism and her love.

She took meticulous notes of all that was happening, wrote long letters to governmental officials outlining the ways things could be positively changed, and to her gratification many of her ideas were put into practice. At other times, her tendencies toward melodrama and exaggeration upset the War Board for she could react passionately and irrationally when she thought things were out of order. She challenged their way of doing things and it was not always well received.

There were times she battled depression, but outwardly she retained the calm presence that inspired those around her. All of England rallied behind her and sent packages when she requested personal items for the soldiers. When Florence appealed to her countrymen for help, they listened, and even Queen Victoria sent packages to the front. The dying were grateful to find Florence at their bedsides, writing their last words for their families, and sending their mementoes and remaining money home.

When the war was over, Florence returned home, but she was determined not to go home as the hero England wanted to make her. The thought of society, her family, and a return to the life she had led filled her with despair. The picture of being some sort of war exhibit, the focus of social intrigue or notoriety, sickened her and she was afraid she would lose her purpose and her way. She had become the most famous woman in England, but she knew these next years when she could affect reform would require true single-mindedness.

She couldn't sleep for seeing images of the dying and she could hardly stand to eat. She would walk the floor at night, wringing her hands, or sit staring off absent-mindedly. She refused all visitors although when an invitation came from Queen Victoria and Prince Albert to visit them at Balmoral Castle in Scotland she went for the good it might accomplish. They were so impressed with her information and intelligence that she was asked to lead the army reform under a royal commission. She and a number of dedicated and powerful upper-middle-class men formed her "kitchen cabinet" that fought for fourteen years against well-established military control which was largely hostile to change. Florence was the chief advocate among them in strategy, statistics, correspondence, and fortitude.

The reports of both 1858 and 1863 were presented with hard facts, tables, analysis, firsthand testimony, and her unique perspective. They presented ideas on sanitation, training, establishing a place for the wounded to be received and treated upon arrival, and even ideas for professional advancement in the British Medical Department.

She went on to involve herself in the training of nurses in the early 1870s where she stressed training, discipline, and dedication, but she did all of this from her private rooms. When she was in her sixties and seventies she was in touch with reformers throughout the world, but she preferred to work in obscurity, refusing any honor. In 1909 when she was eighty-nine, England gave her the Order of Merit, the highest award given to a civilian, but by that time she was blind and mostly unaware of the honor she was receiving.

She was virtually a recluse the last fifty-two years of her life, rarely leaving her home, seeing people only by appointment, and then only one at a time. She barred her parents and her sister from visiting her for years on end. Yet, her greatest achievements were made during this time while she was in pain, depressed, and sometimes thought she was dying. Florence accepted it as ordinary and logical, for she believed had she not been so indisposed, she might not have accomplished her destiny. She was happy to sacrifice anything that interfered with her work, including friends, family, pleasure, music, and society.

Her time in the Crimea had been hard and her life of conflicted emotions, obsessive introspection, lack of solitude, demands at the front, and the turmoil of the scrutiny she had been under had taken a tremendous physical and mental toll. She was done with polite society and the inane small talk and expectations it enforced. She would do what she pleased the rest of her life and no one would tell her what to do or be allowed to get on her nerves. Very likely, she suffered from chronic fatigue. She was so exhausted that she became convinced for a season that no one had suffered or sacrificed as much as she had, and she was angry and resentful.

It is impossible to know what the world owes her for her determination and dedication to reform.

Fortunately, Florence, resilient Florence, came out of her dark tunnel and did resume normal relations with her mother when Fanny Nightingale grew ill and she determined to nurse her until her death. Her sister, Parthenope, finally married when she was forty years old to Sir Harry Verney, a widower of fifty-six with children and grandchildren. Florence allowed herself to share in this family and became increasingly close to her new nieces and nephews and their children. She lived out the final days of her life well loved and content. At the time of her death, she was cared for by a staff of loving servants who held this kind and gentle woman in highest regard. It is impossible to know what the world owes her for her determination and dedication to reform.

Florence Nightingale's frail body lay still in the darkness. The night nurse had put fresh linens on her bed, for she knew Miss Florence would have requested them if she were not so weak. She sat by her side holding the hands which had held hundreds of grateful hands during her lifetime. She felt the old woman's faint pulse and wondered if she would make it through the night. It had been a privilege and an honor to care for this dear woman as she approached the end of her life and to follow in her footsteps as a nurse. She turned Miss Florence's small hands over in her own and considered the impact of their touch in countless lives, the notes she had written, and the changes her meticulous arguments had brought about. She blew out the lantern and left the lady in the quiet and solitude she had always loved, oblivious to the sound of the chariot that was swinging low to take Miss Florence home.

Florence Nightingale had visited the sick as though they were the Lord Himself, cared for the dying, and alleviated suffering out of a big spirit even when she lacked human strength. She had confronted, reformed, and established nursing just as God had asked her to. "Well done, my good and faithful servant," her Bridegroom whispered as they walked through the gate into a place where there would be no more pain.

The man emerging from the Rolls Royce was stepping gingerly through the Chicago snow, taking great care to preserve his Italian leather shoes. He was dressed in a very expensive and stylish black cashmere coat and a black felt fedora, and he had ducked his head to resist the cold, North wind. The building he disappeared into was an antique store, but a doctor's office was also in the building. He didn't appear to be a doctor, but perhaps a very successful business man. Two men got out of the car at the same time, and hurried to keep pace with him, their eyes darting about as though it was their job to be keenly aware of their surroundings at all times so as to protect the first man. The chauffer waited in the car with his cap pulled over his face, preparing himself for what might prove a long wait, but still he kept the engine running while the men went inside. The wealthy man he was waiting on was none other than Al Capone, the most notorious Chicago gangster of all times.

All at once, a huge black car sped down the street from where it had been hidden in a nearby alley, careening in the curve, as men with machine guns riddled the windows of the brick building with bullets. Al himself, barely in the door, was pushed to the ground by his two bodyguards, and was unharmed. The horrified chauffer who had remained in the car dove to the floor of the Rolls when he first heard the screeching tires, but no one seemed interested in him at the moment. Bugs Moran's men were trying to gun down the Big Fellow, and they had almost gotten him. It was a normal day in the neighborhood for the Chicago underworld of the 1920's.

The years from 1920 until 1933 were the years of Prohibition in the United States, a thirteen year period when the sale and production of alcohol was illegal in the country. During that time, entrepreneurs stepped forward to capitalize on the closed market with black market goods for those who had no intention of obeying the country's law.

Many felt justified since they had strongly opposed the amendment. The city of Chicago had voted six to one against it, and that meant that most people in the city, including prominent citizens and government officials were willing to turn their heads while "businessmen" procured the outlawed substance for them. The Windy City would not be told what to do, so it determined not to obey the laws, enabling a lucrative black market to prosper in a flamboyant and daring way. This provided the fertile ground for the emergence of powerful Chicago mobsters whose crime binge prospered for decades, until even Chicago became fed up with them.

The city seemed able to tolerate the worst of the worst, especially if these men tried hard to reconcile their public images with their clandestine underground activities, and they allowed the city to carry on as usual. Truthfully, Chicago didn't merely tolerate the mob's presence, but it was controlled by it. Many public officials from mayors, judges, policemen, and legislators were bought off by the mobsters. Because there was so much money to be made illegally, there was plenty of money to be shared with corrupt officials who would turn a blind eye to the most lucrative capitalism around.

The imposition of the eighteenth amendment provided a rare opportunity for practical opportunists commonly known as gangsters. One of those "business" types who seized his chance at the American dream was the son of Italian immigrants, Alphonse Caponi, a name he shortened to Al Capone. "Scar face," the "Big Fellow," "Big Al," saw it like this: "This American system of ours, call it Americanism, call it capitalism, call it what you like, gives to each and every one of us a great opportunity if we only seize it with both hands and make the most of it." So, that's what he did. He seized an opportunity and provided a service that was lucrative, dangerous, and obviously highly in demand, because his estimated income in the year 1927 was somewhere between sixty and one hundred million. This was merely an educated guess since it was nearly impossible to calculate accurately due to all of his combined activities and his lack of any legitimate accounting. He had no intention of making it for Uncle Sam to claim his share.

He said, "When I sell liquor, it's called bootlegging; when my patrons serve it on Lake Shore Drive, it's called hospitality."

According to Capone, he was no bigger criminal than all the good folks of Chicago who consumed his product. He said, "When I sell liquor, it's called bootlegging; when my patrons serve it on Lake Shore Drive, it's called hospitality." He employed a thousand men, and most of them were killers, just like he was. He had earned his way to the top by ruthless loyalty to former leaders with murder for hire, but he sold himself to Chicago as mostly a nice guy. The city could accept gang murders if "they" were killing each other and not killing ordinary citizens. As long as the two worlds were separated, at least theoretically, everybody seemed able to get along fine.

Capone did what he believed he had to do to protect his market, and gang wars over territory or position were prevalent. He built his organization on fear, and he felt that one needed to be on guard against the competition, ready to instill respect in the hearts of his adversaries at all times. As he said, "You can get more with a kind word and a gun, than a kind word alone." Acquiring wealth and power were his primary goals in life, and he just happened to be in the right place at the right time where he could reap great benefit for his expert business sense and his willingness to be part of a dark underworld. He was a shrewd businessman, and although his business was racketeering, if one looks at the profit margin alone, he was incredibly skillful at making money. As a businessman, he exercised sound judgment, rewarded his loyal employees when they did well, and oversaw details with a keen eye for total control of the market, and he did it all by the blackest means imaginable while remaining out of the reach of the law.

He was known to be diplomatic, always preferring to negotiate, and only if the opponent left him no other alternative would he resort to violence. However, when he resorted to brutality, he spared nothing. He bootlegged liquor, ran prostitution, and established secret nightclubs called speakeasies where illegal liquor flowed, illegal gambling could be found, and up and coming entertainers could find a place to dazzle the law-breaking party goers. One of those musicians who made it to the top of the jazz world by the way of Capone's clubs was a jazz player out of New Orleans named Louis Armstrong. Big Al liked to promote people that he had discovered. It was one of the ways that he shared the wealth at his disposal. He was well connected with some of the up and coming talent of the day, and he provided venues for them to showcase their talents. Louis Armstrong wasn't the only one who owed Capone some thanks for his start; Bing Crosby and Bob Hope both entertained in his night clubs, although Bob Hope said that he always feared he would be shot before the night was over. No doubt about it, Capone was well connected. He knew people from every social sector, especially from high places in government and entertainment.

One of the things that endeared him to the folks of Chicago and enabled him to remain above the law was the persona he created of the "lovable outlaw," which he created through his famous generosity. It was believed that he averaged about ten million a year during most of his reign, and considering the times, that was an almost inconceivable fortune, so he could afford to be generous. There were many grateful struggling Italian Americans, newcomers to the country, who idolized the man for his hand-outs.

He didn't forget the "little people." He bought milk for Chicago's school kids when rickets became a health concern to Chicago's poor, and because he loved operas, circuses, and rodeos, he often bought up blocks of tickets for performances and handed them out to people who could have never paid their way into events like that. During the depression, he established soup kitchens in Chicago and instructed merchants to give people clothes or food when they needed it. Some say he was trying to white wash his image, but Capone believed his own public persona. He kept his world divided into its good and bad components, and he believed he was a good guy, a benevolent father in the city, watching over his children, giving them illicit pleasures to ease their troubles.

The fact that he "bent" the laws to provide for them, he compensated for through his "good deeds" of charity. Capone regarded the laws the mainstream were required to obey as rules for small minded men who needed to be told what to do. He saw a way around most laws, and he lived for a very long time evading any repercussions, because he knew how to beat the system as well as how to manipulate it. He was smart enough to know that if Chicago was sure he was only dishing the "bad" out to the "bad," he could get away with it, and if he had his dirty work done by thugs who were far removed from him, he would remain untouchable. His enemies were the sharks who tried to cut in on his territory, like his arch rival, Bugs Moran. These gangsters all had nicknames like "Bugs," "Dingbat," "Lucky," and "Murray the Hump" and they drove around in Rolls Royces and filled their dead gang members'

Capone always loved luxury.

coffins with orchids, flaunting their wealth in style in the middle of the Great Depression.

Capone always loved luxury. He wore the finest clothes, ate the very best gourmet food, and drank the best illegal liquor. He dressed in expensive suits and raised his son to have impeccable manners. He liked to see himself as a family man and once came to greet a bunch of reporters at the door wearing a pink apron and carrying a pan of spaghetti. He hired a publicist to help him with his image, and at the man's suggestion, he came out of the shadows and began appearing in public, assuring the public he was a legitimate business man and a personable fellow. When Charles Lindberg made his transatlantic flight, one of the first people to push through the crowds and shake his hand was none other than Al Capone.

Chicago was proud, in some sort of perverse way, to call him its own, at least for a season.

He abided by a code of conduct that was one of his own inventions, and he was honorable by his own standards. If it became necessary to shoot a rival gang member, he would send flowers to the funeral, once sending an enormous $5,000 spray to the funeral of a fallen adversary. Then there was the time that an innocent woman was shot during a gang conflict and Capone paid for her hospital stay and all of her bills, to demonstrate his sincerity about not wanting to hurt regular citizens. He enjoyed public notoriety and fame, the things money could buy, and especially the respect and power he could get with its use. At the White Sox's games and the Cub's games, he could be seen, sitting with his son, signing autographs. Chicago was proud, in some sort of perverse way, to call him its own, at least for a season. They knew he was a criminal, but because they didn't fear he would hurt ordinary people, they approached him like he was a tame bear, or at least one on a leash.

Al Capone was the son of Italian immigrants from Naples. He was born in Brooklyn in 1899. The Mafioso which had existed in Sicily was a traditional form of "government" where strong families battled each other for control over the illegal enterprises in a city including prostitution, gambling, extortion, and so forth. American Italians brought the tradition with them, but Capone was not Sicilian, but Neapolitan, so he never quite fit in with that underworld kingdom and the other war lords. While they were unquestionably ruthless with each other, they were usually seen as benevolent protectors by the people, or at the least, by local Italians who went to them for help.

Like the Mafia he had been raised around, Al Capone perceived himself as a fatherly type who watched over his children, using power and control to keep them safe and happy, and coincidentally padding his own deep pockets with the rewards of his labor.

The Chicago chieftain, Al Capone, enjoyed a long run of popularity and tolerance before he became public enemy number one, because he was smart, cunning, conniving, and intuitive. He had an extensive spy network, one that enabled him to be forewarned about any threats that might be coming his way. He was brilliant at hiding his millions from the government by doing all of his transactions in cash. His building had a "front," where he worked behind a very normal looking doctor's office and furniture store. He never filed an income tax return, nor really could he have done so legitimately, because he never made money in any legitimate way. Outraged at his wealth and his lack of legitimate "work," the city once attempted to file vagrancy charges against him. He didn't own anything in his own name, having put everything in his wife's name. He had a very savvy accountant, Easy Eddie O'Hare, who knew how to outfox Uncle Sam, but in the end when Easy Eddie saw Capone's empire coming to an end, he would be the informant who confided to the feds all he knew, sending Capone to jail for tax evasion.

Ironically, the government got him because he had not paid legal taxes on all of his illegal money, which might seem a little absurd, but it's the law. Eddie paid for the "slip" to the FBI with his life one week before Capone left Alcatraz. (As a side note, Easy Eddie had a son, Edward O'Hare, who became a war hero, dying as a fighter pilot at age 29 in World War II, and whose name is enshrined at Chicago's O'Hare Airport.)

Al might have been tolerated in Chicago, but the rest of the country saw Capone as a menace to society. President Hoover wanted him caught and punished, but no accusation of murder ever came close to sticking, he was usually so far removed from the actual crime which was carried out by underlings. The country was coming out of the Depression and Prohibition was about to be repealed, so his procurement of illegal alcohol would soon be unnecessary. Capone's capture and successful prosecution became a high priority.

Still, Capone might have endured longer had he not made a huge public relations mistake in the gunning down of Bugs Moran's men on St. Valentine's Day in 1929, in what became known as the St. Valentine's Day Massacre. Capone hated Bugs and thought he was an unpredictable, maniacal killer, and that he would personally never know peace while Bugs was alive. Capone's men dressed up like policeman, found Moran's lieutenants in a warehouse, and mowed them down with machine guns, although they still didn't get Bugs himself.

The tough inmates refused to give him the respect to which he was accustomed.

When the newspapers began circulating the ghastly pictures of the execution all over the country, Capone's persona as a good guy was beyond remedy. Finally, due largely to Easy Eddie's testimony, and Eliot Ness' relentless pursuit of Capone, he was convicted on tax evasion, fined $50,000.00 and sentenced to 11 years in the federal penitentiary. Al, of course, tried to bribe the jury to escape his prison sentence, but his efforts were thwarted and he was sentenced, at long last, to prison time.

Ultimately he was sent to Alcatraz, which was a maximum security prison at the time, because after he was initially sent to the Atlanta prison, he took over the place by bribing the authorities. He had his room decorated with rugs, mirrors, and made to be quite comfortable, but when higher-up authorities got wind that he had been able to procure luxury for himself, they sent him to the much tougher Alcatraz. Capone wasn't popular there because he showed contempt for the social order of the prison. He was much too famous and too independent to try and fit in, and the tough inmates refused to give him the respect to which he was accustomed. They called him names, put lye in his drink, and set out to abuse him.

The story is told that Capone tried to cut in line for a haircut and a Texas bank robber named James Lucas told him to go to the back of the line. Capone said, "Do you know who I am?" The man replied, "Yeah, I know who you are, grease ball. And if you don't get to the back of the line, I'm gonna know who you were." These criminals were the worst in the nation, and they were unimpressed with Capone, in fact, they made it almost intolerable for him. By this time he was also losing a lot of his vigor due to illness. It was impossible to bribe the authorities and he had no underlings to command, so he was on his own, and the prisoners of Alcatraz went out of their way to diminish him. When the other prisoners wanted to strike or rebel, he refused to cooperate with them, maybe because he was used to calling the shots, or maybe because he had decided to become an exemplary prisoner to earn early release for good behavior, which he did. He was released in 1939, returning to his Florida home where he lived with his family until 1947 when he died.

He had used all of his money to fight his imprisonment. By the time he got out, his power and organization were gone. He had lost his health and some of his mental faculties in prison and died at 48, believing himself to be an American capitalist, entrepreneur, and benefactor. He had a remarkably long run, considering the dangerous aspects of his particular line of work, but seventy-five years later, history remembers him as nothing more than a gangster, a mobster, the most notorious outlaw Chicago ever called her own.

Chapter 4
Emotional, Impulsive, Erratic...and Admired

The thriving fishing business was competitive and sometimes dangerous due to the fact the fishermen were often bombarded by sudden, violent storms - conditions generated by the surrounding hills and because the sea was more than two hundred meters below sea level. Simon didn't mind the challenge or the danger of the sea. In fact, he always felt most alive and happy when the seas were a little rough, dark clouds loomed in the distance, and the temperature began to drop slightly because then he knew a storm was on the horizon.

If he was out in the deeper waters, he never wanted to rush frantically back to shore, since he knew that often the greatest catch could be had - by the most adventuresome fisherman - right before a storm. He was far more likely to turn the boat toward the choppy waves at the first sign of brooding clouds rather than head back to the predictably safe shore. He trusted his sense of timing and, although he loved the energy of the choppy waves and the sheets of wind and water that doused the boat and almost blinded his vision, he possessed an intuitive time clock that warned him when it was imperative to turn back, his boat often filled with fish.

On the contrary, Simon's wife hated the storms. She knew how likely it was that her husband would sail directly into one, driven by his competitiveness to bring in the biggest catch and his reckless certainty that he would not be harmed. Although she had to admit he was a competent sailor and had come home safely every time so far, he both scared and infuriated her. She would sometimes pace the shore in the soaking rain until she could make out the little boat returning, bouncing on the waves like a toy, the bow diving and pitching into the water. She knew her burly, fearless husband would be at the helm, probably laughing uproariously, yelling to his brother, "I love this. This is what I live for." They would soon be inside, wet and invigorated by danger and the feeling they had outwitted the sea once again, while she thanked a merciful God who watched over foolish men who were not tame at heart.

Mending the nets was the kind of tedious and exacting work from which Simon tried to escape.

Simon had always loved the challenge of the unpredictable Sea of Galilee. He had once lived to conquer it and capture its depths, dragging into his boat the daily catch to supply the village which lived largely on its generous bounty. For generations his people had fished in the sea and its warm waters had fed them, rocked them to sleep at night, and provided most of the adventure they had known.

Every day the weather permitted, two hundred boats would dot the seascape, painting the canvas of the ten by thirty mile sea with tranquil and familiar strokes. The fishermen who were not out in their boats could be seen lining the shores with massive nets, dragging the bottom for fish or whirling the nets above their heads in circular motions against the blue sky, dropping them strategically in a place that secretly called to them.

The life of a fisherman could be monotonous, so the storms were a welcome break from days which blended into each other - sunrise and the nets, dusk and selling the fish at the market. They rose slightly before dawn and went down to the familiarity of the lady who had captivated their hearts. Carefully coiled ropes and perfectly folded nets were taken from the places where they had been stowed away but a few hours before. The tools of their trade were precious - life itself - and there was no place for random carelessness when storing them for the night. Every day they were checked for the slightest tear since too many fish and a net that had started to tear would prove disastrous. A little tear would certainly lead to a bigger one. It was an ongoing process to check and repair them regularly. Mending the nets was the kind of tedious and exacting work from which Simon tried to escape. He delegated as much of the boring task to the day laborers as possible, for to him it was the worst part of being a fisherman.

None was more emotional, impulsive, or erratic than Simon, and there was no one the other men admired or respected more.

With nets in hand, the decision was made whether to stand in the shallow water or take to the sea by boat. This strategic decision was made by seasoned fisherman who knew the signs of the sky, the breeze, the temperature of the water, and the habits of more than thirty species of fish. The fishermen were hard at work by the time the first light appeared in the Galilean sky. They shouted greetings and joked with one another, their voices bouncing and ricocheting across the water, for there was a camaraderie among them that had been honed in this day to day routine.

Each had his own reputation and personality, but none was more emotional, impulsive, or erratic than Simon, and there was no one the other men admired or respected more. It would be a long day of toil, demanding strength, endurance, and hope because these were days that taxed them all as they searched the depths for its reluctant treasure.

Today was an ordinary day in every way. While the men mended the nets, Simon and Andrew were in the water with their circular net, a large one measuring about twenty feet across. Dropping the net to the bottom, they would capture a mélange of fish and then drag its contents to shore. Once ashore, they would separate the fish carefully into clean and unclean, according to Levitical law. The scaled ones, predominately musht, were clean. The unclean ones were mostly eels and barbels, a kind of catfish.

When Jesus approached the men, they were busy with the task at hand. Simon was getting his large fingers entangled in the rope, partly because he was distracted that day and could hardly focus on extricating the helpless fish. He had been idly wondering if there was some greater purpose in life than catching fish and living in this quiet little village. He worried that he would never discover what it was or accomplish it, but he never discussed it with anyone anymore. The few times he tried to talk to Andrew about it, Andrew had just stared back blankly. Simon was unwilling to pursue the topic again with him. Now he wandered away at times like this and looked at the sea, moodily preferring solitude for sorting things out.

Jesus stood and watched them for a moment in silence until Simon felt His gaze. Simon turned to look directly into the stranger's eyes. He was average height with dark, wavy hair. He looked fit although He was probably not a fisherman - likely a craftsman or tradesman judging from His complexion which had not been browned and weathered by the sun and sea as theirs had. Nothing about the stranger captured Simon's attention except His eyes, the most peaceful and compelling eyes he had ever seen, filled with encouragement and a sort of merriment. The man was looking at him as though He knew him. Maybe He recognized him from somewhere. Simon racked his brain to think of where he might have seen Him before.

When He spoke, His words had a strong Galilean accent, but despite the familiarity of the cadence they sounded uncharacteristically refined and melodic. "Follow Me," He said quietly, "and I will make you fishers of men."

"Fishers of men!" What an odd saying. *Why would we fish for men,* Simon thought to himself. Little matter, he wasn't about to walk off and follow this stranger. At least that was what reason was saying to him, but his heart had begun to beat wildly and for some indecipherable reason his untamed spirit was clamoring to go.

Simon's impulsiveness was notorious in the village. He might set off to night fish on a whim, even when a storm seemed to be brewing, or give away a boat load of fish if someone had a bad day at sea and his generous heart was moved to help. He also had a reputation for speaking before he thought. The words just popped in his head and usually flew off his tongue quickly before they could undergo censorship or revision or, better yet, get swallowed up all together.

But hadn't he sworn off impulsiveness just this morning and resolved to be content as a fisherman?

Why would he even entertain this invitation? Why was he so motivated to act quickly? He felt like a door was opening that might suddenly close and never open again, that he must walk through it quickly or lose something precious and wonderful. He could not unlock his gaze from the man. He felt this man's eyes were beckoning him into the unknown and he desperately wanted to go. Even the more cautious Andrew was putting down his net and waiting for Simon to make the first move. Simon dropped his net and rushed after the stranger, followed by Andrew who glanced back at their net and the fish abandoned on the shore - carefully arranged into piles of clean and unclean - flopping about, gasping for breath. They could hear the faint voices of their mystified friends calling inquisitively after them, but they dared not reply for they had answered another call now.

But hadn't he sworn off impulsiveness just this morning?

He walked along listening to the stranger's voice and drinking in His words. He had never felt peace and happiness like this before, not even after his best day at sea, nor had the roughest sea filled him with this kind of excitement. He had an expectancy that he was starting the most amazing journey of his life, and it had come out of nowhere on an ordinary day intruding upon the deadening sameness like a beloved storm or welcome rain on parched, dry land. It was odd, but he felt this man was an answer to the questions he had been mulling over when He arrived. What a coincidence!

Simon knew and liked some of the disciples Jesus called but others were far more difficult to accept. On the day they passed the tax collector's booth, Jesus called Matthew and Simon was inwardly vexed. He hated tax collectors. He had paid far too many fees to their kind. All of the fishermen were required to do so. Men like Matthew charged the fishermen exorbitant rates to fish in their own sea, then handed over most of the money to Roman invaders after stuffing their own pockets with some of the fishermen's hard earned profits. He did not want to team up with a thief - a traitorous one at that - who stole from his own people. How could Matthew help them? He had never worked for a living. Just look at his hands!

The thing that always took Simon most by surprise was that Jesus seemed to like everybody, and He would look right past their obvious sins into the hidden place of who they might become. Simon wanted to resent His looking past the tax collector's sins, but he knew he himself wasn't as special as Jesus always acted like he was. He wanted Jesus to believe the best about him, but it was revolting to watch Him give the same treatment to Matthew when Simon knew for certain that he was nothing but a scoundrel and a thief.

Jesus never seemed to blame anyone for being where they were in life. He acted as though they had been captured against their wills. He equated His kingdom with setting captives free, more than setting up a visible structure. Simon was still trying to decipher the strange language, but in the meantime, Matthew surprised Simon by accepting the invitation to join them with the same urgency he had accepted his own invitation. He had to grudgingly admit that even Matthew was different around Jesus.

Jesus confronted Simon on every front. Nothing was sacrosanct. Simon was familiar with the laws God had given His people. He had been taught what God required and he understood that a whole system of rules and punishments had been put in place in order for God's people to be protected and blessed by Him, but he despised the hair-splitting interpretations over what the minute details meant and he was offended by the prestige some men felt they had earned by obeying them.

While Simon didn't have an explanation of the true purpose of the law, as soon as he heard Jesus talk about it, he knew He was right. Jesus made the law seem simple, yet considerably more difficult than Simon could have imagined. He seemed to be talking about a system of laws that were written on men's hearts which only God could judge. Lust was as great a sin as adultery and gossip was now comparable to murder. God hated pride most of all.

God wasn't impressed with people who kept the law but were mean spirited. Based on the places where Jesus was looking for devotees, He really liked the most broken, outrageous sinners in the land. In fact, He had come looking especially for them, and wanted to give them everything at His disposal. He never sounded like He was merely interpreting the law, but as though He understood its very intent.

Then Jesus told people not to sin and told His disciples to forgive sin, bypassing the legal authority of the priests and outlining a theme of repentance rather than sacrifice. Only God could forgive sin, usually by an intricate procedure watched over by the priests. Now he, a fisherman, was acting like a priest, forgiving sin, casting out demons and healing the sick. The more Simon saw Jesus use power to heal and forgive sins, and the more he realized the goodness of this man who truly seemed to care about the broken and oppressed, the more he was convinced about His mysterious identity. With his analytical mind and ability to see how things related, Simon had begun to put it all together. In fact, he thought of little else. *This **had** to be the Christ that they had been promised through the prophets. Who else could it be?*

Something was coming alive inside him and all of his former passion and happiness seemed shallow in comparison.

Jesus performed miracles. Simon was an eyewitness of too many to count. Eyes shut from birth popped open and people saw for the first time. Sometimes His face was one of the first things they saw, and when Simon saw the unspeakable joy and gratefulness in their newly opened eyes, he was always amazed and filled with an awe he had never known before.

Something was coming alive inside him and all of his former passion and happiness seemed shallow in comparison. He saw men's crippled legs straighten and watched lepers' skin turn from blotchy with open sores to smooth and beautiful, glistening with health and youth. Jesus cared about their afflictions, and He said His Father was not a rule maker waiting to catch them in sin and hold it to their accounts, hoping He could spew His wrath and judgment upon them.

Simon felt so convicted in those early days that he thought his heart would break. He realized how little he had understood about anything and how woefully short of Jesus' kindness and love he fell. He could barely control his own competitiveness and jealousy. There were days when John's intimacy with the Master made him jealous and angry and, although he tried to hide it, he knew the Master knew. He found himself having to forgive John over and over, not that John set out to offend him. He just had such an easy affection that it caused Simon to envy.

Everything about Simon surfaced - even the pride that he understood more quickly than the others at times. Jesus was teaching a new world view, rearranging everything and presenting a radical kingdom which would turn the present structure upside down. It was like being part of a revolution and Simon discovered he had within himself the heart of a revolutionary. It felt like "setting things right," and he loved being at the forefront, listening to the ideas, and watching the new model that would create the shift.

While he relished that part, other things surfaced which were sources of ongoing embarrassment for him - jealousy, need to control, and anger. His sinful nature would surface at the most inopportune and humiliating moments, but the eyes that had beckoned him never changed. They still looked to what he might become and didn't condemn him or push him away, although there were times when he hid from the gaze, so great was his own shame.

Then Simon would come out of the dark shadows to stand in the light again, because there was always hope beside Jesus. He felt loved and it was the unconditional quality of that love which changed him more than anything else ever had. Love compelled him to be different. Faith caused him to risk, but love sustained him.

He wanted to please Jesus more than he had ever wanted anything, and sometimes he thought he did get it right. He had been the first to blurt out the truth when he said, "You are the Christ, the Son of the living God." Jesus validated the immensity of that insight by renaming him "Peter."

On the other hand, he thought no one got it wrong more than he did, and no one felt like he had less right to be with Jesus, to be known as His disciple, or to be forgiven more than he did.

In the early days, everything Jesus did surprised him - the way He thought, the things He said, His treatment of the people, His calling of the twelve - everything. He could never have predicted any of His actions, but gradually he began to know Jesus and there were times when he knew exactly what He was going to do.

But even then he never thought He would die, or be betrayed by one of His own, or that the words "I don't know the man!"

would spill from his own lips motivated by a fear too terrible for words. Peter realized at that horrible moment that his own strength and courage had come not from himself but just from being with Jesus. Without Him, Peter was nothing much.

This very morning, the day of Pentecost, everything had changed. A new kind of courage had come from the Spirit. Within him, he felt the power, intensity, and call to action unlike anything he had experienced in the storms of Galilee. He knew it wasn't him. This had to be what Jesus had meant when He had explained that it would be better for them if He left and sent His spirit. Hard to imagine at the time; impossible to deny now.

They were not expecting the mighty rush of life that enveloped their already passionate hearts with fire.

Peter looked confidently into the face of the crowd. The fisher of men looked out over the sea of faces and sensed their hunger. He knew it was time to drop the net. He vibrated with uncommon emotion as he stood with the eleven before the crowd at the Feast of Pentecost.

Or was it really emotion? It felt more like fire burning within his spirit. Peter knew what it was to face a storm with confidence in his soul, but never had his spirit felt so alive, so powerful, so controlled. It had been close to two months since Jesus died, and Peter was about to declare before the crowd what had just happened and what it all meant in relation to the last three years of his own life ... and in relation to eternity.

"Raise your voice like a trumpet." The words of Isaiah the prophet came to Peter as he stepped forward. He had been a

disciple of Jesus and he had been a firsthand witness of powerful encounters, signs, and wonders, yet today in the room where more than one hundred people had waited for fifty days, the Spirit had come in a different way. Tongues of fire had rested above their heads, they were filled with the Holy Spirit, and began speaking in languages they did not know.

Peter felt as if he had been hit by lightning and that when he opened his mouth he would thunder. A surge of faith and power coursed through his body. His passion for the truth of what he had lived and seen could be heard in his voice which boomed mightily, testifying for all to hear. The past fifty days had been a glorious trial as the disciples fought their own logical minds, frayed emotions, and individual sense of loss, fear, and uncertainty. They privately and openly wondered if they would have the strength to go on without Jesus. Their spirits cried out for vision, enabling power, and direction, but they were not expecting the mighty rush of life that enveloped their already passionate hearts with fire.

"In the last days, God says, I will pour out my Spirit on all people. Your sons and daughters will prophesy, your young men will see visions, your old men will dream dreams. Even on my servants, both men and women, I will pour out my Spirit in those days, and they will prophesy. I will show wonders in the heaven above and signs on the earth below, blood and fire and billows of smoke. The sun will be turned to darkness and the moon to blood before the coming of the great and glorious day of the Lord. And everyone who calls on the name of the Lord will be saved."

Peter was shouting and the people were captured by his words and his passion as the electricity of the supernatural riveted them to his voice. He wanted to shout, "I am changed." He was no longer the old Peter. All of the things he had despised about himself seemed new. He who had never been a coward was bolder. The big fisherman was stronger, more sure, more Peter than he had ever been before.

Peter looked confidently into the face of the crowd. "Therefore let all Israel be assured of this: God has made this Jesus, whom you crucified, both Lord and Christ."

He knew.

His own life proved it.

Jeanette Watson awoke, startled by angry male voices, but not even in her first groggy awareness of the conflict taking place in her home was she surprised. *They are at it again,* she thought, as she jumped up, put on her robe, and moved quietly down the stairs to her son's room where the commotion was.

"Just hear me out!" she heard Tom Jr. shout, exploding with angry frustration at his dad's iron fist. Every time he thought that the wound had finally healed, a random brush with his dad's obsessive control would cause passionate emotions to surface. He had learned to stand up to his father, but he despised these conflicts.

Then she heard her husband's thundering reply, "Don't you ever talk to me like that!"

She looked at the clock on Tom's nightstand, ill tempered red numbers staring back boldly: it was 2:00 A.M. It was hard to believe that with the upcoming day, one typically filled with intense drama and stressful agendas, Tom Sr. had chosen to do this again. He had come home late from a dinner party to their New York apartment where he sometimes stayed on the really, long days. He proceeded to awaken his son who also slept there occasionally, ostensibly to say good night, and then decided to ask him a business question or two.

Truth was, one of them had more than likely changed a decision that would cause a dozen other carefully arranged decisions to crash like dominoes, and now the two were yelling at the tops of their lungs. The father's bizarre sense of timing might well have been calculated to catch his son at his most vulnerable. Abruptly awakened and unguarded, Tom faced his father, who was alert and aggressive, while Tom Jr. was not mentally or emotionally prepared for the onslaught. This was no teenager and his dad coming to blows over a dent in the family car: the junior was almost forty; the senior, almost eighty, and it was the multi-million dollar family business the old man insisted was in jeopardy.

Her husband intimidated almost everyone, although he probably rarely noticed as long as they did what he said.

As she descended the stairs, Jeanette's heart was once again both sick and fearful. She stood in the doorway looking at these two men she loved, husband and son, both livid, the old man practically blue in the face. They frightened and wearied her as these fights sometimes ended with both men in tears. "Please get some sleep, you two," was all she knew to say. She had seen these fights more times than she cared to remember.

Tom Jr. needed to be heard and have his opinions valued; Tom Sr. wanted unquestioning compliance, the same kind he always got from his subordinates at IBM where he was the long standing president. She knew her husband had to be "right," so she had learned to let him, as she did not have her son's stubbornness or his need to prove himself. She feared this would end only when her husband was in his grave, and judging by his quivering jowls and agitated demeanor, that might be very soon.

They calmed down when they saw her panicked face, both ashamed they had let it go so far, and she returned to bed again. Now she was lying wide awake in the dark, staring at the shadows of the tree branches calmly dancing on the ceiling. Who better than she knew what living with this legendary man was like? There were times when she didn't think she could do it any longer.

Once she had asked him for a divorce because of all the barking orders and the demeaning way he treated her and the kids, but his surprised and anguished face had been so stricken with pain, that she realized he loved her and, oddly enough, that he needed her. She had decided never to bring it up again. True, a few times she had been found lying flat on her back on the floor in a public bathroom, having excused herself from an event, to take her own desperate measures to calm herself from the very stress her husband thrived upon. She had learned to cope.

Her two daughters had fared well with their father, but he had treated them differently; he demanded so much from the boys, especially Tom, who although he sincerely tried to please his father, never seemed to be able to function in the exact manner his father seemed to want him to.

Her husband intimidated almost everyone, although he probably rarely noticed as long as they did what he said. People could be subservient, or barely tolerate him, for as long as they got the job done, he was happy. He probably preferred to engage with like-kind because he understood them best, and there were plenty of men like him in the marketplace, opponents and champions, circling each other in the arena like gladiators, keenly aware of each other's fear and weaknesses, maneuvering to be the first to draw blood. Control of the market, the customers, the fame, and the power could go to the champion, and if one's opponent lay crumpled in the dust at the end of the match, well, so much the better.

With their eldest, it was different. Tom Jr. was not cut from the same cloth, not that this made him a coward, in the least. He had a different style of management, one that he made work, but one his father could not comprehend. In short, Tom Jr. legitimately cared about people and knew how to draw the best out of his team with a gentler touch. His dad seemed determined to clone himself and remake his son in his own image. While Tom Jr. wanted to please his dad, he hadn't succeeded at willing himself to become someone he wasn't.

Jeanette had watched this painful dynamic all of Tom's life, as her sensitive, intelligent, and gifted son was beaten down by a father who meant well, but who was utterly blind to many useful qualities that he didn't possess himself.

"Come to bed, Tom," Jeanette said to the shadow now standing in the bathroom door.

"I'm sorry. I really am," he said as he climbed in beside her, as though he had no idea how a few minor "suggestions" could have reaped such consequences. She was the safe place for them all, and God knew they needed one. She had little hope that her husband would change, even if he had wanted to. He had succeeded in all the ways that mattered to him, but she knew, sadly, that nowhere in his entire kingdom was anyone at rest.

To the employees of IBM, Tom Watson Sr. was a hero of epic proportions. He stood at the helm for forty-two years, guiding it successfully through two world wars and a depression, creating an empire that ushered in the lucrative information industry. They created company songs about him and rallied behind him to achieve Watson's slogans for success, like: "Make things happen," and "Beat your best!" He rewarded their hard work and their loyalty with generous pay and benefits, motivating them with high expectations. Many did achieve enough to form a thriving 100% club filled with salesmen who met all of their sales goals for the year.

Tom Watson Sr. was often visibly angry with his employees, although he could be deferential and charming when he wanted to be.

He wanted his two sons, Tom Jr. and Dick, to be a part of his team. He especially wanted his eldest son at the top, and so he tempted him, second guessed him, challenged him, and tortured him to get him ready for the position, training him the only way he knew. The son's stubborn desire to prove he could do it was all that held him at IBM in the early turbulent years of climbing the corporate ladder, while his dad stood at the top, shaking the ladder violently.

Watson had been trained by the head of National Cash Registers, John H. Patterson, for whom he had worked at the turn of the century. Patterson was a ruthless tyrant who ruled by pressure and fear, rewarding his favorites arbitrarily, while punishing others by withholding his approval and all financial rewards. He often fired his best men on a whim if they crossed him, and he believed strongly in monopolies at a time when they were coming under serious government scrutiny.

Patterson had devised a simple scheme to drive the competition out of business. He moved into a town and started a business that undercut the competition at a loss to his own company. When the local business was hurting, he would buy them out for an unfair sum. It almost sent him and his team of executives to jail in one of the nation's first anti-trust suits. Watson was one of those executives who were carrying out Patterson's scheme when the crisis came. They barely escaped jail by rallying to help out during a local flood and winning public opinion, but Patterson fired Watson soon after in a restructuring of the company.

It turned out to be the best thing that ever happened to Tom, because a man named Charles Flint proposed he head his company of Computing Tabulating Registers, whose name would later be changed to International Business Machines. Watson brought from Patterson one excellent management practice, however: that of taking green kids and transforming them into super salesmen.

Tom Watson Sr. was often visibly angry with his employees, although he could be deferential and charming when he wanted to be. He might graciously defer, but often it was nothing more than a negotiating tactic, for when it came time to decide, he usually did it his own way. He might read the quarterly earnings report, spot a place of poor judgment on the part of a salesman, and call a meeting of his executives for what he deemed, a well deserved tongue lashing. He would burst into the room, impeccably dressed as always, his temper flaring.

"How many times have I told you," he would lecture, "that you need to study these reports? Look at this! We installed machines only to take them out three months later because the business was too small to need them. This costs money. What were the salesmen thinking to have sold these machines to such a small business to begin with?"

He would soon become even more enraged when no one fought back. He would scream, "I want to be challenged!" However, no one wanted to be singled out for the brunt of the tirade and reduced to an insignificant pile of cinders, so they usually remained silent. Or worse yet, at the meeting's close, he might say; "Now I'm not mad, although you might think so. I am just trying to help you guys get to the bottom of this matter." Finally, the meeting would be over, and the boss' temper would subside, but only after it had come ashore like a tidal wave and traumatized the company executives who exited the room shaken and contrite.

That same afternoon he might call the same group back to his office, after he discovered he had read the dates wrong and what he had thought was a few months turned out to be a year before the company decided the machines were too large for their needs. Now he was really mad. "How could you have let me make a mistake like that and not catch it and speak up? I am not infallible, you know."

His executives stared at their well polished shoes and decided that if Watson truly were fallible, they would not be the ones to tell him. Tom Watson Sr. could be terrifying with his temper and demands, but that was the way he pushed the executives to accomplish his goal of building the IBM empire. He never seemed to run out of energy or vision, as he hired the right people, placed them strategically, and then counted on their loyalty. He paid them well, gave them a multitude of perks, and created an elite club mentality - the culture of IBM.

Often, the engineers could not keep up with his vision, a testament to his incredible energy and his relentless expansionism. He seemed to live by a motto of "Work Harder," and it ignited the company.

He brought the same intensity to those outside the company. Once the comptroller from Bethlehem Steel, a fellow named Shick, along with some of his top executives, were invited into IBM by the head of the IBM's steel industry's account. The objective was to prepare a report on the steel industry's needs, so that IBM could better meet those needs.

Shick, who had always seemed to have it in for IBM, used the opportunity to bring in more than fifty of his best men who prepared a report of 36 problems they discovered at IBM, problems which they insisted needed remedies or Bethlehem Steel intended to dump them. Shick himself handed Watson the secret report at a subsequent meeting. Watson graciously accepted the report with a smile, reading all 36 out loud and appearing to agree with most of them.

Shick had made it appear that he and his boys at Bethlehem Steel were the brains behind IBM. Watson was furious, although he never showed it in the meeting. Once the meeting was over, he threatened to pull all of IBM's machines out of their entire company, a move which would have virtually shut them down, and which he could have easily done because they were rented punch card machines. It was no idle threat. Shick had infuriated the wrong man.

Watson's men reminded him it was war time and IBM might be in trouble for shutting down a company with war contracts, but he didn't care. Faced with their options, Bethlehem Steel pulled the reports and dropped the matter, acknowledging the whole incident to be their error. Even that was not enough for Watson who then made generous job offers to the men who had created the report, seeking to steal them away from the offending company. He dealt decisively with his enemies, and Shick's maneuver to one-up IBM had temporarily moved him to the top of Watson's list.

They could either think him mad or be condemned by their own cowardice.

Tom Watson Sr. didn't concern himself with sanity, if that meant being conservative and cautious. The Watson perspective was this: the right people with the right ideas could push themselves through every obstacle. When Watson tested the direction of the wind, it always seemed like the perfect climate for growth to him. His immediate plan was always expansion and hiring more salesmen, the men whom he believed were the most valuable to the company, because without them there was no need to produce.

During World War II, and the Depression of the 1930's, IBM and CTR its predecessor, grew when every company around them was shrinking. Watson was an optimist, a visionary, and a fighter. Because he didn't believe the war would come or the Depression would hang around, he largely ignored both and that worked to his advantage. Other companies were taking a more cautious approach.

"Still hiring, Tom?" they would ask him, hoping for a "No" to confirm they were doing the right thing.

Then he would shake them by saying excitedly, "Still hiring!" as though patriotism, good sense, and American enterprise demanded it. They could either think him mad or be condemned by their own cowardice.

Tom Watson Sr. was gifted with more than his share of determination, will, and drive. Those three things made him one of the wealthiest and most influential men of his time. In the 1930's he was the highest paid man in the country earning him the title of Robber Baron at a time when some were angry with the very rich who often exploited others to earn their money.

While some were angry, most were also fascinated by these powerful, rich men. He quickly became the very first celebrity CEO, a role he was happy to play because he loved the limelight. He believed that his image and IBM's image depended on living large in the public eye. He never thought he was over paid, because he never thought IBM could have succeeded as it did without him.

While his out of control anger might brand him as a man without a conscience, he considered himself a moral man. He despised alcohol and wouldn't let it on the premises of IBM, even monitoring those who drank outside the company to determine if it were excessive.

On the home front, he treated his children like little IBM employees, demanding high marks and perfect conduct. No one is quite sure what he would have been like without Jeanette there to balance some of his more ruthless side, nor does anyone know how different any of them would have been if their dad had been a softer, gentler man. She laid down her own independence and perhaps a lot of her self-esteem to accommodate her powerful husband, but who knows at what expense.

Tom Jr. suffered depression much of his young life, maybe because he knew what the expectations were and that he could not meet them. He was not a good student, popular or athletic, or really even motivated as a youth. He didn't have much to recommend him, but his father never lost hope that he would eventually turn out to be a chip off the old block if his dad only pushed him hard enough. Watson never doubted that determination would win in the end, and his success proved him right - at least in his own mind - in a hundred different situations.

It was not a problem for Watson to think ahead twenty years or a hundred and twenty years. He guided IBM through World War II by producing more war products and fewer domestic ones. He kept demand high with the cut backs for domestic items, at the same time using the war products to grow IBM, positioning it positively for the end of the war. His ability to think ahead was perhaps his finest gift. IBM helped the allies win the war with the efficiency of punch card machines, an early computing technology; however, he also sold machines to the Germans early on, which reportedly were a help to their war machine too. He had a very hard time letting go of an international sale, even in war time.

Sometimes his ego and his belief that he was as great an influence outside IBM as he was inside, led him down political paths that tarnished his image. He was made the president of ICC, the newly established International Chamber of Commerce in 1937. Taking his entire family along with him to Berlin so that he could preside over the meeting, Watson accepted an invitation to meet with Hitler himself, who deceitfully assured him that he had no intention of going to war with anyone.

Watson, usually astute about character and motivation, believed Hitler. Of course, five years later Hitler took much of the world into war. Watson then regretted accepting the medal he had been given by the dictator, for trying to bring world peace through business, an idea that Watson adamantly believed in. To his credit, he tried to send the medal back, although some felt it was only to shore up his reputation which was tainted by the incident. He had been bedazzled by the light of his own image, fancying himself to be perhaps the only man in the world who could bring about world peace by stopping Hitler with his own daring leadership. It was a vanity and arrogance that the world took note of: Tom Watson believed that his persuasion and power were limitless and irresistible, that he was now a head of state, leader of the country of IBM.

Tom Jr. was assigned to follow in his dad's footsteps. He ran from the "call" like a Jonah.

Being president of IBM was Watson's life, so naturally he wanted both of his sons to grow up and join the company; his fathering was dedicated to getting them ready to join the ranks. Although one of his daughters had more of his personality and would have likely done well in the company which was opening to women in management, he never encouraged them to join IBM, but rather wanted them to marry well. He loved the thought of a Watson dynasty at IBM and groomed his boys for the task. In the case of Dick, he actually created an international department for him to run, because Dick had an affinity for languages, speaking seven well enough to do business in all of them.

Ironically, however, it had been under his leadership, that IBM grew to become the largest company in the world.

Tom Jr. was assigned to follow in his dad's footsteps. He ran from the "call" like a Jonah, and probably would not have succeeded if he hadn't been mentored and believed in by General Bradley, the commander of the First Air Force, during the war. Tom became his aid, indispensable to the general. "Indispensable" was not a concept that his father had embraced, and the relationship was undoubtedly a healing one to young Tom. The lessons he learned from the general in the war and later at the Pentagon were invaluable to him. The general's confidence in him as a leader brought to the front an orderly mind and an unusual ability to zero in on what was really important.

Even when Tom decided to surrender to the family destiny, although his dad was pleased, the old man still fought him all the way holding tightly to the reins. The father gave the company over to the son at 82, just six weeks before he died, apparently unable to perceive himself as limited by age or health, or to perceive his son as competent, groomed and ready. The father still believed he was the singular driving force of IBM. For twenty years his peers had been enjoying retirement while he had remained in charge of IBM.

Tom Watson Sr.'s soul was tied to IBM and when it soared, so did he, and when it dipped slightly, his mood came crashing down with it. He led with the strength of his determination and will, and after his death in 1956, his own family seemed to sort of sadly fall apart without him. Tom Jr. eventually felt compelled to demote Dick, causing Dick to find his way out of IBM, but never out of alcoholism and his sense of failure. Dick died at 55 from falling down a marble staircase in his own home.

Tom Jr. ran IBM for 15 years, until he had a heart attack at age 55. He never went back to IBM after the heart attack, but turned instead to the pursuits he had always loved, especially flying and adventure. Ironically, however, it had been under his leadership, that IBM grew to become the largest company in the world.

One wonders if Tom Sr. would have congratulated himself on his wisdom in making Tom Jr. his successor, or whether he would have picked up some reports, found some flaws and stepped to the plate to help his son become better at his job.

Chapter 6
Maybe God was Disappointed in Him

Mary could feel her heart racing as they entered Nazareth at the exact time of day when it was awash in light and long shadows from the setting sun. The familiar town looked dusty and habitually tired - like she imagined they did. To be home and steps away from her family caused Mary's heart to surge with joyous anticipation as well as panicked apprehension.

She was so focused on not drowning in the river of her feelings that she hardly noticed the whispers of the last-minute shoppers at the market or those who were loitering in doorways. "Joseph and Mary are back!" The word was relayed through cupped hands from doorway to doorway, causing a few of the curious to dart to their windows to see them pass.

Mary looked intently at the back of Joseph's head as he walked just ahead of her. While she enjoyed watching the sun dance on his thick brown curls, there was something deeply symbolic about his posture and she couldn't help but drink reassurance from it.

His shoulders were squared, his face set, his eyes never directly meeting the stares of the townspeople. He intentionally ignored their prying eyes and gossiping tongues as he always had in that remarkable way of his. He appeared oblivious, but she knew him well enough to know that he was not.

To her, he was a hero in every sense of the word.

Humility and determination formed the core of this rock-solid man of simple faith. What a hero he had been! He had earned her respect and gratitude every day with his strong, courageous heart, and his simple, steadfast ways had become a familiar bedrock of comfort to her along their precarious journey. They had come full circle today and through all of their experiences Joseph had proved himself to be unshakeable.

He had been her point of stability throughout their journey that was filled with the kinds of shocking events and abrupt transitions which her soul hated. It was Joseph who brought her peace and security. Hadn't he taken this role that was thrust upon him and embraced it with all that he had within him? To her, he was a hero in every sense of the word.

There had been so much upheaval in their lives in the last three years. He would never understand what a relief it was to her that he had been able to deal with all the change so effortlessly. He had no need to be personally understood, for acclaim or self-indulgence. He never highlighted his own needs or demanded solace for his losses. Waiving his rights as he had, he continually amazed her with his ability to sacrifice his will and his own way.

Mary marveled at his phenomenal inner strength in the face of relentless transition and instability.

Joseph had laid down his life for her in a hundred ways and she praised God, who in His characteristic perfect wisdom could not have designed a better husband for her. She still marveled at how, from the time the angel first spoke to him, Joseph had been able to accept without question his role as protector to her and Jesus. Their journey had cost him dearly. He had to believe the impossible, withstand humiliation, obey angels and dreams, establish his trade over and over again, and demonstrate continually his ability to choose their safety over everything else.

Surely God had known He could trust this simple man, and she experienced deep gratitude that he had been the one whose job it was to walk with her every step of the way. She loved him dearly. More importantly, she trusted him implicitly.

Mary wasn't alone in her high esteem for Joseph because almost everyone liked him. Whatever one disliked in one's own self never seemed to be so glaring in Joseph's eyes. He never focused on the weaknesses in others; in fact, he seemed to ignore their deficiencies completely. Ironically, though, while he appeared to be totally blind to glaring brokenness in another, he could swiftly spot a place of need buried deep inside in what you thought was a well hidden nook. Usually, when he moved to meet the need, he did it with such discreet humility that any initial discomfort passed quickly. He didn't begrudge helping anyone, was not stingy with his time, and gave of himself in such a way that others were able to accept help without embarrassment.

For 30 years Joseph could remember very little happening to him that would have been interesting or exciting to anyone else.

His life had been measured by piles of sawdust on a carpenter's shop floor or by helping his neighbors with mundane tasks he felt were insignificant, but were deemed highly important and desperately needed by those who received his help. Nothing about his life had ever been characterized by impulse, intrigue, or surprise of any kind. These last few years had certainly made up for his slow start. How remarkably extraordinary and unpredictable his life had become, and he had never, not once, looked or wished for it.

Joseph held Jesus' hand tightly as the two of them walked ahead of Mary. He was consciously ignoring the gossip of the townsfolk and was also utterly oblivious to her thoughts about him. What he did feel was an overwhelming love and protectiveness toward this precious child whom God has entrusted to his care - he could not love Him more had He been his own. He moved his hand to the boy's shoulder and gave Him a reassuring squeeze. "This will be home now, son. We've come back home."

After the angel came, his assignment went from being an above-average husband to becoming a protector on a much grander scale.

There is something so amazing about this child, Joseph thought as he looked into Jesus' eyes, alive with light and curiosity. *I have always wanted to give Him the very best.* He cringed inwardly for the ten thousandth time as he remembered the stable and the night Jesus was born. Would he always feel so dismal about that experience? He had been determined to see that his young wife's firstborn arrived with every comfort she deserved, yet nothing had turned out as he planned. He had failed somehow; he was sure of it. Mary had never reproached him, nor had God seemed to mind, but still to this day he wished he could have done better and made it more comfortable and pleasant for her. She had been so vulnerable and trusting, convinced that her husband would provide for her, and he had failed miserably.

When he first decided to marry her, he had felt quite capable of protecting her and keeping her safe. He had his carpenter's trade, so he was confident that with hard work and God's help they would be financially secure. His greatest desire was for her to feel well cared for, resting securely in his ability to provide for them. After the angel came, his assignment went from being an above-average husband to becoming a protector on a much grander scale.

As he watched the drama unfold, he was thrilled to be a spectator.

Travel and life-threatening situations had not entered his mind when he evaluated his ability to be a good husband. Now, with the stakes much higher, his desire to protect her intensified to the point of it being all he could think about much of the time. But even so, it was not burdensome. It was glorious! It became his obsession - a place where God's requirements and his deepest joy became one. What a fortunate and happy circumstance to be commissioned by an angel to do what was already in his heart to do! He would have taken it seriously without the angelic visitation, but now it had been catapulted into the most crucial assignment of his life.

Merely being responsible would never be enough because God was depending on him. Mary and Jesus were his personal life call. It was this passion and dedication to his most serious and holy assignment that had caused that night in Bethlehem to be so utterly humiliating for him.

"No room here."

"Sorry, no more room. You are way too late."

As door after door had slammed shut in his face, he became frustrated and embarrassed. When the benevolent innkeeper offered his stable, it was a crushing blow to his pride. The one thing he had determined to do with utmost competence - make provision for Mary - and he was able to do in only in the most rudimentary and distasteful fashion.

The stable was only one step up from an open field or worse yet, a city street. He remembered it all: the strange darkness, the sounds of unhappy animals disturbed by human intruders, the mingled repugnant smells, and the midwife's rude mumblings about the situation that was as appalling to her as it was to him.

Filling in the background of the memories from that night was Mary's sweet gratitude to God for watching over them and bringing the child safely into the world. He was grateful for God's protection, grateful for the roof over their heads, but he couldn't help but think that maybe God was disappointed with the man He picked for this job.

Dismissing the embarrassing thought of the stable, he relived a more pleasant memory: the night the Magi came. *The angel warned me of what was to come. Why am I still so shocked to be here? It seems like a dream,* Joseph had thought. He greeted the men, invited them in, offered them what little food he had, and stepped back discreetly into the shadows so he could safely and quietly wonder at it all.

One minute he had been at a loss to provide for his wife and the next minute foreign dignitaries were bringing expensive gifts into his humble home. He felt somehow that their visit was right, that the gifts were appropriate, but if truth be told he also felt awkward in their presence. As he watched the drama unfold, he was thrilled to be a spectator. These elegantly robed men with their fine gifts and beautiful beasts had come a long way to find Jesus and worship Him.

Should Jesus rise to power, Joseph hoped that he would be relieved of further responsibilities. *If Jesus becomes King of Israel, I am determined not to let it influence or alter my life!* Joseph thought to himself. He looked into the last rays of the sinking sun and wondered if it was the sun or this familiar street that caused these unbidden thoughts from far away and lofty places to cascade into his mind.

Joseph would never understand why he had been given such a big assignment. Even now he imagined he had been drawn into the plot merely because of his love for Mary. His goal in life had been to marry her, settle down in Nazareth, and live out his days as a carpenter. He had been certain he was meant to lead a conventional, ordinary life.

He did not have ambitions beyond that, nor had he changed his goals and wishes in the light of the unusual circumstances. He was still the same Joseph the angel first visited. None of these strangely dramatic events had really changed this simple carpenter from Nazareth, except that he trusted Yahweh more now than he did at first. Would he be content if nothing miraculous or spectacular ever came his way again? He decided it would be an incredible relief, and he secretly longed for that peace and stability for just a second before he filed the wish under "Impossible."

Many times Joseph had prayed, "Yahweh, help me understand," and had never received true understanding. Did it please God that he chose to obey when he didn't understand, when the facts were so sketchy and the outcome so unpredictable that he had to walk blindly in simple obedience? It never seemed enough to him. Maybe if he could understand more he would have more faith. Maybe then he could set out with the boldness of a true risk taker. In his mind all he had ever really done was stand by Mary's side, not really comprehending the magnitude of the journey but beginning it all the same. There was nothing heroic about that.

Joseph was not an impulsive man who was reckless with decisions, nor did he crave adventure. Maybe the fact that none of this life would have been his choice made him better for the job. He would never wonder if he had chosen this path to suit himself or his own personal ambition. He doubted his own mind and his decisions, but he didn't doubt the Lord's instructions and the reasonableness of obedience. It hadn't been easy to uproot and leave in the middle of the night or go to another country or even come back home, but he could say with some confidence that he had learned to trust the outcome.

Sometimes he felt God trusted him instead of the other way around.

Surrendering to the voice of the angel meant overcoming logic and reason, not to mention fear. But once he realized that the path of understanding was hopelessly closed to him, he merely followed through. When you can't understand, just obey. *Really,* thought Joseph, *it is a relief not to have to find logical answers to every strange thing that happens to us.*

But wouldn't you know it! Just when he had decided that all he ever needed to do to please God was obey, God stopped giving him explicit instructions and he had to make major decisions on his own. It was simple when God told him to leave Egypt. Just obey. His plan had been to go back to Bethlehem, but here he was in Nazareth having determined that this was safer for the boy.

Was he being led even when he didn't know he was? Sometimes he felt God trusted him instead of the other way around. Joseph sighed, thankful to return to the familiar, ordinary life that he had once known. *I am no hero,* he thought, *just a carpenter returning home.*

Father looked down on the little procession entering Nazareth and was pleased with this man and his thoughts. "To obey is better than sacrifice." It had not been hard for Joseph to obey.

It was precisely THAT, not the obedience itself, which made him a treasure to his Father, a perfect choice, just as God had known all along that he would be.

Chapter 7

The Redneck Messiah

Huey Long was shouting from a platform of empty cartons to a small, curious crowd that had stopped their Saturday shopping in Winnsboro, Louisiana to listen to him. His brown curly hair had begun to take off in diverse directions, his perpetual motion enabling it to free itself from the oily tonic meant to keep it in place. With every wave of his hands, he ran his fingers nervously through it, trying to tame it while he was taming the crowd.

"Who is he?" someone asked.

"Says his name is Huey, and he's running for governor."

"Has he ever run for anything before?"

"Says he's on the Railroad Commission."

He wore a white linen suit and a black bow tie, and his suit pants were too short, exposing white shoes and white socks. He never stopped pacing while he talked, expending a tremendous amount of energy that hypnotized the listeners, while his words were delivered like pummeling, shocking blows. He had the crowd stunned, for he had just attacked its leading citizen, and while a number of people were horrified, someone in the group had snickered with approval.

Huey was executing his most masterful charade - acting outraged on behalf of the poor - for he had no idea about the character of the town's leading citizen he had just maligned, since he had only just found out his name from a passer-by. If the victim of his tirade had been standing on the first row, Huey wouldn't have recognized him, but he needed power to accomplish his agenda, and if he played his cards right, these people would give it to him.

He was playing the crowd like a con man.

He was counting on class rivalry, appealing to the poor man's plight and maybe his envy and jealousy, in hopes that the comfortable status of the leading citizen might elicit a sneering response from someone in the crowd. If he could get enough agreement by going for the negative, he could win them over. He was playing the crowd like a con man, except he wasn't selling snake oil, he was selling Huey Long, and he knew just how to do it.

"What is the trouble in Louisiana? Why I'll tell you. The main trouble is that a small percent of the people have all the wealth. Too few have too much and too many have too little."

There were a few "amens" from a couple of men who were used to agreeing with the preacher when he made a good point, and Huey was preachin' for sure. This was a small rural town filled with farmers, many of them share croppers, and these were lean years right before the Great Depression. Times were hard, and many of the farmers felt they had been made even harder by rich land owners who rented them the land they wouldn't sell to them, and then took an unfair share of the profits, leaving less for the man who worked the land.

The way food prices had been dropping lately, people who grew food were hurting. They never seemed to be able to get ahead, and most of the time, they were hardly breaking even. They needed cheap loans to put in their crops and to sustain them in the rough seasons, and although they weren't the type of people who wasted time complaining, Huey was appealing to whatever self-pity and bitterness they did have, and he was calling it "fairness and equality." It sounded good.

"We have every resource we need in this country, and we don't need to ask the good Lord for nothin' else. But I want to ask you, would you have a barbeque and invite a thousand people and then let one man sneak up and run off with all the food? There is plenty to go around, and government ought to do something about sharing the wealth God gave us. Sixty-five percent of the people in this country only got 5 percent of the wealth. How is that fair?"[1]

He could justify anything that took power away from the elite and gave it to him.

He had them in the palm of his hand. Huey was a populist in the agrarian South who believed that government should intervene to insure economic equality. He was demanding reform in a place where poor men and women were working hard but getting further and further behind. His idealistic message of equality gave them hope, and he could expound on this kind of idealism until the cows came home, making him seem like he was the most benevolent guy in the world.

They called him the Kingfish after a character on the Amos and Andy radio show. He liked the name, for it symbolized his place at the top, and it was certain that no one ever made a bigger splash in the proverbial, muddy, shark-infested waters of Louisiana politics, or swam with more flair than Huey did. Once he convinced the people of Louisiana to give him power, he wielded it like a dictator, causing historians to label him The Redneck Messiah. He could justify anything that took power away from the elite and gave it to him.

According to Huey's mother, he had walked at nine months, but even before he was able to walk, she claimed he would roll right off the porch, crawl across the yard, and somehow unlatch the gate, in order to sit on the side of the road and watch the passers-by. No one doubted her story, because people were his obsession, whether they fell into the enemy camp or the friend camp. There wasn't much that Huey let stop him, and he had a reputation for never doing anything he didn't enjoy, and that included farm work. He grew up in a family of farmers and enraged his siblings who weren't as good at escaping their chores as Huey was. He was known as the show off in the family, the bossy kid who was always belligerent and ornery, and who usually butted in where he wasn't invited, arguing his point whether it was welcomed or not.

Huey graduated from law school by the time he was twenty one, taking the bar after only one year of classes. He made a good lawyer, practicing for a number of years in Shreveport, Louisiana, fighting big corporations such as Standard Oil on behalf of the little man. However, he felt politics was the place he could put all of his skills to use, for he was a natural born influencer, orator, and schemer. Huey was a mover and a shaker, a Robin Hood trying to take from the rich to give to the poor, but he was also shamelessly ambitious for power, unencumbered by the kind of basic morality that usually keeps politicians from being too brash. He thrived on attention, positive or otherwise, and he was audacious enough to believe that he should run the whole country.

He ran for his first office, railroad commissioner, in 1918 when he was twenty-five. The Public Service Commission, as it was later called, became the platform from which Huey fought Standard Oil, since that committee had oversight of the regulations enforced on utilities and transported goods. He became something of a hero when he went up against Cumberland Telegraph and Telephone Company and prosecuted them for unfair rate hikes and forced them to refund $440,000 to its customers. He was already earning a reputation as a champion of the little guy and people were impressed by his sharp legal mind.

Politically, he was a Democrat and a populist. He wanted government to intervene and make prosperity more attainable for everyone. He wanted to see shorter work days, redistribution of wealth, salary caps at the top, and greater economic equality. He believed in sharing the wealth, and felt there was no better man to divide the American pie than he. Huey would be called a socialist by his adversaries, and many other things less kind, but he had despised the rich and the powerful all of his life and he didn't care what they called him. There was nothing like the right set of enemies to attract the right set of friends, and Huey was an expert at making enemies.

While Huey never minded an enemy or two, he was at the same time hungry for the admiring acceptance of his supporters. He was a natural orator, one who would do or say anything to win the crowd over. He was dramatic, fiery, and able to shock his audiences in order to manipulate them, which he customarily did by attacking one of the town's leading citizens and appealing to the man's foes.

Even if his listeners had nothing against the man he attacked - which a few always did - the majority still couldn't help but be impressed with Huey's sheer audacity. People often felt unable to say what they thought in small rural towns for fear of ostracism or reprisal, and here was an outsider, as bold as a rabid dog, saying whatever he wished. They were shocked by his candid opinions, and that usually won him respect of some kind.

His lust for power was never really satisfied.

Few realized how insincere he was in his tirades, or recognized that he was manipulating them in order to seize power for himself. He wanted his supporters' approval as much as he wanted their votes, and while he got plenty of affirmation, no amount of allegiance ever seemed to fill his bucket, at least not for long. His lust for power was never really satisfied, and when his opponents realized how far it might take him, he was already well on his way.

Huey was not discouraged by the fact that almost every town and city in the state was accustomed to being run by powerful individuals who were part of a well controlled political system. The parish bosses owed their allegiance to a New Orleans machine that ran the state and united the parishes under its umbrella. It was an entrenched political system that no one had either the guts or the desire to challenge.

Huey recognized that the sheer number of disenfranchised citizens could overcome its power with their votes, but an enforced poll tax in Louisiana kept the poor away from the voting booths. Before he could change that, he would have to beat them first at their own game. He would wrestle the power away from them by going straight for the people who were able to vote, but were being ignored by the corrupt system, and he would do it by exposing the culprits, by name if he knew them. These local bosses were about to meet their match, and if they wanted to stop him, they'd have to outwit him. While in the beginning, some of his ideas might have been idealistic, his methods never were.

Huey never minded a lie if it served his purpose because he always figured his good plan outweighed his shady means of securing it. He told the Protestants up north about hitching up the wagon and taking his Baptist grandparents to church on Sunday, and he told the French Catholics in the south about hitching up the wagon and taking his Catholic grandparents to mass every Sunday. When questioned about the discrepancy, he answered, "Heck, we didn't even have a horse."[2]

To hear him tell it, he grew up poor and understood the raw deal the poor got. Nothing could have been further from the truth, for he grew up as the son of a wealthy farmer, but he never aspired to fit in with wealthy men. He would remain too common for the upper class, even while he was governor. He always acted like he didn't care that they snubbed him, for he was dedicated to ousting them from their position of privilege anyway. He had his following, people of his choosing, and he was impervious to the enemies he made along the way, especially if a new high class enemy made him a new low class friend. It was us against them to Huey, and the "us" he chose were the downtrodden, who seemed happy enough to accept him as a leader and a voice. Huey was determined to lead and to change things, and making allies of the lower class came easy to him; they handed him power with childlike trust.

Louisiana politics at the time was different from other states, even other Southern ones. There seemed to be a psychological dynamic to politics in Louisiana that accepted corruption as a distasteful but unavoidable part of the game. There was usually a tolerance - or a disgusted resignation - about corruption, and the politician who could out bluster, out maneuver, outwit, and demolish the competition was often even admired, despite his tactics. If his shenanigans had certain flair and made a humorous story, it would probably bear repeating hundreds of time and pass from parish to parish.

Stories about Huey Long went ahead and behind him, ricocheting from one town to another. The Anglo-Saxon North and the French Canadian South had always been politically of two minds, but oddly enough, here was a man that both sides seemed to appreciate, one who was a political genius, part bully, and part hero. They told themselves that he was no worse than the rest, except he was looking out for them and the other crooks only cared about themselves. In some ways it was true, and there was plenty of injustice to rail against. There were those who had inherited privilege and wealth, and their secure positions had never been challenged. Huey knew full well what he could get by with, and he exploited every wound and slight that the rich had ever given the poor, including his own wounds, and used them to gain personal power. He did the impossible: he united the North and the South, but he did it by dividing the poor from the rich.

He was as flamboyant, diverse, flexible, and mystifying as the state itself. He knew where he was and he never apologized or cared who knew about his strategies. He claimed to have ancestors from every country he thought might help him influence someone today: French, English, Irish, Spanish, and Italian, and he would have claimed African heritage if he thought he could have gotten away with it.

Louisiana was ripe for a Kingfish. When he adopted "Every man a king, but no man wears the crown" as his motto, he was appealing to desperate people who needed a champion and who dreamed of equal opportunity. He was an opportunist who saw himself as a gift to the state, and while he was realistic about injustice and about how vulnerable and pliable men had become all around him, he was grossly unrealistic about the consequences of making so many powerful enemies, or the repercussions of his extreme tactics.

He used the strategy all over the state, and just as he predicted, it worked.

"I'm going to run for governor, and I'll tell you how I'm going to win. In every parish, there is a boss, usually the sheriff. He has forty percent of the votes, forty percent are opposed to him, and twenty percent are in-betweens. I'm going into every town and cuss out the boss. That gives me forty per cent of the votes to begin with, and I'll hoss trade 'em for the in-betweens."[3] People watched, intrigued and amazed, as he went from parish to parish and did exactly what he said he would do. He went into town, got up on a stump, and went after the sheriff. Then he would head to the hotel and wait for the sheriff's enemies to show up. That bunch would become his grass roots organization in that town and then he would move on. He used the strategy all over the state, and just as he predicted, it worked.

He appealed to the downtrodden, the powerless, and the voiceless, and although they didn't have individual power to give him, when they handed him all of the combined power of their votes, he had all he needed. Did Huey use the poor for his own ambition and his need to be powerful and admired? Sure he did, but then they set their hopes on him and he didn't forget them. To Huey and his followers, it was a win-win, for he did what he said: he fought big business, gave them free textbooks, provided better educations, built roads, and overhauled the court systems, all while trimming fat off state spending. He told himself that he was helping the little man, but he gloried unabashedly in the power and fame the Kingfish got for his efforts.

Huey was always on the attack, and one of his favorite targets was the New Orleans political machine which never bowed to Huey. It remained his arch enemy until the bitter end, because it always knew there was nothing to be gained by giving in to Huey. It stubbornly refused to hand over control to Huey, and while he had taken much of their parish muscle away from them, it remained more organized and powerful than the rural machines. They were insulted by his gall, his manners, and his supporters, and they developed a particular loathing for his rise to power.

When he attacked newspapers who insulted him or big corporations, his victims howled in protest, but their protests only served to make them appear guilty because they were usually so vehemently outraged. Although Standard Oil officials referred to him as a "braying ass" and "loco coyote," they were powerless to shut him up. He spoke for the little man and he went after the big boys that the little man was entirely powerless to confront.

Huey had a surprisingly vulnerable core where he allowed these men to go.

He promised a new day in Louisiana, a solution to the way things had always been. What he gave the people was a class war and he felt righteously proud to be on the side of the underdog. While he was pious about the dark side of human nature that divided men into classes and kept them there, he was entirely unremorseful about his own dark side of political maneuvering and calculated divisiveness.

The first time he ran for governor in 1924, it was a political leap from the Public Works Commission, especially since he had no big endorsements. No one had ever been elected before without an endorsement from the sugar interests, the railroads, or the banks. It was an outrageously daring move for Huey to go for governor. Although he was an unknown, he came close to winning anyway.

Not to be humiliated by the outcome, he spread the story that rain had caused his defeat. Rain, according to Huey, kept the poor farmers home and that cost him the election. That lie brought little comfort to his opponents, who realized they would never be able to keep him out again, and they were right. Four years later he would become governor, even though he was bawdy, loud, egocentric, and often ridiculous. He seemed to be a caricature of a simplistic Southern redneck politician, but his moves were complex and calculated, and his success is a testimony to how many people he impressed with his larger than life persona.

He had a group of associates from all over the state and nation, many of whom were close friends. He counted on those closest to him for emotional support. The group of men who rallied around him and supported him were called the Longites and they were exclusively "his men." They traded on their complete loyalty to Huey for places of influence and positions in government. Whether they were as convinced in their minds as Huey was about the price of reform is questionable, but they were, nevertheless, appointed to high positions in the state and local government. They were called "suckling pigs" by their adversaries, a derogatory picture of their willingness to take what they could get from Huey while clinging to his power. His organization used gang politics to intimidate and coerce when they deemed it necessary. Huey went so far as to take money out of their state salaries to sponsor his organization, if those positions had been gifts from the governor.

He was so thoroughly disliked that anything he touched died on the floor.

Huey depended on his allies and those closest to him who were men he was very vulnerable with and whose opinions he actually listened to. Betrayal or rejection at that level would have been extremely devastating to Huey emotionally, but it would have been politically suicidal to them, so his friends usually remained his friends. Huey had a surprisingly vulnerable core where he allowed these men to go, and they prided themselves on being close enough to Huey to know his needs and meet them.

Huey was elected the governor of Louisiana in 1928, but when a U. S. Senate seat became available in 1930, he ran for it and won. He had no intention of giving up the governorship before he had enacted many of his reforms, so he refused to step down and go to Washington. He did that for fourteen months until proceedings were about to force him to step down, so finally he left and appointed his man to take his place. When chided for not assuming his congressional seat, he responded that the former Senator had done so little that his seat had been vacant for a long time already. The senate seat was his calculated stepping stone to the presidency of the United States, because he planned to oust Roosevelt who was too conservative to suit him. Although Huey was popular with many people in the country, he was not a beloved senator among his peers. He was so thoroughly disliked that anything he touched died on the floor.

Although Huey eventually moved on to Washington, he still kept Louisiana in his back pocket, making return trips to the state when important votes were on the floors of the legislature. He would cheerlead the vote, running up and down the aisles, sometimes shouting out the vote for his men, if they were too slow to suit him. It was such a time in early September of 1935 that Huey showed up to see that New Orleans got the punishment it deserved for its long, adversarial relationship with him. New Orleans was in a position to receive federal aid, but he planned to intervene and make it impossible for them to get it, by getting a bill passed maintaining that federal intervention would violate state's rights. It was a ploy to squeeze them into submission.

A special session had been called to pass the bill, and Huey had showed up. He was well aware of an organization that had vowed to stop his antics one way or the other, the Square Dealers. They had been meeting secretly, had already stormed the East Baton Rouge Court House once in an attempt to take over, and they had made it clear that they were fed up with Huey. Although he had been warned by his men not to appear, Huey didn't fear the Square Dealers. He would not be intimidated when he was finally in a position to destroy the New Orleans power base. He was not about to miss that triumph.

When a usually mild-mannered local doctor who was known to hate Huey approached him in a corridor before the session, no one perceived the danger that Huey was in, not even his body guards. Huey responded to the man with his customary arrogance, there was a physical struggle, and to everyone's complete amazement, the doctor pulled out a gun and shot him. Huey was mortally wounded, and although he was coherent for a few hours, his chief reaction was utter dismay. He kept asking "Why did he shoot me?" Apparently Huey had believed enemies were his own manageable creations, figments of his imagination, to be used by him for political means, not actual enemies that might turn on him and destroy him. In his own mind, he had been an indestructible hero, an intrepid legend: the Kingfish.

In his own mind, he had been an indestructible hero, an intrepid legend: the Kingfish.

Huey died surrounded by the people who loved him, men who would attempt to carry out his vision for many years ahead.

Friends and politicians filled up the hospital, even the operating room, and then the private room to which he was moved after the surgery. No one was able to get them to leave, and they remained with him to the end.

His last words were, "God, don't let me die. I have so much to do."[4] He had always thought that time was his only real enemy, and in the end, it was. He had planned to run in the next presidential election, and he had just finished his new book, My First Days in the White House, incredibly confident that the future he dreamed of was close enough to touch. He had already plunged himself into it in his imagination.

Mystery clouded the assassination, for a proper investigation was never really carried out. The coroner was not allowed to examine the body, statements were not given by all of the body guards, and no autopsy was done, plus the assassin was killed immediately and could not be questioned. Some have concluded there was a conspiracy, or that a random shot by a body guard seeking to defend him, might have mortally wounded him.

Huey was only forty-two years old when he died, still full of ideas, his powers of persuasion in tact. One hundred thousand mourners made their way through the new state capitol building he had built, in order to pay their respects to Huey, more than four times the population of Baton Rouge itself.

His ability to influence masses of people had carried him so far that it became the very thing that his enemies feared the most.

However, his ruthless tactics had reaped ruthlessness, and he had died by the sword.

Chapter 8
He was a Mystery to the King

The carefree, young prince skipped happily toward the old woman, jumping into her outstretched arms and covering her wrinkled face with his kisses. He plunged his chubby, little fingers into his pocket and retrieved a precious treasure he had found for her on the way: a gray rock with faint red veins, which he offered her proudly.

"It is lovely, little one," she said as she sat down to study it more closely. "You brought it for me?"

He nodded, his wide eyes sparkling. Jehoshaphat adored this old woman, who of all the people in his life, always had time for him and his childish games. She preferred to be touching nature, just like he did, and she too was moved by mystical colors, the smells of the flowers, and the textures of rocks, along their quiet walks. She shared a respect and a yearning for the world's beauty with her delightful great-grandson, a precious little boy who expressed his heart in countless ways beyond words.

She allowed him to be quiet, not growing impatient when he stopped to study an outstanding rock or a scurrying beetle, or to peer into the face of a flower expressing his approval of its fragrance with an explosive sneeze. She listened intently when he explained to her what he heard the beetle say on his way to "the place where he was going in such a hurry," and although she sometimes wanted to laugh, she did not, rather accepting his inspired translation with affirming nods of her head and a curiosity that equaled his.

Because he was a tender child who could be hurt easily, she was troubled when her grandson, King Asa, demanded that the child act perfectly or answer quickly. The little boy usually thought about things carefully for awhile before he gave a good answer, and that did not suit his father. Queen Maacha was the one person who seemed to understand him completely, perhaps because she tried, or perhaps because they were very much alike. She was an entirely safe place for Jehoshaphat, since she was always happy to see him running toward her, never spoke harshly to him, and always protected him. He would curl up in her lap and she would brush the hair from his forehead while he drank in the acceptance in her eyes, and then he was perfectly at peace.

His father, King Asa, was a completely different story. Although the king had vowed to serve God and had rid Judah of its idols, he sometimes exploded into angry outbursts, and to Jehoshaphat nothing was more terrifying. When his formidable father was focused on a task, he was totally driven to see it done, brutal to anyone who opposed him or slowed him down, and oppressive to the over burdened workers with his ever increasing demands for perfection and productivity. Jehoshaphat's temperament was a mystery to the king, for he sincerely believed that nothing could be accomplished without loud and abusive oversight, and that a leader who was not demanding was weak.

Privately, to Azubah, his wife, he would say, "How will such a strange, shy child ever govern the kingdom?", and then he would redouble his efforts to make a "man" out of his dreamy and sensitive son. Jehoshaphat was told repeatedly that one day he would be king, and far from inspiring him, it overwhelmed him and made him want to escape to some other place, one that was safe and happy, free of problems and demands. He would have preferred being a musician, for it was music that carried him away on its wings, but of course, his father would not hear of such pursuits.

He knew if being king meant becoming like his father, he was surely doomed to fail. He really hoped his childhood would go on indefinitely, for although he tried to please his father in every way he knew how, rarely did the "right way" come to him. He was in no hurry to grow up, although it did happen, suddenly and sadly in a single day.

On a particularly beautiful summer day, before his tenth birthday, Queen Maacha took the little boy with her to the hills to show him her secret place. There, she showed him a pole she was having carved to the goddess, Asherah. The pole had the figure of a nude woman in the center, two ferocious lions standing beside her, and flowers and snakes in her hands. Jehoshaphat's immediate reaction was to cover his face from the grotesque image, for the pole terrified him, and then inexplicably, he shivered with fear. He had heard that some people thought the goddess brought forth life and there were those who secretly worshipped her, flagrantly insulting their own God and behaving like the pagans they were meant to conquer, but he could not imagine Asherah's connection to life, for all he could feel was death all around him.

Just as quickly, he shuddered a second time, this one prompted by a flash of his father's face. He knew that his great-grandmother had become increasingly stubborn and defiant in her old age, and more than a little senile, but he also knew that what she had done was strictly forbidden by God's laws. If his father found out, she would be in terrible trouble. He couldn't bear to look at it, because the goddess' eyes were staring menacingly at him, and even the beautiful grove of trees started to feel strange as if the wind had shifted or the temperature had suddenly dropped. It was a hideously ugly pole, and yet his beloved great-grandmother was regarding it with a strange pride, as though it were a thing of beauty.

He knew this was a serious quandary, and his conscience burned within him.

On their journey back down the mountain, Jehoshaphat was lost in his thoughts trying to decide what he must do. He knew this was a serious quandary, and his conscience burned within him. He loved his great-grandmother, but he feared his father. He didn't want to betray his great-grandmother, his truest friend, but to be discovered by his father and thought to be her accomplice was a frightening and sobering prospect.

Then there was the whole matter of God himself and what he required; he certainly didn't want to offend God. What should he do? When they returned, he learned that a soldier, who had been informed by a spy up in the hills, had already told his father and there would be terrible repercussions. His great-grandmother was immediately whisked away by a guard and later his father deposed the Queen Mother, and gave instructions to keep Jehoshaphat away from her. He was dismayed and heart broken.

That had happened twenty-five years ago. The Queen Mother had not lived long after the incident, but he had never stopped missing her, especially now that he was about to be crowned king of Judah at his father's death. He wanted to be a good king, and he determined to maintain all of his father's beneficial policies. Although he never attempted to mimic his father's style of leadership, he did many things he was sure his father would approve of, the chief one being to strengthen the military, placing troops in all of the cities where Israel might attack Judah.

He proved to be a good listener, able to accept wise counsel, and faithful to seek the Lord's instructions.

He acquired great wealth and honor, and the people spoke kindly of him as a man of compassion, devoted to the Lord, and able to rule without anger or malice. He was compassionate to the poor, and provided for the widows and the orphans, organizing the distribution of food or clothing with precision, when it was necessary. In one respect, however, he was entirely different from his father in that he was rarely seen among the people. Jeshoshaphat hated crowds, and he avoided them when he could. He preferred to rule from behind the scenes, but there he proved to be a good listener, able to accept wise counsel, and faithful to seek the Lord's instructions so that he prospered on every front.

Jehoshaphat believed that if his people were properly instructed in the law and if they lived with integrity, they would be much safer and happier, so he sent teachers throughout the land to instruct the people. Because he hated conflict and chaos, he was willing to see that the nation was protected from her foes, but he understood that the people needed to heed God's instructions or there would be no peace from within.

He removed the high places and stopped the worship of Asherah, for he never forgot how he had felt the day his great-grandmother led him to the vile place in the grove. For Jehoshaphat, it was much more than God's law that kept him from foreign gods; he had seen their power to influence and divide and to destroy. He wanted no part of the delusion that false worship would produce good results, for he knew it would cause God, their only ally, to refuse to come to their aid and he had no confidence that he could rule without God's mercy.

Jehoshaphat's heart wanted to please God, and because he did not just obey in external rote ways, a true fear of God permeated the land. Even foreigners, Arabs and Philistines, brought tribute to him because they enjoyed the peace of his reign, and they respected him and his devotion to his God. He continued to build; fortifying Jerusalem with even more fighting men, for Jehoshaphat's greatest worry was for the country's safety. He did not want his subjects to suffer while he was Judah's king, and so he worked hard to insure peace on every front. He, although no one knew, also lived accountable to a hidden standard of his father's approval. He did not want to fail, and especially not in military valor. He did not want Judah to suffer pain because of his blunders,

Even the workers and builders who had despised his father thrived under his command.

and he was well aware of the weaknesses his father always believed he had. He faced the place within himself that hated conflict and determined to see that the nation was ready to defend herself against its strongest enemy, because he knew his own tendency to deny that it might come one day, and the thought of suffering a bloody defeat sickened him.

Making allies came easily to the king because he made friends effortlessly, motivated by sincerity and caring. In fact, he found a way even to align himself with the king of Samaria - the notorious and irreverent King Ahab - by marriage to his daughter. King Ahab's daughter was beautiful, decisive, and fearless, and Ahab was a powerful ally, so Jehoshaphat willingly overlooked Ahab's history. Jehoshaphat had few enemies anywhere, and he thought with pride that of all people, he would be able to get along with King Ahab. Jehoshaphat's style was without threats and control, since he preferred to secure friendly allegiance with his pleasant and gracious personality, respecting others, not offending anyone with outspoken intolerance or brutal honesty. Even the workers and builders who had despised his father thrived under his command, because he regarded their well being as important to the overall peace of the kingdom.

When his wife asked to return home to visit her father, he gladly obliged. Although Ahab treated him well upon his arrival, Ahab was perpetually looking to use anyone to further his kingdom and his acquisitions. He made a proposal to Jehoshaphat to help him attack Ramoth Gilead, a proposal he knew full well that Jehoshaphat would have a hard time declining, since the request was coming from his father-in-law. Just as Ahab had assumed he would, Jehoshaphat agreed, adding as an afterthought: "We must seek the counsel of the Lord."

It was Ahab's custom to surround himself with prophets who always courted him by telling him whatever he wished, knowing that any other "truth" was bound to be an aggravation to him. It was a nod at faith and reliance on God, although because of the way that Ahab controlled the outcome, it was simply a manipulation of the system resulting in a pseudo-blessing that completely lacked God's authority. Predictably, all of Ahab's prophets assured them they would win the battle, but something didn't sit right with King Jehoshaphat's spirit.

He continued to probe until Ahab was forced to call the one prophet who told the truth in the kingdom, a man whom the king despised, and his word was that Ahab would be killed in the battle if they went forward with it. Remarkably, Ahab chose not to listen, believing that he had could manipulate the outcome like he always did. He decided that he could outwit his enemies if he disguised himself in the battle and sent his son-in-law into battle in full kingly robes, a ludicrous proposal to which Jehoshaphat politely agreed.

Exactly as the man of God had said, Ahab, though disguised, was killed by a random arrow in the battle, and Jehoshaphat although dressed in his kingly attire was protected by the Lord and left unharmed. The trip back home was a tortuous one because Jehoshaphat felt remorse and confusion over what had transpired. He was stricken with the pain and sadness his wife was feeling at the loss of her father, and he kept defending himself against it in his mind, remembering that he had not wanted to go into the battle at all and only did it to please the king. Surely that didn't make all of today's events his fault. Wanting to be done with all of it, he was happy to see the palace ahead. Home at last, he stepped wearily down from his carriage, only to be greeted by the flashing eyes of a prophet waiting for his arrival with a stinging message spoken in uncompromised conviction: "Should you help the wicked and love those who hate the Lord?"

Should you help the wicked and love those who hate the Lord? The words hurt. Jehoshaphat always liked to believe he did what he did out of love, and that going to battle with Ahab was a way of honoring him, and that somehow his act of kindness would lead to a change in the king's heart if he continued to love him unconditionally in a submissive and sacrificial way. Truthfully, it was always easier for him to do what people asked of him than to stand up to them and endure their displeasure. He did not like to think of himself as a coward, but his father-in-law was dead, his wife was distraught, and God was not happy with him either, sending him a cruel messenger and a harsh word to bring this sad day to its unhappy conclusion.

In the days that followed, Jehoshaphat determined that he would not offend the Lord again. He went into Ephraim and Beersheba and turned the people's hearts back to their God. He established judges to oversee them and to hear their disputes, and he admonished them to judge rightly, not taking bribes or meting out injustice, but to act courageously in all situations.

Things went very well for King Jehoshaphat until the day that the Moabites and Ammonites and some of the Meunites decided to attack Jehoshaphat. United they were more powerful than all of his defenses, and they were already marching toward Judah when he got the word. There was no way to make any further preparations and no place to run. Quickly, the king proclaimed a fast and asked all of the people to come to the city to seek the Lord as to what they should do. The king himself stood up and sought God in front of the whole assembly saying, "If calamity comes upon us, whether the sword of judgment, or plague or famine, we will stand in your presence before this temple that bears your Name and will cry out to you in our distress, and you will hear us and save us."

An army was coming that was so vast that none of Jehoshaphat's careful preparations were going to insure a victory, and so he defaulted to his vulnerable and contrite heart, invoking the presence of His God, whose heart, if touched, would surely annihilate his fiercest foes.

The answer came when the prophet, Jahaziel, stood to his feet to speak for God: "You will not have to fight this battle. Take up your positions; stand firm and see the deliverance the Lord will give you." A cheer erupted from the people. Jehoshaphat fell down with his face to the ground, and the priests who were standing behind the king began to shout emotional and thankful praises to God.

The next morning, as they set out, Jehoshaphat appointed singers to lead the army, and so men went ahead, singing joyfully, "Give thanks to the Lord, for his love endures forever." They had nothing except their faith and their assurance that God would deliver them as they marched to the battlefield relying on His word.

When they came to the place that overlooked the desert, there was a strange stillness in the air. Not knowing what to expect, for the armies should have been marching below, they approached the ragged cliff. In the gorge below lay hundreds of dead soldiers from three different armies, not a soldier was left alive. The Lord had caused the men of Ammon and Moab to destroy the men of Mount Seir, and then to turn and destroy each other. There was not one left alive, only a hushed valley filled with carnage, shields, armor, and swords strewn carelessly about glistening in the sun, while birds of prey circled lower and lower over the dead.

There was not the slightest doubt Who had won it for them.

The men of Judah descended the mountain to collect the plunder, an activity that lasted three long days. On the fourth day, they assembled and praised the Lord, entering Jerusalem with deafening shouts of praise, laden with treasures, triumphantly parading into the Temple with a joyful symphony of harps and lutes and trumpets. They had experienced a miraculous victory that had not cost them pain and suffering. They had been made victorious and were handed the spoils of war, and there was not the slightest doubt Who had won it for them.

Their God was pleased with their dependence on Him and with their king. The kingdom was at peace at last, and Jehoshaphat had won peace for his people on every side, not through might or power, not through imitating his father or employing methods that were trusted by other great rulers of his day, but with an uncompromised, contrite heart that knew how to align itself with the King of kings.

Chapter 9
She Insisted on the Truth

No one who watched Katie as she walked onto the tennis court could have guessed that she had not grown up as her daddy's "little princess." She was slim and athletic in her tennis whites. Although her hair was casually pulled back in a long ponytail, it only served to make her look younger than her 50 years, accenting her graceful features. She had the stride of a formidable adversary, which in truth she was. She could second-guess the ball and, with quickness and agility, effortlessly arrive where it would land as though she knew its destination beforehand.

She abandoned herself to the game in the same way she did almost everything in her life, working with the fierce intentionality and diligence which often secured her a win. None of her friends minded losing to her, nor did she really mind losing to them when the tables turned. To Katie, it was always about the way she played the game. She was a good player, but she didn't need to win nor did she gloat, and her friends just hoped she would carve time out of her outrageously busy schedule to play because something about her presence made the whole experience richer for each of them. For some of the women their time with Katie was the thing they most looked forward to all week because she had an ability to make them feel they belonged and were extremely valuable.

She had time for only a couple of sets today because she was rushing to get home and prepare for the dinner party she was giving in the evening. Invitations to Katie's dinner parties were coveted due to her legendary hospitality and extravagant gourmet meals. It was the best of both worlds at her house: guests were treated to mouth-watering culinary surprises while their souls were warmed by her genuine acceptance of them as people and her particular way of making them believe the best about themselves. Her friends admired her on many levels and the ones who knew her whole story were amazed by her confidence and caring.

She had four children, three of them grown and out on their own. Everyone agreed Katie was a great mom, one who shared her children's sorrows and celebrated their joys. She and her husband had raised them to be responsible and hard-working but, more than that, they were straightforward and open about how they felt because she had always insisted they face life honestly.

She gladly rearranged her life to be there for them when they needed her, supporting them through all their activities, encouraging them, and sometimes embarrassing them with terms of endearment like "Darling" or "Sweet Peach."

Although her family came first and lived in the security of knowing that, she expected each of her children to walk in reality and was relentless about speaking the truth to them when they edged toward denial even a little bit. Her personal core value was authenticity and her family was not allowed to opt out of it, even had they wanted to.

Her husband was a dynamic leader, but he too took solace in the haven Katie had created, and he was well aware that her prayers had calmed many a treacherous storm that might have threatened their family's safety.

* * *

"Hey, everybody, watch out! Here comes Lizard Face."

"Hey, Lizard Face, Tommy loves you."

Katie ducked her head and pulled her books close to her chest in an effort to protect her heart. She kept her eyes down, hidden behind her massive bush of unruly brown curls. She looked at her feet, pretending to study the floor while she walked as fast as she dared, hoping somehow the speckled black and white tiles would open up and swallow her and never spit her back out. No matter how she determined not to let those words assault her spirit, they always did. She would map an evasive course to her next class hoping to avoid the boys who tormented her, but invariably out of nowhere the words would find her.

Reading had enabled her to cope with the ugly reality of her life.

She pretended that not being pretty, popular, or loved made no difference to her. She longed to be like the brave heroine in a Jane Austen novel who had been abandoned by her true love. She often wished she could live within the pages of her beloved books where she could be a delicate creature, given to extreme moodiness. Then she would languish wistfully in front of the fireplace somewhere in Northern Scotland, or maybe spread her fine skirts under a magnolia tree in the deep South - Charleston, perhaps.

Regardless of the place she dreamed of, she would cast herself, of course, as the most cherished member of her imaginary family. Once she imagined herself to be the youngest daughter of a devoted and handsome father who bought her a pony, like Rhett Butler's Bonnie in Gone with the Wind. Then again, she might pretend to be young Amy in Little Women, whose father had gone off to war and left her with three older sisters and a devoted mother.

It was as if everyone in the world who had been assigned to protect her went AWOL, each at the most inopportune time.

Reading had enabled her to cope with the ugly reality of her life. She could go so deep inside the pages of a book that she would be startled if someone spoke to her, causing her to return abruptly from a faraway place or disengage from a heroine who made suffering seem beautiful. Inside a book she could bathe in melancholy or ride the wings of hope, but best of all she could escape the hell that was her reality.

Lizard Face, that's all you are, a voice in her head often told her, and sometimes she agreed with that voice. She remembered the day it had become her dreaded name. It was spring and her English class was doing descriptive writing. Tommy had asked the teacher at the beginning of the assignment, "Can we write about **anything**?"

"Yes, anything," Mrs. Sloan had answered in encouraging tones, her mood obviously enhanced by the sound of chirping birds and fragrant blossoms on the trees.

Katie had long finished her own assignment and was lost in the beauty outside the classroom window. The grass was so green that she longed for the day to be over so she could walk slowly home, basking in the glorious return of the first warm days. She was hardly listening to the oral reports, but suddenly she heard her own name spoken from the front which drew her back into the cold reality of the classroom.

When Tommy started reading in front of the class, she realized that he had chosen to write about her, specifically about her complexion which had recently begun to suffer from an explosion of hormones, more embarrassing to her than her wild hair.

It was one of those moments when there was no place to run, no way to stop the laughter in the classroom, and no chance in the world to save an ounce of dignity. She looked to Mrs. Sloan for help, but unbelievably she was laughing too. It was the most awful nightmare imaginable. It seemed like the few minutes it took Tommy to read his paper went on for hours and her teacher never tried to stop it.

Mrs. Sloan was not abusive or cruel to the other kids, just to Katie, and no one knew why. Emotional brutality by the students was often tolerated by the teacher unless a child had a parent who would go to bat for them and Katie certainly didn't have one of those. Tommy was the most popular kid in the class, so whatever he said or did was always considered clever, even by Mrs. Sloan.

Katie had liked school until then because it was her one safe place, but that day yet another authority stepped over into the enemy's camp and she had no vestige of safety left. It was as if everyone in the world who had been assigned to protect her went AWOL, each at the most inopportune time.

Sadly, the nickname stuck.

It stuck year after year all the way from junior high right through high school. When the guys could drive, they would cruise by Katie's house at night and yell "Lizard Face" in chorus and then screech off, cloaked by the darkness, laughing uproariously. She wondered sometimes what her parents thought about that name ringing in the night - hurled through the air like a rock, falling with a thud just short of the picture window, doing no real damage to anything important.

If they wondered, they never asked.

In fact, no one asked Katie how she felt about anything. She assumed everyone knew how she felt. It wasn't like things were secret because Katie was quite sure Mom knew what Dad was doing to her. Apparently no one cared about "Lizard Face."

This was the shameful way a young girl could be treated if the people who were meant to protect her had all gone away into some wretched, sinful place and these shadows were left in their stead. No young heroine in any novel Katie had ever read endured this kind of fear and trauma. They had proper problems, mentionable ones that could be discussed with mothers, priests, neighbors - not dark ones too horrendous to mention. Any of their difficulties, even their most painful ones, paled in comparison to Katie's world and made them seem almost like balm to her heart and sweet ointment for her pain.

* * *

In time that never went quickly enough, Katie grew up and was able to escape from the place she had called home. It was then that God intruded into her life, saving her and restoring her by coming into her pain and shame, taking it away as if it were His own. He made her brand new again. Although it took time and was hard work on her part, He was faithful to her and had the power to heal her hurts.

It was often excruciatingly painful to face the past honestly. He required her to let go of every false identity and a hundred different coping mechanisms, but she discovered that each time she surrendered to God instead of to her own fears she became stronger. Freedom was extremely expensive for her, but in the end it was worth every bit of the price of being honest. The girl who had been a master at escaping reality became an expert at over coming self-deception every time God revealed a new one to her.

Katie fought hard to understand forgiveness. In the beginning, the concept seemed almost absurd: ***I** should be the one to forgive and release the guilty? How could that be fair?*

She began to see, however, that it was her only path to freedom. She could no longer escape to her once precious and safe thought that there were places too dark to visit and people too guilty to forgive. She had to come out of denial and visit those places and people again, painfully and slowly forgiving each player, one by one.

She forgave the boys at school. She forgave the teacher who didn't defend her and the classmates who joined in the cruelty. She forgave her landlord and her boss and even the car salesman who sold her a car with a dozen things wrong he forgot to mention. She forgave the neighbor who wouldn't control his dog when it repeatedly ripped open her garbage.

She sometimes thought that God lined people up to hurt her just to keep her in practice forgiving, but none were ever again as hard as the first ones had been. Because she knew with blessed relief that her own sins had been forgiven by God, she could not withhold forgiveness from others. Forgiveness was sweet freedom to her. She learned to consider what had happened to her as a kind of joy because every time she forgave and called upon a grace she didn't naturally have to do what she could never have done on her own, she changed. The painful process changed her for the better and the result was joyous.

She had mercy for people, but mercy didn't drive her.

The day Katie pulled into her parents' driveway with forgiveness in her heart, she was shaking all over. They opened the door and knew immediately that something immense was about to happen. Not only had they not seen her in ages, but here she was unexpectedly - no phone call ahead, no warning at all. They braced themselves for the tirade of accusation they had anticipated and feared for years.

Katie began softly. "I've come to ask your forgiveness for my attitude toward you," she said. "I need your forgiveness for my anger and my rebellion. I need you to forgive me for not honoring you and loving you. Would you please forgive me for wanting to leave you out of my life completely?"

She looked up to see two familiar people staring at her as though she were a total stranger. Her words had caught them utterly off guard, but the spirit in which she had spoken moved them despite their habitual walls of resistance. They both managed to mumble forgiveness, not fully understanding why she wanted it or needed it. She had disarmed them enough that they had not been able to retreat into defensiveness or evasion. She had long since forgiven her parents for the molestation and the cover-up, but what she needed today was to own her part in the fractured relationship.

Katie found healing and then went beyond it into a place where she was used by God to heal others. Beliefs, behaviors, and demons she had known personally were easily recognized when she saw them in other people. Rather than cover up her past, she chose to be open and transparent about it as she determined that she would find a way to redeem all the pain. People began to find their own freedom in her words of wisdom, drawn from her own deep well of hard experience.

She was direct and confrontational with truth because no one hated darkness, deceit, and cover-ups more than Katie. She had mercy for people, but mercy didn't drive her. What motivated her was to bring cleansing and healing to others by dismantling lies and reestablishing truth with proper boundaries.

She understood tough love, because she had embraced it herself in order to recover, and she knew there was no other way for victims to be free.

This afternoon, between tennis and the dinner party, she was squeezing in a ministry session for a friend of a friend. She had a string of people who wanted time with her because her life and words were so transformational. Unlikely people came from many different places, sent by this or that acquaintance. When a problem seemed too difficult or a person had been stuck in the same place for years, they would often wind up on Katie's doorstep.

Many of them had horrific pain and intense brokenness, but she didn't turn them away because she believed nothing was too difficult for the God she relied on. The woman who was coming this afternoon was one she had never met before, a lady named Andrea.

When Katie's doorbell rang, Andrea stood there, clearly nervous. It had been difficult for her to come to a complete stranger's home planning to talk about the intimate details of her sordid past. She had absolutely no intention of "telling it all" but hoped she might find enough compassion here to get her through another month of her hopeless, pain-laced life.

Dim hope began to burn within her heart.

Katie welcomed her still dressed in her tennis outfit because she had barely made it home in time. Andrea took one look at her and the beautifully decorated living room and moaned inwardly, *Why did I ever fall for this? She will never understand where I've been and what I live with.* She had learned to draw life from the compassion of those she went to for help, but pity from those who did not "get" her only added to her pain.

Katie fixed her a cup of tea, sliced her a piece of luscious, buttery pound cake, then ran upstairs to change into jeans, leaving Andrea desperately trying to figure out how to share just a few scraps of information, get the token Bible verse, and make her escape.

When Katie returned, she seemed slightly less intimidating. Once the small talk was over and their mutual friend had been thoroughly discussed, Katie began to ask a few questions, fishing for the real reason this woman had driven three hours to see her about her marriage.

Unaccountably, Andrea felt herself relaxing. Although she couldn't exactly explain why, she felt safe here, and when Katie, quite out of the blue, began relating her own story of sexual abuse, Andrea couldn't believe her ears. Andrea's childhood abuse had only recently begun to surface in her life, haunting every facet of her world, sending her into rages, and driving her husband away, right up to the brink of divorce. They were both at their wits' end.

Katie talked about her own childhood misery with incredible transparency and vulnerability, which in itself seemed unbelievable, yet Andrea recognized to her shock that there wasn't a trace of pain clinging to any of her words.

She listened in disbelief. *Jesus could do that? He could leave the memory and remove all the pain from it?* There was no need to ask the question or have Katie answer. It was obvious that He could, because a living, breathing person was telling her stories that were all too familiar without flinching, crying, or even wincing. Katie was a real testimony. She was unmistakably healed. Obviously, unbelievably, it WAS possible to heal and if it was true for Katie, could it then be true for her? Dim hope began to burn within her heart.

She had been to counselors who were sympathetic and compassionate, but this was different. She didn't sense that Katie felt sorry for her. She knew how crippling the victimization had been for her life, but she had no clue how to change her thinking. She would have been happy to stop being the victim just as soon as other people quit victimizing her. Right?

Even as Andrea crafted that excuse, she knew it wasn't going to work with Katie. She had already gained some vague sense of her ongoing penchant for being victimized and she knew that hanging onto her rights as a "victim" had cost her something. She knew an adjustment was needed but Katie was demanding nothing less than turning her back on all her victim thinking.

Fear fought fiercely against the hope that rose within her. She recognized that Katie would hold her accountable and was flat-out calling her to face her own contribution to staying trapped in yesterday's pain. She didn't want to stay stuck, but embracing an entire mountain range of pain by walking in truth and transparency was absolutely not what she had come here to do. Katie's proposition was overwhelming and preposterous.

Andrea scrambled to regroup and find a graceful exit.

As Katie talked to her about boundaries, she recognized how poor she was at maintaining any of her own and had to admit it was a constant source of heartache. She had always found it impossible to enforce limits on others, perhaps because of the early violation, or possibly because of her lack of self-worth, yet now she was furious when she was taken advantage of. Sensing that her anger of late was her spirit crying out for healthy boundaries, she found herself listening intently to Katie's explanations.

She was surprised when the hope rose that maybe she could start to establish some in spite of her fear of more pain. She had never heard anyone explain the need for boundaries so clearly and rationally. Her fear began to subside. *Was this what the Bible meant about truth setting us free?*

Andrea and Katie worked through a number of issues in the two hours she was there. When she left, she could not believe how quickly Katie had dove in and gone right to the heart of the matter. This woman knew how to unravel the threads of a life and weave them back together in a pattern that wasn't the same ugly blanket of shame she had draped around herself in the past.

When Andrea had gone, Katie rushed into the kitchen and finished the preparations for her dinner party. She was serving prime rib with a parsley rub, herbs grown in her own garden, new potatoes, green bean bundles wrapped in bacon, a wonderful romaine salad with her special homemade dressing, and Crème Brule for dessert.

On her way upstairs to the shower, she stopped and fussed over the fresh flowers on the table, then bent down and smelled them. Katie loved the smell of fresh lavender which she had mixed into the flower arrangement. Maybe she would fill the bath with her lavender salts and, while she soaked in the perfumed water cleansing her mind and spirit from the day, give herself ten extra minutes to "chat with Poppa" about His heart toward the dear friends that would arrive in a few hours.

Yes, she decided, that is what she would do. She was worth being pampered.

In the middle of the nineteenth century, a group of gifted men were born in the United States at a most opportunistic time - the coming of the Industrial Age. Although they would pursue varied business ventures, they possessed the same abilities to make money by seeing the time in which they lived for what it was - a window of huge opportunity for the forerunners and the risk takers. By the turn of the 20th century, these men would become rich and powerful, demonstrating by their hard work and success that the American dream which had prompted their parents and grandparents to leave homelands behind, had kept its promise of prosperity to their offspring.

They had names we still recognize, like J. P. Morgan, Andrew Carnegie, and John D. Rockefeller. These three, along with a handful of others, were destined to prove the ability of capitalism to drive a nation's expansion, and to reap their own personal rewards as risk takers and gamblers in business before heavy taxation and laws against monopolies attempted to curb capitalism's excesses.

Today they are known as Robber Barons, a term denoting their ruthless use of power, as well as their acquisition of wealth at the expense of the laborers who did grueling work that generated vast profits for others. The common laborer was paid $2.50 a day for working twelve hours a day six days a week. These were the men who built railroads across the nation, drilled for oil, and produced steel.

New industries grew rapidly making millions in wide open national markets, but even then, the men who were at the top of these enterprises were not overnight successes. They worked throughout their lifetimes, steadily inventing, investing and accumulating, holding on to enough ownership in their individual industries to eventually profit grandly from their abilities to keep pace with an expanding nation.

The interesting thing about many of these rich men was that while they worked hard to accumulate wealth, many of them worked equally hard to give it away at the end of their lives. Carnegie claimed that accruing money was the most dangerous and idolatrous of practices, yet he couldn't help but acquire it, whether because of his personal financial genius or because of destiny. Because of his beliefs, he spent the last twenty years of his life overseeing its distribution. Rockefeller and Carnegie both invested heavily in the arts and education. Carnegie established libraries throughout the United States while Rockefeller poured money into

Men who gambled everything over and over on the American dream.

medical research, hospitals, and the arts. J. P. Morgan helped finance the Metropolitan Art Museum and establish the Federal Reserve Bank.

Some argued that these men were simply trying to redeem their images, but each appeared to be as driven to use his resources for influence based on his own concept of what was good for the nation, as he had been to earn it. They appeared to believe that their ability to make money was a stepping stone to its proper distribution, or perhaps as others suggested, they were simply conflicted men, as good as they were bad.

Whatever the drive, they were entrepreneurs, quintessential American capitalists, gifted enough to realize that the times in which they lived were rich with opportunity. They worked hard and dreamed big, becoming the wealthiest Americans to have ever lived, easily outdoing moderns such as Bill Gates, Warren Buffett, or Sam Walton. Rockefeller is said to have been the richest man in world history, earning two hundred million dollars in one year, when the entire GNP for the United States was only 1.5 billion dollars.

It was a time when the oil industry, the railroads, and the steel industry were being birthed, and these men stood in the right places at the right time to capitalize on the technology of the industrial revolution and an expanding nation. They had the "Midas touch" - a genre of "wildcat capitalists," men who gambled everything over and over on the American dream, losing big at times but winning often enough to become staggeringly wealthy.

There was another man born in the same time period who was just as talented as the Robber Barons, who also made and gave away a fortune, yet whose name does not appear on the list of the infamous millionaires. While he became a wealthy success story and left much of his money to causes which are still thriving today, he marched to a different drummer.

History has not accused him of earning money tainted from the abuse of the workers; in fact, they called his first California drilling operation "Christian Hill," and mocked him for discouraging profanity among the roughnecks. He was known to be a gentleman and a man of integrity who left most of his fortune for the purpose of alleviating human suffering and equipping men to teach the Word of God. His detractors claimed he suffered from "compulsive piety," and that he used his wealth to further his fundamental Christian beliefs, an attack he would have no doubt enjoyed.

His name was Lyman Stewart and his game was oil.

* * *

Lyman read through the document a second time, laid it down on the table, and stared out the window into the busy street below. As he watched the people busily winding along the city street, each hurrying somewhere compelled by the day's demands, he felt certain that he was doing the right thing. He had determined to leave his children only one hundred thousand dollars each and nothing more from his vast fortune, although he was grooming his eldest son, Will, to one day take over the business when the time was right. He knew the power of money to corrupt, or equally as important, to limit one's need for hard work and perseverance. This was especially true of money that came too easily. He wanted each of them to develop the character that struggle and sacrifice created, and not to live an easy life squandering their father's inheritance. When it came to making and spending money, Lyman Stewart was usually right. His children inherited his ingrained values and watched him model frugality and an astounding work ethic. They lacked for nothing.

In the economy of the early 1900's, Stewart was leaving his children an inheritance that most Americans would have seen as incomprehensibly large, but it was only a tiny fraction of the money that he had made in his lifetime. Wealth had come to him from huge oil finds, but he had fought hard to earn every penny. He had won and lost, invested and run risks, some which paid off and some which left him flat broke. He prized every experience for what it had taught him and where it had led him, and he didn't want to deprive his children of the same kind of reality-based training in the game of life. Every venture had required a measure of hard work and sheer stubbornness that most men had in much smaller measure than he. In the end those character qualities had been the primary source of his wealth.

God seemed to be on Lyman's side.

God seemed to be on Lyman's side, guarding over his financial journey with a keen eye, providing just the right opportunities while also permitting occasional failures to teach him just the right lessons. Lyman reached a place where he was finally getting the hang of it, doing things God's way in God's timing, demonstrating character and trust that had been molded by the Potter Himself. When he reached that place, it seemed like God then overtly invested in Lyman's ventures, although there was never anything about the risk of the oil field that was smooth or predictable. The structure Stewart helped create shook and swayed throughout the decades, going through periods of vast expansion and rocky finances, in-fighting for control among its top leaders, and an ongoing conflict of ideas about what success meant and when expansion should stop or new markets be ignored.

Acquiring and managing wealth teaches a man many lessons about others and himself, about listening to his gut instinct. No matter what, it places an extreme test on his character. He always felt like he could sniff out a good investment or a bad one, but sometimes, even though he got that familiar "sure" feeling, he could still be dead wrong. Even then, he never quit, because he always believed that a new opportunity was on the horizon. He assumed that even his failures were lessons of some kind in financial wisdom, or opportunities to persevere and do better next time and make even more. Setbacks usually increased his drive to find the next opportunity.

Along the way he had accrued a set of principles he lived by, one of which was that giving people money didn't solve their problems. He knew that people thought he was stingy when he sometimes refused to give to popular causes, or to lavish his wealth on friends or family, but he enjoyed the wisdom of frugality. Frugality in some areas and generosity in others made good sense to him, and he acted on what he felt each called for. He tried not to ignore his instincts when he felt no compulsion to give money away. Lyman knew that God Himself could not be manipulated to give to his children without being sure that they could handle it or that it wouldn't

He was humbled by his losses, but not defeated.

cause them heartache; he believed he had God's mind when it came to money.

At eleven years old in 1851, Lyman had dropped out of school to help his father in his tanning business. He was a hard worker and a bright kid, and although he could hardly stomach the smell of the hides, he was ready to work hard and save every cent he could, because even at that age, he already had investing on his mind. Some people say he had the mindset of his frugal Scot ancestors, but he was not just able to save well, he could spend it just as quickly on an investment.

Oil fever was spreading throughout his Pennsylvania homeland, and he had caught it. He saved one hundred and twenty five dollars, an impressive sum by the age of nineteen, and he gambled the entire sum on an investment in an oil well where he lost every penny. The irony was that six years later a well would be drilled on that same spot that would produce 300 barrels a day for someone else, proving that something about the prospect was right. Although he had bad equipment, he did have intuition - a natural ability to see an opportunity and take it.

The Civil War came and went and Stewart, a Union soldier, served three years in a Pennsylvania regiment before returning home at 25 years old to find the oil fields alive from the war boom and Civil War expenditures. He was amazed to see the advances in technology: new explosives were being used to fracture the rock; new piping had been developed; and improved drilling rigs were sturdier and more reliable.

Equally astonishing was seeing the sleepy town of 6,000 people which he had left, hopping with the energy of the oil boom in the Venango Valley. Stewart was ready to jump in with both feet and was as enthusiastic as any man returning from a war in his twenties full of energy and glad to be alive. He had spent the years of his youth wandering the valley and watching the dark crude seep from the ground. He knew it like the back of his hand, and something told him that he would find a place in this amazing and exciting new enterprise. The oil field can destroy a greenhorn quickly, and Stewart learned the price of the gamble just as fast.

Not having any capital himself, he started out by helping investors negotiate oil leases with farmers. By 1868, at 28 years old, he had earned respect as a businessman in a hard field due to an amiable personality and his ability to negotiate. He was a natural in the business world and he focused on staying at the forefront of a new industry. Oil was being used to fuel the railroads, factories and steamboats, and while no one could have predicted the coming automobile boon, the product already had enough markets to make it a winner.

A year later, he invested in drilling again and he lost everything for the second time; while he was learning a lot about risk and timing, it appeared he was learning it all the hard way. For the next ten very sobering years, he had to take hourly jobs on the rigs just to feed himself and his family, for by 1872 he had married. He was humbled by his losses, but not defeated, for he had faith that at any minute it would all turn around, that some circumstance would appear and he would find the door of real opportunity open to him once again. Faith and stubbornness marked him, as he once said he never had the sense to cut his losses and get out. The monotonous work and the steady paycheck which meant security to some, was bondage to Stewart, but he endured it because it was the opportunity of the moment.

Finally the day came when Wallace Hardison, a Californian with money, came to visit his brothers in the Pennsylvania oil fields and was introduced to Lyman Stewart. Wallace had been searching for a man to partner with him who understood the business from the ground floor, and he decided that Lyman was his man. He immediately liked Stewart and was confident he had found a man who was trustworthy, hard working, and who had enough experience and perseverance to make it happen.

"Stewart, if you will run this company, I'll back you," Hardison told him, and although Stewart had no capital to invest, he gladly agreed to the opportunity and the partnership. He had been waiting for just such a break, and he had learned his lesson of hanging on through the hard times by working on the rigs. Circumstances had changed, just as he had thought they would, and although he and Hardison began to prosper in the Pennsylvania oil fields, they decided to sell out to a man who had taken control of the market there.

There was no reconciling these two strong minded men.

The man, John D. Rockefeller, was squeezing everyone else out because he owned the pipe lines and the shipping. He had paid them cash, a little over one hundred thousand for their company, so they headed for the dream of discovery in California, although they kept some investment in the Pennsylvania fields. Stewart gladly went West with his teenage son to get the lay of the land, and when he got down off the train in 1883, he looked more like a conservative preacher than a wildcatter.

For the next ten years, Hardison and Stewart combined their energy and insight and drilled for oil in California. Although they prospered with impressive regularity on their own, finances were hard. Lyman received five dollars a day for all of his labor, and even when they merged with two smaller companies and formed Union Oil Company in 1890, things remained difficult. From the inception of the company, Thomas Bard, president, and Lyman Stewart, vice president were in a tug of war over the infant company each trying to take it in the direction of his vision. Stewart who was the oil finder, land buyer, and producer of the product was also the only one who tried to sell the product and find new markets. Hardison and Bard seemed more interested in politics and land interests. Bard would have preferred to sell the crude quickly for a profit, but it was Stewart who wanted to accumulate land and develop a company that could do it all from discovery to refining for generations to come. Men quickly divided into Bard's camp and Stewart's, and while Bard made a whopping five thousand a year income, Stewart was still paid five dollars a day.

His lack of accountability to anyone else seemed to produce two more decades of financial turmoil.

Each man would run the company with a high hand, making decisions without the other when he could. Bard would overturn Stewart's purchases and promises. Board meetings often turned into showdowns, from which Stewart would emerge victorious. There was no reconciling these two strong minded men, so there was the ongoing struggle for control and the winning philosophy of how to do business.

Finally, Stewart's land obsession paid off and Adams No. 28 hit a gusher of 40,000 barrels a day of crude before it settled down to a respectable 200 barrels a day. It would touch off a new frenzy for oil just as the gold rush had, only now men came and fought the land and each for the black gold. By 1894, Stewart had won the fight with Bard, for all practical purposes. Bard would leave for good in 1900.

By this time the company was under Lyman's control, but his lack of accountability to anyone else seemed to produce two more decades of financial turmoil. His ambition was control of the market, and by 1920, Lyman could still not rest comfortably since Union Oil was, as usual, oil rich and cash poor. It owned three hundred wells.

He still had investments back East that his family lived off of, plus enough extra to share with the downtrodden. As early as 1891, when Lyman Stewart was fifty years old, he began to invest in the city of Los Angeles, which he called "a great city of the future." He decided to call in Christian singers, evangelists, and preachers and sponsor them to start a mission for the poor. He wanted them to preach the gospel and give out food and clothing in what was the beginning of the Pacific Gospel Union. He imagined not only holding revival meetings in tents, but afterwards he envisioned preachers and singers riding through the streets in gospel wagons handing out food, clothing, and offering salvation to the downtrodden.

He enlisted a man named George Hilton to head up the mission and run it for him, while he underwrote the costs. He was a businessman who made money, but he was never satisfied until he had invested it in the right place. There was always an element of taking his wealth and investing it in God's kingdom. He differed from other philanthropists who wanted to see men's souls enlightened or their bodies healed, because he wanted to see their hearts and lives changed. He was an evangelist at heart, and his instincts about investing in the kingdom were even sharper than his striking oil. His instincts in the marketplace made him wealthy. His instincts about the soil in which to plant his seed produced a phenomenal increase. Had Jesus not promised a hundredfold increase for good seed in good soil?

Stewart was a ruling elder at Immanuel Presbyterian Church which he also helped organize. He helped that congregation build a beautiful $50,000 building in the late 1800's in Los Angeles. He also helped other Christian laymen in the city to start the YMCA, and helped fund the Catholic restoration of the old California Missions.

One of the most significant endeavors of his life was the co-founding of what is now Biola University, a Bible centered liberal arts campus with three graduate schools. Stewart observed the fast growth of the Los Angeles area and the inability of the church to be able to keep up with the vast urban growth. The Bible Institute of Los Angeles, which became known as Biola, was founded for that purpose. Stewart was a friend of T. C. Horton, a pastor with ability to inspire and organize, and Stewart sponsored his early efforts to put together a Bible Institute. Still, these two men

Stewart believed he was in a cultural war.

wanted something that would earn credibility on a national and international scale, and they knew that their early efforts were good, but not as polished as what they wanted. They solicited R. A. Torrey who was a Yale educated, well known evangelist, to be a faculty member, recognizing the esteem he would bring to the fledgling school. He agreed to come if they would build a church big enough for him, so they also founded the nondenominational Church of the Open Door and gave him full control of the Institute's leadership, including hiring, doctrine, and curriculum.

Stewart could let go of control once he had laid the foundation, at least outside the oil field, and when he had a person to hand off to whom he trusted like Torrey, he was ready to finance that man's vision. Torrey was able to make Biola an excellent choice for conservative Protestants of all denominations because of his ability to focus on fundamentals. People poured into the school from everywhere. He was both dean of the school and pastor of the Church of the Open Door, which as its name denotes, welcomed everyone. It thrived under his leadership.

Stewart saw potential easily, but he primarily gave into what he believed would last. He gave money to sponsor the endeavors of two prominent theologians of the time. One was Cyrus Scofield who wrote the famous Scofield Bible, a Bible which contained commentary with the text, cross referenced scriptures around topics, and attempts to date scriptural events. Scofield believed in pre-millennialism, namely that Christ would reign for 1,000 years on earth after His second coming, and the Scofield Bible included his interpretations of events according to his theology. It had sold two million copies by the end of World War II.

The other project he sponsored was one by William Blackstone who was also teaching pre-millennial theology and wrote a popular pamphlet called, "Jesus is Coming." Lyman also sponsored Chinese missions and held the lofty hope that each Chinese would receive a copy of the Bible.

He and his brother, Milton, were concerned about America's movement away from fundamental Christianity into modernism. He felt an urgent need to give a warning to the nation not to be seduced by ideas that were causing many to drift away from the faith and accept a watered down liberal version of the truth.

After hearing a man named Amzi Dixon preach a fiery sermon in Dwight L. Moody's church, Stewart felt compelled to underwrite a work on Christian fundamentals of belief. The twelve volume set was called <u>The Fundamentals: A Testimony to the Truth.</u> The books were written by 64 different contributors from various Protestant denominations with Dixon heading up the project. It was published and sent to every pastor, evangelist, missionary, theology professor, theology student, and Sunday School superintendent, as far as was possible in the English speaking world.

Stewart believed he was in a cultural war and that as a Christian layman whom God had blessed with finances, it was part of his duty to try to turn the tide. He provided fundamentalist teaching to thousands of churches and institutions in America emphasizing the fundamentals of the Christian faith. Since Christian Fundamentalism today has been maligned and grouped with other fundamentalist teachings throughout the world that are feared or despised because of their violence, intolerance, and extremism, it is interesting to note what the tenants of the beliefs were that were outlined in the volumes which Stewart sponsored:

1. The divine inspiration of scripture.
2. The Trinity.
3. The creation of man, the fall into sin, and total depravity.
4. The universal transmission of spiritual death from Adam.
5. The necessity of the new birth.
6. Redemption by the blood of Christ.
7. Salvation by faith alone in Jesus Christ.
8. The assurance of salvation.
9. The centrality of Jesus Christ in scripture.
10. The true church made up of genuine believers.
11. The personality of the Holy Spirit.
12. The believer's call to a holy life.
13. The souls of believers go immediately to be with Christ at death.
14. The pre-milliennial second coming of Christ.

Lyman Stewart's legacy lives on in the many lives that he touched with his investment skills. One hundred years later Union Rescue Mission, as it is now called, is the largest private Christian homeless shelter in the United States. It provides food, clothing, shelter, medical help, dental care, legal help, counseling, education, job training, and programs for recovery. It has a guest chapel to rest and pray, and church services on Sunday in the main chapel and can sleep up to 1,000 people a night.

For over a century, Immanuel Presbyterian Church has left "its gentle and devoted mark on the hearts and souls of thousands of Southern Californians of all races, backgrounds, and lifestyles."

For over 100 years Biola has trained Christian leaders with excellence. Union Oil Company remained a major petroleum explorer and marketer having influence which spanned the late 19th century into the beginning of the 21st century. Unocal became the new holding company for Union Oil in 1983, and the company celebrated 100 years in the 1990's, one of only 22 companies to have survived since the turn of the century.

Institutions dotted the landscape of Los Angeles for many decades that were symbols of Lyman Stewart's enterprise and vision. After the automobile's arrival, the first "gas stand" in the state was created by his company and eventually there would be 400 others to accompany it. One could not drive down a city street without seeing the modern image of the bright orange and blue Union '76 emblems on the gas stations. The Union Rescue Mission remains a symbol of hope and encouragement to the downtown poor, and although the neon "Jesus Saves" sign which topped the Bible Institute of Los Angeles for decades is no longer there, the school has educated 50,000 men and women to teach and preach throughout the world.

After the automobile's arrival, the first "gas stand" in the state was created by his company.

It was all part of the legacy of the vision and stewardship of one man: Lyman Stewart, oil man. He held himself to the highest level of responsibility for the use of his fortune and he carefully selected the places to sow his seeds, and like a good businessman, he expected to earn the hundredfold increase on his investment that he had been promised by God.

In 1995, more than one hundred years after Lyman Stewart formed Union Oil Company, the giant corporation, Chevron, bought Unocal for 18 billion dollars. It had weathered more than 100 years, having been birthed and watched over by a visionary, a "wildcatter," who was never conservative when it came to business ventures or risks for God's work, but who was grounded by a deep and fundamental faith.

Once the insatiable thirst for gasoline for the automobile came along, Union Oil was doing sixty million dollars a year in business. Toward the end of Stewart's life there was a huge fight to save the company from being bought by foreign investors, a fight which Stewart helped to win. Petroleum World published the following after his death in September of 1923.

> The life of the revered veteran of oil, ended by an attack of acute bronchitis and bronchial pneumonia, was the longest record of oil achievement which can be credited to any American. Sixty-four years he served petroleum, twenty-four in Pennsylvania, forty in California. Eighty-three years old when his gentle soul was called, his name was known wherever oil was spoken of and his three-score years of square dealing in business and kind personal interest in all around him had earned the friendship and respect of thousands. On October 1, when his funeral services were held at the Bible Institute in Los Angeles, for which he labored so hard the last fifteen years of his life, thousands of people paid their final respects to his memory.

Long recognized as the father of oil in the Pacific Coast region, long given the honored title of 'dean of western oil men,' consulted by the oldest and the wisest and held in respectful awe by the younger element, Lyman Stewart had been the outstanding figure in California oil for forty years.

Chapter 11
Lawlessness Based on Principle

Mattie and Sam Clay were dressed in their everyday clothes - simple homemade garments, slightly tattered but clean - because they didn't own any fancier ones. They had just witnessed the presidential inauguration and now decided to attend the party at the White House since President Andrew Jackson, the great American hero, had been kind enough to invite the public. Word had passed through the streets that this would not be a party for the "elite," and from the looks of it they weren't the only common people taking the president at his word. A crowd of folks was making its way down Pennsylvania Avenue toward the White House to catch a closer glimpse of the people's president and partake in his gracious hospitality.

It was exciting to the couple to be part of such an historic occasion and to celebrate the coming of age of real democratic ideas and freedoms. American presidents had been heroic before, like Washington, or scholarly like Jefferson or Adams, even aristocratic like Monroe and Madison, but never had one been born in a log cabin in "the West" (which with only 24 states denoted either Tennessee or Kentucky) or been an obvious symbol of the average American like Jackson.

Here was a man who understood their struggles, who was for them, who would not be swayed by aristocratic ideas or a privileged position in life - a real American, "Old Hickory." When he spoke about "the people," they were sure they were the ones he was talking about.

When Mattie and Sam arrived, they saw that the lawn of the White House was brimming with folks like themselves. Servants were carrying out huge tubs of punch and setting them on the lawn for the masses in an attempt to accommodate the visitors who were just arriving at the White House.

It already appeared to Sam and Mattie that gaining entrance would be impossible, when suddenly there was a crash and glass fell out of the huge front windows and shattered on the porch. Word came there were so many people in the parlors of the White House that someone had broken out the front windows for ventilation.

But it was a bittersweet moment, like every other victory he had ever experienced.

At that point they wisely decided to stay put on the lawn. They had obviously arrived a little too late to catch a glimpse of President Jackson, for there was no pleasant or civilized way to make their way through the swelling crowd into the house. They stood on the lawn in the cool March air and drank punch, chatting with some folks next to them, and congratulating each other on the outcome of the election of 1828. Their candidate was the very first to be nominated by a political party - the newly organized Democratic Party.

Many believed that Andrew Jackson should have become president four years earlier, since he had received the majority of the popular and electoral votes in the election of 1824, but the close election was thrown to Congress to decide. Congress had given the election to John Quincy Adams, since he was one of "them." Although he had been full of new political ideas which might have benefited the country, too many people were angry that they had been robbed of their "say" and they resisted his leadership.

Now, four years later, Jackson was enjoying the revelry of the night, the promise of tomorrow, the vindication of his name, and the accolades of his loyal supporters.

But it was a bittersweet moment, like every other victory he had ever experienced. His wife, Rachel, had died from heart failure only a month after Election Day, causing his victory to be laced with pain. Not only was she gone, but he blamed his opponent, Henry Clay, for her death. Rachel had been married before and believing the divorce had been legally finalized, she married Jackson. When they discovered the divorce had not been executed properly, they were forced to remarry. His political opponents had used the story to smear him and malign Rachel, humiliating her and, in Jackson's focused mind, causing her death. What had already been a hostile political campaign had evolved into a deep personal grudge and he rarely forgave an enemy.

Andrew Jackson had blue eyes, like cold steel, that sank despondently into their sockets with a look of both sadness and determination. His face was surrounded by a mass of thick, white hair. Amid the lines on his face there emerged a noticeable, ugly scar and there was another on his hand. They always reminded everyone who saw him that he had been a soldier almost all of his life. When he was only 13 years old, he fought in the war to defend the colonies against Great Britain by serving as a messenger for the troops.

He was captured, starved, and then insulted by a British officer who demanded that young Jackson clean his boots. When he refused, out of both principle and pride, the outraged officer slashed his face and hand with a sword, leaving deep scars. Jackson never forgot the humiliating and painful experience or any of the pain the Revolution had brought to his life, for during it his mother and two brothers died. After bravely securing his release from a war prison in exchange for British soldiers, his mother left him to heal from his war wounds, while she traveled 160 miles to seek her nephew's release. During the journey she contracted cholera and died, leaving Andrew shattered and alone, for his father had died before his birth in a logging accident. He was now an orphan, except for the extended clan who sought to look after him.

Andrew Jackson often authorized himself when he felt the cause was just.

He came from Scots-Irish ancestry in Western Tennessee, a close-knit, proud family who were hard-working, self-reliant, and quick to defend their honor. Andrew was known to be rough, unpretentious, rowdy, and heroic - a fighter to the core. When he believed in something, he was singular in his focus and fortified by the "rightness" of his perspective. If his perspective was tainted by bitterness, he felt even more justified in wreaking vengeance on his adversaries.

At 15, after his mother's death, he was a quarrelsome, lonely adolescent. At 17 he began to study law and after two years became an effective Tennessee attorney, although taking the law into his own hands appealed to him too. He had a reputation for defending his name in duels and bar fights alike, demonstrating a fierce aggression toward anyone who dared to belittle him.

Jackson was usually a friend or an enemy, rarely anything in between. He became a romantic figure to a portion of the people after he took on the two groups that were the most frightening to many Americans: the Indians and the British.

He first took his men into Florida to chase the Creek Indians although he did it without authorization from the government. Andrew Jackson often authorized himself when he felt the cause was just, and securing safe lands for American expansionism was always "just" in his mind. While he maintained that he was a friend of the Indians, enlisting peaceful groups to aid him in his Indian wars when it suited him, he could turn on them in a minute when he no longer needed them. The Cherokee who fought with him against the Creek would soon suffer the brutality of his infidelity to their nation.

His military victories were probably less genius and more bloodthirsty vengeance fired by his own ideology.

After the Revolutionary War, Britain did not immediately disappear from America's list of adversaries. England was heavily embroiled in the Napoleonic Wars and did not want the new nation trading with France, a restriction the Americans felt was an unreasonable assault on their rights as an independent nation. Furthermore, the English had been impressing sailors to man the ships of the Royal Navy and as many as 11,000 sailors had deserted by 1805, a number of them turning to America for both citizenship and jobs in the American Navy or merchant fleet.

The British regularly stopped American ships, taking the liberty of searching them for deserted sailors. Occasionally, due to poor records and inaccurate proof, they took away a few legitimate American citizens along with the belligerent deserters. Most American sailors felt the British deserters had a right to choose which nation they sailed for and the sailors' cry became "free trade and sailors' rights."

Jackson would finally rout the British in the Battle of New Orleans. He was a tough soldier known for his military bravado and, because he had never really forgiven the British for his childhood scars, was happy to wage a personal vendetta against them. He would earn the nickname "Old Hickory" in this campaign because men said he was as tough as a hickory nut - the notoriously hard-shelled fruit of a native tree back in the Tennessee hills - and as stubborn and relentless a soldier as America ever called her own.

His military victories were probably less genius and more bloodthirsty vengeance fired by his own ideology that demanded he protect the ideals of the hard fought Revolution while wreaking a little personal vengeance at the same time. His own pilgrimage and sacrifice were inextricably entangled with that of the nation and he fought like a mother lion would fight to protect her cubs, acting out of his own accumulated grief, personal loss, high ideals, and certainty that he was on the side of right and justice.

In his handwritten plea for Americans to fight in the War of 1812, Jackson said, "Are we the titled Slaves of George the third? The military conscripts of Napoleon the great? Or the frozen peasants of the Russian Czar? No - we are the freeborn sons of America, the citizens of the only republick [sic] now existing in the world." He was passionate about liberty and righting wrongs, whatever he perceived them to be.

The Battle of New Orleans was a testimony to Jackson's courage and downright audacity. He had information that the British planned to take the port city with 10,000 men and that they were entering the Gulf on their way up the river. When he arrived with only 700 men he had no guarantee that anyone else would come to his aid, so he began to problem solve Jackson style. He created an unlikely army of pirates, free slaves, and Indians by teaming up with Lafitte, the Haitian born pirate, whose men were close by. Then he enlisted two outfits of free black men and a group of loyal Creeks. Two of his old friends arrived with 2,000 men between them and another 100 showed up from Mississippi.

He was ready to defend the city from behind mounds of mud, bales of hay and sugar barrels. Another 2,000 men arrived from Kentucky before the battle began, so Jackson now had about 5,000 soldiers to England's 10,000. With a little skill and a lot of luck, the Americans held the city and "Old Hickory" moved into national prominence, becoming the most popular American general since George Washington.

He had a burning desire to rid the world of its unfair system of favoritism, which he deemed aristocracy to be, and he had an innate ability to change with the times while never shifting from his basic ideals. He reworked the same ideas of representation for the common man, his best democratic ideal, into every new situation.

He was able to profit from his mistakes although he never seemed to learn or grow from them personally. He remained stuck in the past, always looking backward rather than forward, letting it define the present. For all that, he did a great deal to create democratic ideals. As a forerunner, he had many dedicated followers and was able to advance his principles despite his volatile style of leadership. Whether opinion was for or against him - and it was usually polarized - he won most of his battles one way or another and left his mark on the nation.

Though the founding fathers worried that equality might be too democratic and idealistic, Andrew Jackson felt that inequality was engendered by those who used privilege to benefit themselves, and those particular men and their systems were his enemies.

While he was perhaps not progressive enough to impress a modern egalitarian, limited by the times in which he lived, not a champion of women, slaves, or Native Americans, he expressed more democratic ideas than his forebears had. He has been scoffed at by some as being a man of democratic ideals who was also a slave owner and responsible for the removal of Native Americans from their land, which contributed to many of their deaths. He was all of those things.

Regardless, the Jacksonian democracy changed American politics. His ascension to the White House saw the very first smear campaign in America because he demonized his opponents as being the men who stole the previous election from the people. They were the "elitist insiders" who had a death grip on governmental processes by keeping them out of reach of the common man. He was the first candidate to give out campaign memorabilia such as buttons, hats, and canes bearing the image of a hickory tree. He was also the first candidate nominated by a political party, one that saw the advantage of organizing and promoting a single candidate, and he was probably the least prepared to be president of any before him.

He wasted no time advocating that the Electoral College be done away with, maintaining that popular vote was the trademark of a true democracy. He hated the college for costing him the election of 1824. He increasingly widened the power of the Executive Branch, ignoring those who insisted that the founding fathers had intended the Legislative Branch to be the strongest. He advocated rotation in office, so that no corrupt leader would be able to stay in office an interminable length of time, and he advocated the public election of federal judges.

Jackson wasn't interested in the role of watchman over the Constitution. He ruled with an iron fist, obeying the Constitution or the other branches of government when it suited him, and ignoring them when it didn't. It is a testimony to his popularity with the common people and his powerful persona that he wasn't impeached. There certainly was enough evidence of lawlessness to warrant it.

At the time Jackson took office, the Second Bank of America held the nation's money and enjoyed a monopoly sponsored by the government's treasury and tax revenues. Jackson hated the concept of a national bank and he hated this particular bank for backing his nemesis, Henry Clay, in the past election. The bank's president, Nicholas Biddle, was just the type of "aristocrat" Jackson hated - a well educated, rather arrogant man who disdained the thought of public oversight of his institution.

Because of the massive amount of capital that had gone into the War of 1812, the United States had reveled in a financial boom and was loaning almost anybody money to buy land, creating a bubble that was bound to burst. Having overextended its lending capacity, the bank began to call in loans, thereby creating the panic of 1819.

Although Henry Clay was able to get a bill through Congress to extend the bank's charter in the 1830s, Jackson was determined to destroy the Second Bank. He not only vetoed the bill Clay had supported, but made a scathing speech denouncing the rich investors and foreign stockholders in the bank. Ultimately, the Second Bank shut its doors which led to another panic, this one in 1837. Another Jackson enemy had gone down as he brought in his personal verdict and meted out punishment, once again focused on his personal sense of right regardless of the national consequences of the bank's failure.

The first presidential assassination attempt against a U. S. President was on his life.

The Native Americans were another problem for Jackson. He had befriended them at many points in his career. In fact, he would never have defeated the Creek without the help of the Cherokee who fought beside him in the Indian Wars, but their presence was unwanted by most Americans. Farmers wanted to seize their fertile land and be rid of living under the threat of conflict. Jackson was more of an expansionist than a loyal friend to the Indians who had been loyal to him.

Although the Cherokee were civilized, had adopted Christianity, and 90 percent of them could read Cherokee or English, he used the argument that they were too "uncivilized" to peacefully coexist with Americans, maintaining that they were but a few "savage hunters" on the land anyway. They fought his Indian Removal Act of 1830 in the courts, where the Supreme Court ruled (Worcester v. Georgia in 1831) that they were indeed a sovereign nation and not subject to the laws of a state; consequently Georgia could not remove them.

It became a short reach into lawlessness based, of course, on principle.

Jackson was not intimidated by the court's ruling. He replied that if Chief Justice Marshall had made that decision then he could enforce it himself. He turned his back on the Supreme Court ruling and acted on a treaty that a small number of Cherokee had been deviously manipulated into signing by some of Jackson's men. The Cherokee nation cried out against the unlawful treaty maintaining that those who signed it did not speak for the nation and their wishes, but Jackson had a legal document to move the entire Indian population west of the Mississippi by force and he had every intention of using it.

He acted as though he was being paternalistic to the Indians by moving them to places where they would be allowed to live in peace and rule themselves. It was not what they wanted, nor did he finance the moves in such a way as to make them humanely plausible. The worst of the moves was the brutal and shameful "Cherokee in the Trail of Tears" from North Carolina to Oklahoma in which more than 4,000 died along the way.

That Jackson had enemies is an understatement because he was a fiercely polarizing agent. The first presidential assassination attempt against a U. S. president was on his life, but he was able to take his cane and beat the assailant badly. The man who fired his gun twice at Jackson's chest was a mentally deranged unemployed British immigrant and if his gun had not misfired he would certainly have killed the president. Andrew Jackson showed no fear and, had onlookers not aided the assassin, no doubt would have beaten him to death. The newspapers called it a "sign of the times" for Jackson was unpopular in many circles.

After the bank showdown with his old enemy, Henry Clay, Jackson went on to win his second term with 56 percent of the popular vote. In his mind, the magnitude of the popular vote gave him even more carte blanche because his passionate reelection by the common people was the kind of endorsement that to him legitimized his style of leadership. He could ignore the ramifications and consequences of his decisions, convinced that the people appreciated his adversarial style.

It became a short reach into lawlessness based, of course, on principle.

His Vice President, John Calhoun, was from South Carolina. Calhoun began to support the Southern cause of nullifying any tariffs that were not in the South's best interest. The tension between the Federal Government and the Southern states was particularly strong at the time and every infringement of the rights of the states caused the South - with its cotton and farming interests and its fears about slavery - to shudder at the callous attitudes of the North in dictating their rights.

The tariff system was uneven, for the South was selling cotton in a free and declining world market while having to buy goods from the North which were manufactured at highly taxed rates. They watched as their exorbitant tariff money went into the improvement of roads in the North and they were angry over the inequality.

Talk of secession was already brewing over the tariff issue. Jackson decided to punish the South for the talk about secession because they struck a chord that outraged him. To speak of dissolving the Union that had cost him so much to see established made him explode with anger. The one thing he lived for was the protection of the Union, be it from the Indians, the British, or the Southern elitists.

To Jackson, Calhoun typified the rich Southerner who wanted to protect the interests of the plantation farmers and cared more about their money than the Union. He was so focused on his own sense of "right" that he failed to see the big picture - the Civil War looming on the horizon - and the legitimate cry from the Southerners who were feeling powerless about the unfairness of the tariffs.

Jackson parted ways with his own vice president, rejecting him completely and having nothing to do with him. Then Jackson turned to fight the Southerners over their attempt to nullify tariffs they didn't want. He was always quick to personalize any conflict and Calhoun became a symbol for him to fight. Had Henry Clay not stepped in and presented a compromise of lower tariffs, bloodshed was imminent. Clay was trying hard to stop the war.

Jackson was once more lost in his singular focus of preserving the Union, but by trying to preserve it with his narrow perspective, he contributed greatly to its imminent dissolution.

Jackson was a man of principle and ideas and he held to his democratic notion that the job of America was to insure opportunity for the common man. A strong expansionist believing that more land would be necessary to secure the American dream for its citizens, he wanted to rid the nation of the influence of England and Spain. Hatred for inherited privilege was bitterly entrenched in his psyche. He had learned at a young age to fight and defend his honor - that nothing was too strong a punishment for an enemy who should be hunted down and confronted, perhaps with a dueling pistol. His principles, which were demonstrated in the way he dealt with his enemies, guided him through two presidencies and helped to shape America's democratic process.

He created the popular notion that a man who comes from the "common people" is one who best understands how to govern. He elevated the Executive Branch to the highest power and grabbed lands from Native Americans while maintaining he was doing them a favor. He drove back the British and fought for the annexation of Texas which occurred after his presidency. He picked the man to succeed him, Martin Van Buren, and campaigned for him until he saw Van Buren in the president's seat after his own term ended.

Old and broken, Jackson retired to the Hermitage with relentless dysentery from the Indian campaigns, war wounds, dueling wounds, chronic insomnia, and a persistent hacking cough. He died on June 8, 1845, with his slaves weeping on the porch, his last words reassuring them that they would all meet again in heaven.

Historians, critics, and admirers still experience considerable polarization over the positive and negative legacy of the seventh president of the United States, but no one disagrees that he was America's most rugged reformer who stepped in from the outside and imprinted ideas of democracy on the people, giving them the vocabulary of democracy that still remains. They called him a "jackass," and the Democratic Party still carries the symbol of that legacy. The party would survive the Civil War, only 20 years away at Jackson's death, a war that would seek to define more clearly what democracy truly meant.

The high ideals of equality could not endure without the institution of slavery being challenged and Jackson had paved the way for popular politics and the voices of the people to be heard. His mother always believed her youngest son had a special destiny that he would somehow escape the obscurity and limitations of the backcountry, and would become a community leader - a man others would respect.

His picture graces the twenty-dollar bill and it is said that to this day a Cherokee prefers to carry two tens rather than have Jackson's picture in his wallet.

Chapter 12
What is the Most Certain Thing?

As the queen listened to her chief merchant, Tamrin, describe the spectacular temple King Solomon was building in Israel, and then declare the king to be the wisest man on earth, she was both enraptured, and a little perplexed. According to Tamrin, Solomon's every decision was just, resounding with wisdom and authority like no ruler he had ever heard before. That was saying a lot since Tamrin had contact with rulers in every part of the world where he traveled.

Tamrin was the leader of Queen Bilquis' trade caravan and she was the legendary Queen of Sheba, so he had been as far as India - and to most of the places in between - securing and trading goods for her. He knew his way around every important trade capital, but never had he raved about any person with such extravagant praise as he had King Solomon and his temple, a building that boasted of 700 carpenters, 800 masons and would take seven years to complete.

He spoke with obvious pride of his own procurement of the ebony, gold, and sapphires for the king. Apparently, dignitaries from many nations were already sending their congratulations to Solomon for his accomplishments, but Bilquis balked at that idea. From the moment Tamrin began to speak, she knew that nothing short of a personal visit to see this extraordinary man would suit the queen's fancy.

Nothing fascinated her more than people did, and this man might turn out to be the most fascinating person she had ever met. He certainly had her slightly jaded chief merchant ablaze with excitement, which was remarkable since he was not easily impressed. Heretofore, she had always derived quiet pleasure in his comparisons of her palace and her leadership with that of other rulers, for he ordinarily assured her that hers was the finest he had seen, but today he completely shattered that, and though she would never admit it, this had shaken her confidence.

Remarkably, he seemed oblivious to the effect his words were having upon her.

Bilquis was impulsive, acting without much forethought; after all, she had a kingdom at her disposal, a vivid imagination, and very little experience with failure. Her wealth and power had insulated her against the cold, hard realities of life in general, not that she would have been inclined to dwell on them regardless of her circumstances. She had also, of course, been catered to since she was a child.

However, this journey was a grand endeavor, even for her, for she lived in the southwest corner of Arabia where the Indian Ocean and the Red Sea met. Her nation was Sheba, well known throughout the world for its aromatic spices which were needed for many purposes in the ancient world, among them medicine and food. There were well established trade and sea routes to all the major trade cities in the world, so traveling by camel the 1400 miles necessary to reach Jerusalem, tracing the Red Sea along the Incense Road was done by caravans regularly.

The greater consideration was the time it would take her to arrive in Israel. She knew from Tamrin's past travels that it took about six months, since the camels could only travel about 20 miles a day. The caravan would make its way through the difficult Arabian desert, follow the sea coast into Moab, and then cross the Jordan River into Jerusalem. She could also travel by sea, but that journey might take up to three years because of the monsoons, or so her traders told her. She determined to go by land, but she wanted her ministers to agree with her plan.

She relied upon their counsel, but she blatantly measured their loyalty by how swiftly they approved her ideas.

Bilquis was an excellent ruler, intelligent and well spoken. She was also known for her infectious laughter, her happy disposition, and her unfailing optimism. The people she ruled adored her, enamored with the way she had kind words for everyone in the kingdom, even the lowliest servants. She thrived on admiration, and she also knew she needed their good will to rule properly. She liked people from every social sphere, and she didn't want anyone to dislike her.

Her mother had cautioned her that a ruler would not be able to please all the people all of the time, and while she saw to it that her daughter understood protocol and the necessity of not becoming "too" familiar with her subjects, she never restrained her lively energy or spontaneity. Bilquis was accustomed to having things her way and being doted on by everyone in the process. Her privileged life had enabled her to explore life's limitless possibilities while facing few of the worries that most people experience. Consequently, she never troubled herself with thoughts of how things could be accomplished. Her ministers or her staff made the necessary arrangements and she was free to think of parties and grand occasions of state, new trade opportunities, more palace gardens, or intriguing journeys. One did not tell the queen "no," and as long as no one did, all was well in the land of Sheba.

However, she did have a small trusted group of men in whom she confided and from whom she received wise counsel. She assembled them often, because she relied upon their wisdom and wanted their approval to move forward. She wanted to know what each of them had to say and they were free to disagree with her, unless they became "too disagreeable" and then they had to be replaced.

Her ministers were well aware of the paradox. She relied upon their counsel, but she blatantly measured their loyalty by how swiftly they approved her ideas. They were often in a quandary about how to be diplomatic, truthful, and loyal all at once. They were also well aware of how wounding she found disapproval by them to be on any level, so they risked speaking any negative words at their own peril, for the slightest dismissive attitude or harsh questioning would upset the queen.

They maneuvered these discussions as carefully as they might have avoided a desert scorpion, because the queen always heard misgivings of any kind as overt criticism and the crushing of her dreams. She wanted the truth, but it had to be palatable to her taste, and preferably, agreeable to her ideas. At the same time, they did not want the responsibility of being nothing more than puppets who allowed her to rush headlong into danger, so their dilemma was a very real one.

Often she rode out into the villages and visited with the townspeople, or wandered into the kitchen and spoke directly to the cook while he was preparing dinner. She loved the easy camaraderie of the kitchen staff, and she seemed to be at ease in any setting, words coming to her effortlessly, putting the most pretentious in their place or the most humble at ease with a smile and a reassuring word. Rumors of her sense of equality spread throughout her kingdom, as she devoted herself to being happy and having happy subjects.

Until the news of Solomon, she had never considered envying anyone, anywhere.

If he were as wise and as rich as the merchant said he was, she wanted to find out first hand. If he knew things she didn't know, she was eager to know them. He just might turn out to be a peer who could answer questions she had no one to help her answer. The possibilities of the friendship were endless and exciting, so she brushed aside any misgivings she had about the journey, and called in her ministers to determine whether the trip was diplomatically and logistically feasible. After she explained her desire to establish trade between their countries and they realized how excited she was about this trip, each agreed that it would be beneficial for the kingdom and gave her their blessing. In an explosion of emotion, she gushed out a jumble of instructions to each of them, then rushed off to micromanage and to irritate her own highly competent staff.

"We are traveling to Jerusalem," she told her chief of staff. "I have decided to go visit King Solomon. We will take a caravan of the finest gifts." She tried to use her most nonchalant authoritative voice, but they were not fooled in the least about her level of excitement over this venture. Her staff was accustomed to decisions that never seemed to take into account the colossal preparations necessary to carry out her whims. They had learned to nod in agreement and then to scurry frantically in order to accomplish her requests. They were without question the best and most able men in the kingdom, the most accomplished at making the impossible go smoothly and flawlessly. They knew their jobs depended on the good favor of her Highness, because the queen openly withheld favor from those who had not pleased her, and it was very unpleasant for them when it happened.

It must be nothing less than a breathtaking triumphant extravaganza.

They covered each other's short comings and pulled together for the sake of peace and the sake of the queen. To stand in her special favor, which she also had a myriad of ways of demonstrating, was highly coveted. Also, each had a measure of national pride, and their desire was that she be admired everywhere and be seen as wealthy and generous. That was the most important thing, they told themselves, as they labored furiously to get ready for the trip.

They knew that when her emotions were high, as they were now, she would want to leave immediately, but they also understood she expected to make an unforgettable impression on arrival, so they held her off for weeks while they worked to get everything in order. She pestered them to hurry, but they knew that she would wait, if rather impatiently, for them to get it right down to the last detail. When they finally did depart, the entourage needed to be equivalent to the queen's flamboyant imagination. It must be nothing less than a breathtaking triumphant extravaganza, so they held her off until they were satisfied with the preparations.

Perhaps she should have been fearful at crossing borders and entering strange countries, but she felt invincible. There were good trade routes and good relations among the countries she would travel through. There were always robber bands to be considered, but she planned to take 300 men with her, which would serve as a small army should she need one. She would travel through different countries in her grand parade encountering many people along the way, and then she would arrive in Jerusalem where Solomon, in all his glory, would be waiting for her arrival. It was the stuff tales were made of, containing all the excesses she could conjure up in her vivid imagination, and she thought nothing of the discomfort of the six months of travel she would have to endure to arrive at her destination.

Before she left, she worshipped the sun, the moon, and the stars in the traditional way of her people. She asked these celestial bodies for guidance and protection as she traveled. Her people charted the stars and studied astrology and astronomy with passionate zeal, trying to make sense of God's handiwork, for they felt it held keys to the universe and proclaimed mysteries about future events, although they didn't know Who had created the heavens. She consulted the astrologers for the exact time to leave so she would be in proper alignment with the heavens, and they calculated the movements of the stars, watched for significant patterns, and gave her some windows of time they deemed propitious.

When the Queen of Sheba finally set out, there was no doubt that she was on an unprecedented mission. As the spectacular caravan began its slow procession, the sights and sounds were as captivating as a circus. She had nearly one thousand camels, each roped to the other, outfitted with elegant golden chains, and rich tapestries woven with symbolic crescents meant to please the gods. The wooden saddles were covered with soft padding and beautiful fabrics of rich, vibrant colors, the colors of gemstones: garnets, sapphires, topaz, and amethysts. Each camel could carry approximately 500 pounds. While some carried supplies for the trip, and the staff rode on others, many were loaded down with a broad array of riches that the wealthy queen had at her disposal: gold, spices, fine woods, and samples of all the craftsmanship of her people.

She was accompanied by her own entourage of wild animals as well. Giraffes and hippopotami marched along in the caravan, as well as fifty elephants, and several lions which were sometimes pacing and roaring from inside their cages.

A magnificent white camel was led by one of the servants. The queen would ride it through the gates of Jerusalem when she arrived. It was outfitted with a brilliant saddle which was adorned with precious stones.

The queen herself spent most of the journey being carried on an engraved gold four poster bed with a roof-like covering, outfitted with brilliantly colored silk pillows, complete with draperies that she could close if she wished. She was dressed in scarlet and gold, veils and scarves covered her face and gold jewelry glistened from her arms and her ears. Her dark eyes were usually dancing with merriment, and when the wind blew, her scarves blew around her face and hair. She rarely closed her curtains, because she wanted to be seen and admired by the people she passed. Admiration always lifted her spirits, and there was never too much to embarrass her or make her self-conscious.

There was a sense of excitement among all the travelers, a sense of destiny that this meeting would be very important, that perhaps it might change history. Every detail of the caravan pointed to her as the star of the spectacle, and she rose to the occasion with her most elaborate theatrical presence. She had never been happier.

As they traveled along the Incense Road, people everywhere ran to see her and her traveling companions. From out of the dust, seemingly out of nowhere, her caravan appeared. People along the way had never seen such a magnificent display of ceremony, pomp, or wealth. She nodded to the people she passed and occasionally reached out to touch the hands of children. Often she gave trinkets, coins, or precious stones to the children. She smiled at the looks of amazement and disbelief she encountered along the way. It was thrilling to her, because her own people had become somewhat accustomed to her pomp, but these strangers seemed awed by it.

Upon arriving in Jerusalem, the queen entered the city gates in the dramatic fashion she desired, on the back of her white camel.

The sheer magnitude of her entourage, her wild animals, and the dazzling countenance of the queen herself made a spectacle that interrupted life as usual for everyone who saw her. Often older children ran along beside the caravan as far as they dared and shouted to her as she passed or announced who she was to the onlookers once they knew. Those who witnessed it spoke of it for years, recounting the day: "She looked like a vision, a desert mirage, for she appeared out of nowhere in the midst of the dust of the desert and the loping gait of the camels."

"Who is she?" they asked.

"The Queen of Sheba," someone answered.

"Where is she going?" they asked each other.

"To see King Solomon," others answered, and everyone said, "Ah," as though they understood the need for great people to meet and then they felt as though they had been especially invited to witness this momentous event.

Solomon had been told of the caravan coming to see him by more than one merchant who had passed the procession, and he had been preparing for her arrival. He would reciprocate her generosity with opulent gifts of his own: silks, linens, tapestries, beautiful garments, and all the very best food she would need for her camp of servants who had accompanied her. The queen herself would be taken to luxurious rooms which had been prepared for her.

Upon arriving in Jerusalem, the queen entered the city gates in the dramatic fashion she desired, on the back of her white camel. She stopped to marvel at the city gates, pretending to be oblivious to the people who were marveling at her and the spectacle of her train. After six long, hard months of travel, she had arrived and was most honorably welcomed by King Solomon's staff.

When she had been shown to her rooms, her eyes took in every detail, as she traced her fingers along the gold inlay in the tables and on the chairs at the palace. She touched precious jewels surrounding golden mirrors, and felt the exquisite silk coverings on the pillows. It was grander than anyone had described to her, and far from being intimidated, she congratulated herself on coming. This journey was already worth the effort.

When she was ushered into the presence of King Solomon himself, she stood speechless for a moment. Never could she have imagined a more commanding man, for not only was he majestic, but a glory truly did seem to surround him. He looked as though he could easily and effortlessly rule the world. When she greeted him with formal protocol, Solomon held her gaze, unlike most people she had ever known who dropped their eyes at the last moment when greeting her. She realized that no man or woman on earth was his equal. She saw wisdom in his eyes, an ancient wisdom, that startled her, as though she was looking into the eyes of a very old man.

She felt a sudden rush of deep insecurity at the thought of the immense favor he had.

Music played in the background and torches were lit all around the courtyard. Huge trays of delicacies were whisked around by brown skinned young men carrying them skillfully. She was offered dates, goat cheese, salted fish, lamb, grains, and figs, and every morsel was succulent and delightful. There were smells in the room, enchanting smells, and all at once she felt dizzy, overwhelmed by the grandeur, the opulence, the sights and sounds. She recognized that King Solomon had received blessings of such a magnitude that it was stunning to her, which was amazing since she herself was probably the wealthiest woman alive.

She felt a sudden rush of deep insecurity at the thought of the immense favor he had. The limelight to which she was accustomed seemed to move away from her, as even her own loyal attendants seemed awed by the king. She had never stood in the presence of one that she was sure was greater than herself, nor had she ever lost her own sense of confidence before. If she could not compete with her wealth, then maybe she could compete with her intellect. Tomorrow she would test him. She had spent much of her life observing the intellectual sparring that went on between great men. She knew exactly how the game was played.

In the days that followed, she tested her new friend with her knowledge and all of her training plus she explored with him deep and sincere questions of her own. Servants who were privileged to wait upon them were caught up in the competition as their two rulers went head to head in daily intellectual combat. Eyes darted back and forth between the servants of the two households during the king and queen's debates, and when there were moments for discreet interaction among the servants away from their respective ruler's ears, they goaded and sparred with each other as well, filled with pride at their own monarch's antics and wit.

For six months they all lived together in one household and the atmosphere was alive with laughter and intense discussions on many subjects. She asked him the most puzzling questions, the greatest mysteries, and the riddles that could only be deciphered by the greatest mind. He was justifiably impressed by the depth of her questions and the intensity of her desire for knowledge, but he was never overwhelmed by her. She became comfortable in his presence, but her admiration of the depth of his wisdom grew daily.

The Queen asked, "What is evil?"

Solomon: "Evil can only be defined by the Lord, for it is only His eyes that know what evil is."

The Queen: "Which is greater, a man's eyes or ears?"

Solomon: "You can not measure which is greater for the Lord has made them both. Deafness and blindness belong to man and they may be measured."

The Queen: "What is the most powerful organ?"

Solomon: "The tongue, because it can kill or heal."

The Queen: "Seven leave and nine enter; two pour out the draught and only one drinks."

Solomon: "Seven are the number of days of a woman's time; nine the months of pregnancy; two are the breasts that suckle the child; and only one drinks."

The Queen: "What is the ugliest thing, the most beautiful, the most certain, and the most uncertain?"

Solomon: "The ugliest thing is the faithful becoming unfaithful; the most beautiful, a sinner who repents; the most certain, death; and the most uncertain, sharing in the world to come."

The queen paused and studied the king's face. He had talked much about his Hebrew God, but he had never said that she might be among those chosen. She felt the king had become her friend and he had given her material treasures during her six months in

Jerusalem, but she had a secret desire to be one of the chosen ones, to secure for herself the everlasting blessing of the Hebrew God. She envisioned herself influencing others to follow this God, if Solomon would but speak and invite her to worship Him. He had confided in her that his wisdom had come from his God, and she wanted wisdom like Solomon's far more than his gold. She could hardly bear the thought that she was not worthy of acceptance by his God; the rejecting thought was deeply painful to her and ate away at her usual good humor.

"How happy your officials must be and the men who stand before you and hear your wisdom day and night! Praise be to your God who has delighted in you and placed you on your throne. Because of His eternal love for Israel, He has made you king, to maintain justice and righteousness," she announced one evening. Could he not see how desperate she was for this kind of happiness? She hid the disappointment she felt in her heart that God had not chosen her and her people to be His own. No amount of manipulation through her words or pathetic sighs appeared to move Solomon's heart.

The atmosphere of the palace had never sparkled so magnificently before.

"What is it that goes first in a storm at sea?" she asked, changing the subject and seeking to evade Solomon's astute eyes upon her.

"It is flax," the king answered, "for it is woven into cloth to make the ship's sail." He never took his eyes from her, for he sensed she was troubled.

"What when alive does not move, yet when its head is cut off, moves?" she retorted to divert his gaze.

"It is the timber used to build a ship." His quick answer brought little gasps around the room of people who had been searching for the answer and were amazed by his quickness.

"No more riddles tonight, my Queen." Solomon said, for she looked tired and weary and he saw through her contrived gaiety.

In time, the visit came to an end, and she prepared to leave. The servants of King Solomon's household mourned the parting, because the atmosphere of the palace had never sparkled so magnificently before, and the queen's servants wondered if they would ever feel satisfied in Sheba again. They all dreaded the monotony of the return to their normal lives. As she said her good-byes to King Solomon, she repeated a final riddle: "What is the most uncertain thing?" He did not answer her, choosing instead to bend down and kiss her cheek and embrace her one last time.

As she made the long journey back along the Incense Road, bearing the treasures of Israel on her camels' backs, she turned her heart back toward her land and her people. She would have the most wonderful stories to tell, beautiful clothes to wear, and many new riddles and knowledge with which to astound and amuse her people. She would not dwell on any parts of her journey that might in any way tarnish its brilliance. It had been entirely glorious.

In the years to come she relived those amazing days in Solomon's courts many times. Her expansive vision for trade was limitless, and she sold her country's vast wealth to many nations. Throughout her life she was well loved, relating to people everywhere, networking them together, while brilliantly courting their favor. She enjoyed easy acceptance from almost everyone she met, and she used it to form alliances and further

her trade routes. There were quiet moments, however, when she remembered painfully that she was not one of the "chosen ones," and that somehow, although she had impressed the world, she had failed to impress Solomon's God.

That thought found its way to a vulnerable place deep within her heart and made her feel small and insignificant, despite the unusual power she wielded or the self-confidence that others assumed she always had.

She would have rejoiced to know that one thousand years after her reign, while astronomers from Sheba were searching the skies for answers, an invitation from the Hebrew God would come at last. They would be the ones to discover a brilliant star beckoning them to travel to celebrate the birth of the world's greatest King, the Son of Solomon's God. They would make the identical journey she had made, but to Bethlehem instead of Jerusalem, and they would bear gifts, as she had, Sheba's finest treasures: gold, frankincense and myrrh. These future wise men would represent the very first ones who would be welcomed from afar and received by the Messiah. This King would receive every heart who sought Him, and to each one would be given the certainty she had coveted and the promise of everlasting joy in His enduring kingdom.

"What is the most certain thing?"

"Sharing in the world that is to come."

Chapter 13
Hauntingly Beautiful, Distorted, Illogical

The crowd of mostly young people stood on the mall in Washington D. C. swaying together in harmony as they repeated the chorus of John Lennon's song, "Give peace a chance," over and over again. "We just want to say, give peace a chance." They offered with their song a simple solution to the war in Vietnam. The year was 1969, the welcome end of a turbulent decade.

One half million people had rallied in Washington, D. C. to march for peace, protesting the war in Vietnam which had become extremely unpopular in much of the country. The deaths of leaders John Kennedy, Bobby Kennedy and Martin Luther King; race riots and angry protests about the war; anger toward authority; peace, love, and the hippie movement; and a call for young people to drop out of society, had shaped a decade and stunned a nation just settling in to enjoy the fruit of twenty years of peace since World War II. The children of veterans were protesting everything their fathers had worked to establish; a generation seemed to be discarding their parents' values with breakneck speed.

The times were unpredictable, and alarming, wearing heavily on everyone's emotions. A youth culture, united and powerful, was becoming vocal and influential. Protests on college campuses, drugs, Haight-Ashbury, and a growing mistrust of adults - especially leaders - was intensified by violent political deaths, disappointing decisions, scandals, racial unrest, and a war where young men were drafted to go, unsure if they were being sent as heroes or fools. Americans had always answered a call to arms when her liberty was threatened, and now the young were either unconvinced of the reality of the threat, or were unwilling to submit to the wisdom of their elder statesmen.

Phrases like "generation gap" became commonplace, signifying and justifying rebellion against the status quo. Illegal drugs and "free" sex were touted to be liberating, or available to the "liberated" who had thrown off societal restraint. A society whose conservative ways had supposedly led only to war, materialism, and an "establishment" made up of corrupt systems simply could not be trusted.

The message of the day was that a complete turnaround would be needed to rectify the mistakes of the past. Women's rights and civil rights were bursting forth with new energy. Anyone who felt stifled by conservative America stepped forth to stake their claim on the future.

What had happened to so divide a nation, and why were the young suddenly the people with the loudest voices in all the land? The counter culture revolution of the sixties had its leaders, voices which united the youth and appealed to idealism, fears, and their sense of justice, at the same time granting them permission to engage in open rebellion. There arose voices in the land that railed against order, justified rebellion against the system, justified dress indicative of the rebellion, justified "dropping out" and finding a radical new way of thinking and doing things. The voices were found in the lyrics of the rock music of the day, which played in the background of the 60's like the theme music from a movie, pointing out the flaws of society and suggesting rebellion as an alternative.

One of those at the front of the revolution was not even American, but British, John Lennon, a sensitive misfit, whose influence over a generation helped to shape a counter culture.

* * *

John Lennon sat at his grade school desk, drawing as usual. He filled pages with characters that came out of his vivid imagination. Mostly they were crippled and deformed, and he made up funny stories about them; it helped the time go more quickly and he enjoyed his own bizarre, irreverent sense of humor. School was such a bore; his teachers could never understand him and he felt he was different from the other kids. He recognized that what he had was a kind of genius, but what difference did it make? His father had deserted the family, and now his mother had moved out, leaving him with his aunt. His aunt never liked his drawings or his stories. He wondered if his mother would have liked them. Perhaps he could save them for her to see one day.

The days of school came and went until finally they were over. Glad to be free, he began to devote his time to his real passion:

music. He played with a band which had been together since 1950. It was now almost 1960, and although they were developing a sound of their own and a style of their own, they were only playing in small British clubs. For John, it was not a bad lifestyle. He had everything he needed: quiet, a few close friends, some people who appreciated his talent, and a girlfriend. Although a tidal wave of change was almost upon him, he could never have conceived how gigantic it would be. A man named Brian Epstein was about to discover the group and recognize their marketable potential. He saw their appeal, recognized the uniqueness of their sound, and began to promote them. They changed their name to the Beatles, and almost overnight became a phenomenon.

At first their songs were innocent love songs.

The fame and notoriety were fun at first. John was the group leader; everyone called him the "smart one," and it was true he was witty, intelligent, and sensitive. In the early years of popularity, "the boys from Liverpool," an English seacoast city, seemed to demonstrate the carefree exuberance of youth. They influenced style with their long hair and their sound was imitated on both sides of "the pond." At first their songs were innocent love songs, but gradually with their step into drugs and the times that were changing everything, the songs became darker and sadder, more introspective and ultimately, for John anyway, more politically inspired.

Nine years saw lots of changes for the group as musicians, and their popularity gave them an influence that affected society. Music and public sentiment, politics, and serious questions became entangled in the period. The United States was enduring many social clashes and ideological battles during that decade, and the timing of the popularity of the British group, and rock music in general, coincided with the social upheaval, or perhaps in some ways contributed to it.

The Beatles had no real Christian foundations, and although they pursued Eastern religion for awhile before dismissing it and declaring it a "phase," what John really came to believe in was a sort of nihilism, a state where there were no moral absolutes. Drugs became the destructive path to peace, or at least escape. Peace was always a major theme for him. He desperately sought his personal peace in eastern religion, yoga, drugs, sex, and music. John craved intimacy more than anything, and he soon realized that he was able, through his music, to connect people to a place inside himself - broken though it was - and to whatever powerful message his lyrics suggested.

He was impressed with her confidence and her ability to make things happen.

He was not happy, and the road he was on was causing him to be even more miserable. As the popularity of the Beatles chaotically increased and their privacy was constantly threatened, he felt increasingly overwhelmed. He became more self-protective, more withdrawn, and colder. "The fans are sucking the life right out of me," he began to say. He decided that the fans had no emotions of their own and no way to express them, that they were only able to feel through his lyrics. He was growing painfully weary of feeling for the whole world. It all felt like a burden from which he couldn't escape. His temper flared when fans crossed the line; although he never liked confrontation, he could blow up in a quick burst of temper.

Soon the Beatles began to have internal problems. Paul was taking over leadership of the group, since he had begun to stand out as the most popular one. The sense of betrayal and rejection were getting to be too much for John. When he met Yoko Ono, a Japanese artist living in New York, he was impressed with her confidence and her ability to make things happen. She would become a radical peace activist alongside John. Hoping it was a relationship that could endure, he was willing to give up everything to have it: his own wife and child, and ultimately his career with the Beatles.

According to John, the Beatles refused to accept her. Some people felt they were prejudiced against her race, but perhaps it was the huge influence she had over John which no one liked. The whole way he ditched his first wife without any dialogue or concern may have been too much, even for their "live and let live" sensibilities. He was fed up with Paul anyway, so it was easy to walk out in 1969. He was deeply hurt by the way things were evolving, as he was hurt by criticism in general. When the Beatles rejected Yoko and Paul stepped to the front, he would no longer take the rejection. He walked away, clinging to the one relationship that he felt would last for him.

He cared deeply and he wrote simple and direct lyrics that spoke to youth.

John had always used his music to speak for him, to express his soul. The music went from simple love songs like, "I Want To Hold Your Hand," deeper and deeper into drug songs, "Whatever

Gets You Through The Night," and political songs, "Revolution," and "Give Peace A Chance."

When John and Yoko decided to settle in the United States, they were political activists in earnest. They were so overtly opposed to President Nixon that Nixon ordered proceedings to have John deported, using his drug charges as the excuse to send him home. Much of the country's youth seemed to idolize him completely, but the leader of the same country despised him. Nixon never succeeded in getting him deported due to his own involvement in the Watergate scandal. The victorious Yoko and John were happily present in the room during the court proceedings against the president.

John had popularity, fame, power, and influence, and although he used them, they were not what he cared about. He was always very much in touch with his own pain and the pain of a world gone wrong. He cared deeply and he wrote simple and direct lyrics that spoke to youth. He felt the system had failed, as had religion and government which led him to a simplistic conclusion: if we did away with all of those things, and entered a kind of "nutopia" (his own word) where there were none of those things, all of a sudden we would be united in peace because the things we fought over, primarily boundaries and religion, would be gone.

In his and Ono's song, "Imagine," still the most beloved Beatle song in England, he outlines the plan. The song is sung as a ballad, one that has been called a secular hymn, outlining his proposal for world peace. It is sung with all the tenderness and faith of a hymn, outlining escapism and nihilism as the way to peace. In the song, John touches his own brokenness. The song feels like a plea for an escape from the way the world is: an escape into a nihilistic vacuum where nothing exists but man, breaking free from all the defiling systems he has created, new again. Maybe it was the Garden of Eden before man's fall that John was longing for, as it is a song that contains a melancholy yearning for that kind of peace:

> Imagine there's no heaven; it's easy if you try.
> No hell below us, above only sky.
> Imagine all the people living for today.
> Imagine there's no countries; it isn't hard to do.
> Nothing to kill or die for and no religion too.
> Imagine all the people living in peace.
> Imagine no possessions; I wonder if you can.
> No need for greed or hunger, a brotherhood of man.
> Imagine all the people sharing all the world.
> You may say that I'm a dreamer, but I'm not the only one.
> And some day I hope you'll join us, and the world will be as one.[1]

He hated conflict on every level, and doing away with all government, even the government of God, seemed like a logical way to escape it all. He hated war and sadly, every organized system from family to church to a group of musicians called the Beatles had been disappointing failures for him. Because he never knew the peace of God, he couldn't imagine His peace. All he could imagine was peace apart from every system.

He poured out the emptiness of his soul through his musical gift, and it came through a spirit that God designed to connect with people and bring them into intimacy. In a very real sense, he was able to achieve it. He gave the world a song to sing about an ideal state of peace, albeit with no God or devil or man's authority of any kind. It was a hauntingly beautiful, distorted, illogical and impossible hymn of anarchy that is still loved and sung throughout the world. At its heart is a longing for peace and brotherhood, and that part of it resonates with man's spirit.

It was perhaps his finest achievement, a testament to his powerful gift of music and his God-given ability to move people into a place of intimacy and unity, despite his own wounded spirit and ignorance of his Creator, and despite the distorted and deceptive lyrics.

Chapter 14

What Else Could I Have Done?

Eli bent over with difficulty, steadying himself with a hand against the wall, as he searched under Samuel's bedding trying to find his cup that the boy had hidden. When his fingers touched the cold metal, he snatched up the prize and shoved it inside the folds of his robe. The child's mischievous tricks were a source of mild frustration to the old man, but he couldn't begrudge the boy this little amusement. Samuel's childhood had been so unusual, growing up here in the Tabernacle, so it was little wonder that every now and then, Samuel needed to act like the child he was. The boy preferred games of his own design, especially hiding objects from Eli, and whenever something went missing, the old priest had learned to look for it in some odd place.

At first, he had scolded the boy, but his mercy got the best of him and he relented, deciding that the child needed the diversion, not to say that an old man couldn't use a bit of it himself. The game had been going on for years, and the rules had evolved to what they were today: each one played his part without the need for words. It was enough for the boy to know that the old man had to search for things he had hidden. It tickled him to think of the fat priest scurrying about and bending over to find the objects, muttering under his breath about the awful punishments he planned to inflict on the villain who had taken his things.

After he had recovered his beloved objects, Eli pretended not to notice the glint of satisfaction in Samuel's eyes. It was a game of nuances and ever so slight body language; it was communicated by two people, generations apart who understood each other very well.

Samuel loved Eli like a grandfather, while Eli cherished the little boy who had been a comfort and a help to him for almost a decade. Samuel was close to twelve now; he was fast becoming a young man, growing tall and lean, able to do countless tasks that were once beyond his reach. Samuel was probably outgrowing these games, yet he was clinging to them fiercely, in the way of a youth who is debating if leaving childhood behind is truly wise.

A little distraction from the elaborate duties of Tabernacle life did lighten things, especially if Eli had recently clashed with his own sons who were a disgrace to the priesthood and an equally poor reflection of his fathering. His sons were much older then Samuel, grown men who could not seem to mature and be responsible like the twelve year old was.

Eli preferred not to think about his sons' behavior, but he could hardly escape it. Scarcely a day went by without some wagging tongue telling him more than he wanted to know about their misdeeds and demanding that he discipline them. Eli could never bring himself to administer the degree of painful discipline that would be needed to actually stop what they were doing. He knew they were an affront to God, and that time was probably running out for him to intervene. Most of the time, he chose not to think about it at all, or he cherished some private hope that God would continue to be longsuffering. Diligently, he kept busy with his priestly duties. There was always plenty to be done and the whole priestly role enabled him to live in another world, one set apart from ordinary life.

He liked being part of God's plan for dealing with sin.

Down the hall the boy ran into the room where he slept to find his bedding disheveled and the cup gone. He giggled out loud. He really loved it here in the Tabernacle. Every year when his mother came and brought his new linen ephod, she recounted the story of how she had moved God's heart with her tears and He had given her Samuel. "I cried so much that Eli thought I was drunk," she would always say. "But I wasn't drunk. I was just overwrought with grief that I had no child, so God gave me you." Then she would hug him fiercely, kiss his face and cry all over again. This was Hannah's story.

It was Samuel's story too. His mother had brought him to the Tabernacle as a young child and presented him to Eli; he was her gift of gratitude back to God. Now he ministered before the Lord in this place, which had always felt like a safe and secure home to him. He slept with the priests in the small rooms built for them inside the Tabernacle courtyard. At night there was no sound of anxious, noisy animals or people, just a quiet stillness so intense that it drew Samuel into deep sleep or deep thought.

He would snuggle under his covers and imagine what the Ark might look like, because all of the work had its crescendo on the Day of Atonement when Eli himself entered the Holy of Holies where the presence of God dwelt. As High Priest, Eli stood before the Ark itself. All of Israel's heart and soul were centered here in the Tabernacle, preserved by the faithfulness of these priests. By God's grace, he was one of them.

His mother had been right to bring him here where he could study and learn how to mediate between the people and God, just like Eli. There was nothing more important to be done in all the earth, no other job he would have preferred.

Everything about Tabernacle life suited him. As he grew older, he especially loved the Law. He liked being part of God's plan for dealing with sin, watching the people come with repentant hearts to sacrifice, determining to stay in harmony with their God by washing away a myriad of sins with the blood of slain animals.

His heart was torn between the reverence he had for the things of God and his respect for the High Priest.

He was always amazed by the precise requirements of the sacrifices for specific sins and the parameters for different freewill offerings, each one outlined by God. Mediating between God and man - the rituals of the Law - had special significance to Samuel, and he felt privileged to represent God by participating in the daily routine and the special days.

Obedience to God was the most logical thing in the world to Samuel, so he could never understand Eli's sons or their disregard for the essence of the Law. Because they were a mystery to his way of thinking, their behavior troubled him. He was certain Eli didn't know some of the things they had done. *How could he know and allow it to continue?* He debated telling Eli about them himself, because he feared that God would punish them all one day for mocking Him when they took the best meat off the altar for themselves according to their own appetites and desires, disregarding the Law on what portion was rightfully theirs and when it should be taken. *How could the people fear God if His priests did not?*

His heart was torn between the reverence he had for the things of God and his respect for the High Priest, but ultimately he decided he was not the right one to tell Eli. Instead he would pray for Eli to notice and stop his sons. When it appeared that Eli never would, Samuel made a monumental decision. He made his own personal vow to God that, although he loved Eli and emulated him in almost every way, he would never run his family like Eli did. If he had sons, he would teach them the truth and then he would walk in integrity before them, so that he would never find himself in Eli's predicament.

After he vowed to himself that he would avoid Eli's mistakes with his sons, he then promised God that He could count on him to live by the truth and inspire others to live by the truth. While his vow didn't change Eli's sons, Samuel felt that at least he had done something.

Samuel lay down in his room as usual at the close of the day. This day had been ordinary and predictable in every detail; the same as many other days, yet comforting in its order and richly satisfying to Samuel. He did what he was told with a profound sense of responsibility, observing details with alertness.

If Samuel had a fault, it would have been leaving his other chores undone or rushing through them sloppily in order to get to his Tabernacle duties sooner. Eli would scold him about the mess he sometimes left of his bed, or the fact that he often hurried to the Tabernacle before he washed his face or put up his cup. The Tabernacle was where he wanted to be, a place where he was useful and the work was significant, not wasting precious time performing some meaningless task.

It was on such an ordinary night that he was awakened from his sleep, startled by the sound of his own name, a loud and reverberating: "Samuel."

The voice which awakened him did not sound like Eli's voice, but then it had to have been. He jumped up and ran down the hall to Eli's room, saying, "Here I am. You called me." When Eli insisted that he had not called him and sent him back to his bed, Samuel could only assume he had been dreaming. Finally he went back to sleep, only to be awakened the second time, the same voice calling out his name. Surely this was Eli.

Was this a new game initiated by Eli? When Eli sent him back a second time - this time slightly annoyed with him for the second disturbance - he lay wide awake, fearful but expectant, convinced that it might happen again. The third time the word, "Samuel," filled the room, he practically flew down the hallway to Eli's room, his bare feet hardly touching the cold stones. The old priest was wide awake himself by now, and he struggled to swing about and put his feet on the floor and stand up to face the boy. "It is the Lord who is calling you, Samuel. When he calls again, say this: 'Speak, Lord, for your servant is listening.'"

Samuel returned to his bed and did exactly as Eli had instructed him. The words that answered his timid voice were bold and clear like the sound of the shofar in the hands of one who has blown the instrument for many years. They were precise and irrefutable, alive and true. They were so powerful that when he listened to them he was absolutely certain that each one would be performed exactly as it was being spoken.

Only once did he allow his mind to wander from the words, wondering if God might accept a sacrifice to atone for Eli's sons, but at the very moment he thought it, God said there would be no sacrifice or atonement accepted on their behalf, as though He had read his mind. His heart felt sick and he trembled for the old priest and his sons. He would have tried to cry out the rest of the night on their behalf, just as his mother had once done before his birth, but he knew it was of no use. He lay curled in a ball on his mat until morning light, hoping against hope that Eli would not ask him what the Lord had said to him in the night.

How could Eli be so calm and so resigned?

When morning came, fresh and cool, he felt a chill. Maybe Eli would not presume to ask what God had said to him. God had never spoken to him before and so he had no idea how Eli would respond. Entering the room where they took their breakfast, Samuel felt Eli's eyes on him as he cut a piece of bread and picked up some figs. He ate the bread and the figs slowly, while the old man waited patiently, never taking his eyes off of him. When he was done, Eli said, "What is it that He said to you? Do not hide it from me. May the Lord deal with you ever so severely if you hide anything from me." So Samuel swallowed hard, and then told him everything, every word exactly as they had been spoken to him.

As he spoke he watched Eli's eyes, thinking he might be able to predict his reaction and brace himself for whatever would come next. He could not, for the priest's face was inscrutable. All Eli said in return was "He is the Lord; Let him do what is good in his eyes." *How could Eli be so calm and so resigned?* Part of it, he realized, was because the Lord had spoken. He had not personally known the impact of those words before as he now did, and so he could understand Eli's resolve, but there was much more to Eli's mysterious response.

As he watched Eli hobble out to set up for the day, his shoulders stooped, his jaw set in fierce determination, the boy recognized an even deeper sorrow in Eli's eyes than the one he had grown accustomed to seeing. That, maybe, was to be expected. What puzzled Samuel more was Eli's calm resignation. It could only mean that Eli had known about his sons all along and had been expecting this day to come. He had known and he had done nothing or said nothing. Samuel had never been more perplexed about Eli's behavior than he was at that moment. "I will never be in his place," Samuel reiterated his inner vow to God and to himself.

It was not too many years before God's prophecy to Samuel came to pass, and Eli, horrified that the Ark had been taken in battle by the Philistines, died in the aftermath. Although the words God had spoken to him were true, the outcome was one he never would have wished. Samuel could not stop thinking that perhaps with a little more time and a little more instruction, these men could have changed. He knew that God was not hasty or cruel in his decision to execute judgment exactly as He had done. It was just that in himself he found it more comfortable to stay in the most patient part of God's nature, although there were times when even he could be pushed out of his mild mannered restraint and lose his patience over flagrant disobedience to God's explicit instructions.

When Samuel grew to be a man, he became a judge in Israel, and just as he had vowed, he was truthful and faithful to the Lord. He went out regularly among the people, traveling from Ramah to Bethel to Gilgal and then to Mizpah where the Israelites waited for him to settle their disputes and instruct them in the ways of the Lord, leaving them to act on his instructions once he was gone.

On his return trips he was often disappointed to see that his teaching had fallen on deaf ears and nothing much had changed, despite his best intentions and his godly example. God listened to Samuel's prayers of intercession for the people and the people listened to Samuel's instructions about pleasing their God. He mediated peace between the Father and his children. Day after day he lived a life of faithful obedience before them.

He understood, at last, the paralysis that Eli felt when he came to confrontation.

When Samuel grew too old serve as a judge any longer, he appointed his sons, Joel and Abiah, to take his place, but they were not like their father who ruled with integrity; sadly, they were both greedy for wealth which prompted them to accept bribes and pervert justice.

He remembered his vow to himself when he had witnessed the corruption of Eli's sons as a boy, that no such a thing would ever happen to him, and yet it had. He had lived his life devoted to the priesthood, meticulous in his execution of God's commands, an obedient and faithful priest, and yet, his sons were no better than Eli's. He was ashamed of them, and there were times when he wished he could tell Eli how sorry he was to have judged him. He understood, at last, the paralysis that Eli felt when he came to confrontation. *Why was it so difficult?*

It was difficult because he was a reasonable man and he believed that if his example, one they had witnessed their entire lives, was not enough to convict them, then what possible effect could his words have upon them? When the people began to demand a king to rule over them, he couldn't help but take it personally, because he knew that their discontent with his own corrupt sons was at least part of the reason they wanted the king, although there were other deeper reasons. Samuel prophesied to the people what the result of having a king would be, accurately describing Israel's future with her young men as soldiers and her daughters serving in the king's household, all the nation bowing to the king's agenda. He saw into the future reigns of Saul, David, and Solomon, and those beyond, but the people would not listen to him: they insisted on their king. Samuel felt they were rejecting him, but God knew they were really rejecting Him.

He mourned the sad reality that men often start well, but often do not maintain ongoing righteousness before God.

Although Samuel had grown old, he was God's pick to anoint Saul to be the king. It grieved Samuel and God both to give the people what they asked for, because each knew what was ahead. While Saul began his reign well, in the end, he failed miserably. The day Samuel went to him on the battlefield to offer sacrifices to the Lord on behalf of his army and help him seek instructions for the battle, he arrived to discover that Saul had been impatient and offered the sacrifice himself.

Equally as alarming, on another occasion, he had also spared the life of his adversary, King Agag, and kept choice animals alive, despite God's explicit instructions to the contrary. Samuel went into a rage, for he could hardly believe that Saul understood so little about God's ways as to ignore God's instructions and then justify his reasons for doing so. He was outraged at Saul's flagrant rebellion and perhaps also the rebellion of his own sons and Eli's sons - all of the sons who could not follow the simplest instructions from their earthly fathers or their heavenly one. He had Agag brought to him and demonstrating to Saul what obedience looked like, Samuel himself killed the king, executing judgment for God and venting some of his own frustration at watching Israel's disobedient sons cost the nation God's blessing.

Unfortunately, no amount of obedience on Samuel's part could atone for Saul's lack, and God tore the kingdom away from Saul that day. When God rejected Saul as king, Samuel mourned for him, although he agreed with the wisdom of God's decision. He mourned the sad reality that men often start well, but often do not maintain ongoing righteousness before God. He could not understand why it was so difficult for most men, even men who had seen God's power and served Him well, to continue in a path of submission and obedience. He was depressed by what had already transpired with Israel and her "king," and he was not comforted by the thought that he had spent his own life preaching, teaching, judging, and prophesying to the people, and yet in the end his own truth had failed to penetrate their hearts.

Samuel often stood before the people and confronted them from a place of his own integrity, not with harsh judgments or emotional outbursts, but with irrefutable truth and evidence of God's righteous acts and benevolent history with His people. He felt compelled to emphasize his own integrity to the people, for Samuel believed that a man's life was the best picture of his beliefs, and too, he knew that iniquity in leaders had been costly to the people's faith.

He kept his oath to God, as far as he was able on his part. He had walked with integrity before the Lord. "Whose ox have I taken? Whose donkey have I taken? Whom have I cheated? Whom have I oppressed? From whose hand have I accepted a bribe to make me shut my eyes? If I have done any of these, I will make it right."

The people answered him that he had done none of those things, he was respected by one and all, and yet, even then, his obedience had not caused them to obey. God had kept His word and given the people a faithful priest, one who had lived his life righteously, honoring God and His word, incarnating truth and principle throughout his life, yet there was rebellion everywhere he looked, in the country and in his own household.

Samuel recounted his life before the Lord and the people, and then he sat down and mourned. "What else could I have done?" he asked, of no one in particular.

The country of Pakistan is tropical, hot and humid with a long rainy season following the monsoon and temperatures soaring well over a hundred degrees. Two rivers, the Ganges and the Brahmaputra, meet within its borders and empty into the Bengal Bay. It is a country of 75 million people on 51, 000 square miles, a place about the size of Wisconsin. Although in 1970, East Pakistan had 56% of Pakistan's total population, it was ruled by West Pakistan, which held the political power. In a bizarre geographical configuration, East and West Pakistan were split, separated by 1100 miles of the nation of India.

The people of the two parts of Pakistan were dissimilar in every way: they didn't look alike, eat the same food, dress alike, have the same customs or enjoy the same culture. They shared the Muslim faith, but that was where their similarity ended. The East Pakistanis were Bengalis, slender brown skinned people who were quick, intelligent, and sensitive. As a people they were familiar with natural catastrophes including deadly cyclones, tidal waves, reoccurring famines, floods, and mudslides. But natural catastrophes did not prepare them for what happened in 1971 when West Pakistani troops invaded their land, destroying their homes, raping their women, and killing three million of their people.

What prompted this slaughter? Initially it was a national election where East Pakistan won more representative government seats than the West for the first time. Planning to insist on more control of their portion of the country, the East Pakistanis were infuriated when President Yahya Khan refused to convene government for fear they would exercise their new power.

Since West Pakistan had embraced a posture of lawlessness, East Pakistan seceded from the nation, declaring their region to be a sovereign in its own right. West Pakistan proved their lawlessness by attacking them. In the ensuing conflict, three million Bengalis would die, and ten million more refugees would cross into India seeking asylum. The burden on India ultimately prompted that nation to step in and offer Indian troops to the Bengalis, and with their help, East Pakistan ended the conflict on March 26, 1971. The concept of East Pakistan was destroyed, but there emerged a new and better idea, a Bengali nation: Bangladesh.

Dr. Viggio Olsen, who had served as a missionary in East Pakistan for the previous ten years, remained in the country for much of the war. He was in his American homeland on furlough when the news came that the Bengalis had prevailed. Joyously, he phoned his friend, the former East Pakistani ambassador to America.

"Congratulations, Ambassador," Vig said enthusiastically when he heard the ambassador's voice on the line.

"Daktar Olsen, thank you. We are all very happy that the war is over, but our country is in terrible condition. I have had you on my mind lately," the ambassador replied as though he had expected Vig to call. "What would you think of returning to our new nation and meeting with our prime minister? We could provide you with documents signifying your true friendship to the nation and our debt of gratitude to you for helping so many survive during the horrors of the war."

Vig was surprised, but he had years of practice in seizing opportunities when they came, so he did not hesitate. "What can I do to be of help?"

Before Vig and three of his team returned to Bangladesh to meet with the prime minister, he was invited to the State Department in Washington where he related what they had seen in East Pakistan. As he was leaving the U.S. for Bangladesh he received another phone call which surprised and encouraged him. It was from a representative of the government of the United States, asking him to be a secret diplomat to the new nation, offering humanitarian aid and the promise of recognition for Bangladesh as a nation. He was instructed to tell the prime minister that the process of recognition was already underway, quietly.

Before state diplomacy could be initiated with a recognized government, this missionary medical doctor who had fought to win respect in East Pakistan was already being sent as an ambassador to that country from the United States. He had gone ten years earlier as an ambassador for God, and God was now granting him favor with the rulers of both nations.

Returning to these people he loved was at once a great joy and a tremendous shock. The conditions which had been horrible when he escaped had grown much worse. The second phase of the war had ravaged the country, leaving many just wandering about, often maimed and homeless, without food or shelter. Sometimes entire villages had been burned, vehicles destroyed, and even sacred mosques lay in ruins. There were people wandering helplessly with very bad injuries and no one to treat them. Many of those injuries were from land mines which were still an ongoing problem. The people seemed joyful that the conflict was finally over, yet they also seemed dazed from grief, shock, and pain. The strange mixture of emotions saddened the doctor, but only heightened his determination to help.

His heart was broken for the people when he returned.

When his team met with the prime minister, they discovered that he was a likeable and competent man who was completely overwhelmed with the task before him of rebuilding his nation. Three million of his people had died, thirty million houses were destroyed, the monsoon was coming in a few short months and his people had little shelter. They desperately needed medicine, food, and shelter, and they had no hope unless aid came to them from somewhere outside their broken nation.

The prime minister was angry with the United States government for supporting West Pakistan during the war, but when Dr. Olsen told him of the message of good will from his government and its plans to both recognize and help his nation, the prime minister was able to respond with gratitude and begin to hope for the first time. No doubt the personal letter which Olsen's mission team had sent to President Nixon detailing the horrors of the conflict they had witnessed had played a role in the United States' change of heart.

Dr. Olsen had gone back to the United States on furlough in 1971, not foreseeing the second phase of the war. His heart was broken for the people when he returned, and he felt he had to do something to help them, even though he had no resources. Where would he get finances and labor to begin immediately? He could think of little else other than the urgency as he prayed for a strategy.

He had recently spoken at Wheaton College missions' week in the States. Many of the students' hearts seemed to have been touched by the needs of the people in Bangladesh. Could he recruit Christian college students to spend a few months in Bangladesh? The work had to be done immediately, between March and mid-June before the monsoons started. Since the United States planned to give millions in aid, he decided to ask his government for money immediately, sending one of his team to Washington to plead with the Agency for International Development.

There was no way an American's desire to "hurry" easterners would be received.

In the meantime, realizing that Wheaton College was on the quarter system and that students would be able to forego school for one quarter during the time period that was necessary, Dr. Olsen began recruiting, interviewing, and eventually accepting a group of students to travel to Bangladesh for this unusual construction project. About two dozen people formed the Bangladesh Brigade, as he called them, including a few trained nurses. Their lofty goal was to build 4,000 houses, but it was not long after they arrived in the country that the team began to feel entirely discouraged and overwhelmed by the task.

Dr. Olsen went imploringly to the Bible for answers on how to organize the project, searching for some method that would work. He looked especially to the passages about builders such as Ezra and Nehemiah. In those passages, especially chapter three of Nehemiah, he found the answer he was praying for.

Nehemiah had carefully listed the people who were working on the wall, and while it might seem like a tedious chapter to read, Dr. Olsen immediately understood its significance to him. Nehemiah did not have skilled laborers! He used ordinary people, priests, women, and farmers, yet in fifty two days the wall was rebuilt. The same God who had championed Nehemiah was on their side! He sought out the young workers to tell them to put their confidence in God and that this task was entirely possible: he had proof!

He also found another principle in Nehemiah that helped him. As he read about the work on the wall he felt he should resist assembly type work and instead send out small teams who would be responsible for every thing in a village from start to finish. Once he hit upon that idea, the plan came into focus. He would send one student and an interpreter to each village and they would supervise the work from start to finish.

There was no way an American's desire to "hurry" easterners would be received, so rather than do the work themselves or manage the work, he decided to appoint village people to supervise the reconstruction of village-style homes made of bamboo like the ones they had lived in for centuries. The village leader was also responsible to provide food for the laborers while they were building their own homes and to secure all the supplies for them. Dr. Olsen funded the project and offered them bonuses and incentives to keep the work moving quickly.

He was careful to find villagers for the oversight who were respected among the workers. He found two other competent Bengalis to travel from village to village sharing the concept, and he used his Bangladesh Brigade of Americans to see that all of it was flowing smoothly and to distribute the "incentives" which Dr. Olsen secured by steadily cashing checks that were flowing in from the United States to buy supplies and pay bonuses to every villager who completed his house on schedule.

To his delight, the work progressed just like it had for Nehemiah.

At the end of their few months, the Brigade had been responsible for restoring and building ten thousand homes, not the four thousand that were budgeted. They had put together a three million dollar project in a few months, money had poured in, and what they had done was nothing short of miraculous.

As the young workers were preparing to leave the country, the American ambassador to Bangladesh made a confession to the team by saying, "I did not want you to come here. In fact, I opposed your coming to authorities in Washington. While I felt that you were 'good hearted Peace Corps types,' I did not feel you had enough time or experience to be of much help. I did not want you to get hurt or sick, and truthfully, I thought you might outrage the citizens, or violate the customs. I must apologize to you, for I have heard nothing but praises for you and your work here. Thank you. You have brought honor to your country."[1]

The young men went back home in June, but they had seen the power of God move and the ability of a fathering leader to execute a project by using biblical principles. He trusted each of them as sons, granting them their own leadership duties. They left with faith that they could accomplish whatever task God assigned them in their lives, and that He could impart His method right along with the vision. They had been part of a team where the leader had hand picked them, watched over them, and asked no more of them than he gave himself. He trusted them to lead, stretching them beyond what even they believed they could accomplish.

He was not too busy to relate to them personally, or to the Bengalis, who would often run up to the tall doctor who stood a head above the rest, shouting "Daktar Sahib," a term of honor and respect for him. So many had a touching story of how he had saved their lives or the lives of their loved ones. The young men and women discovered they weren't "Peace Corps types" at all, but Christians who had been given an opportunity to build God's way, and it was something they would never forget.

One of the students penned a poem on the bus returning home after a hard day's work. This is part of what he said:

> For I have confronted you with an impossible task and problem to solve, filled with countless widows, never-ending need, and a pleading so often it soon becomes a duplicate of the one before -
>
> Feel them, touch them, my son - for as they touch you, they touch me. As you touch them - so too - it is I that you touch.[2]

Bangladesh had won, and Dr. Viggio Olsen had also won. He would be granted the right to live freely among the Bengalis as he labored for both their physical and spiritual well being, sharing the gospel along with all of his skills as a surgeon. He would remain in the nation for an additional twenty years.

* * *

What had brought this man to Bangladesh in the beginning, and how had God equipped him for what he would face there?

When Vig Olsen had graduated from high school in 1944, he decided to see if he could qualify for a special Navy program rather than enlist for what remained of World War II. If he were able to pass a V-12 exam, he could have his college tuition paid for at Tulane University in New Orleans. It was a fast track program completing four years of college in just two years. He passed the exam and was given three options of careers the Navy wanted these young men to pursue at its expense: career Navy, engineering, or pre-med. Since Olsen didn't want to be career military, wasn't interested in building bridges or roads, he reasoned that medicine would be the right choice for him, mainly because he liked people. Never again would he make such an impulsive decision about something so crucial, yet he never regretted his choice.

Olsen, however, was scientifically minded and a world class skeptic.

At Tulane he was a popular student who didn't differ much from the other 900 Navy recruits who were his roommates in the large facility where they were housed. He said, "We were full of cold, scientific ideas, compassionate feelings, unhealthy habits, idealism, vain ambition, and a sincere desire to alleviate suffering."[3] From that paradoxical mix, one thing began to emerge in Vig, and that was his organizational skills. He had an ability to see to the root of a problem, to devise a method to overcome the problem, and to implement a system to solve it in an effective way. Once he discovered this ability, he claimed that "all sense of humility left him."

After pre-med at Tulane, he was accepted at the University of Nebraska Medical School, which enabled him to return to his home state. He did well in medical school, deciding on internal medicine rather than surgery, because he enjoyed the problem solving aspect of searching for a diagnosis. He graduated cum laude, was president of the student council, and president of the student body in his senior year.

He married his sweetheart, Joan Baur, after his sophomore year, earlier than they had planned, because the school had recognized his abilities. They gave him an opportunity to teach freshmen while he worked on his own degree, giving the Olsens enough finances to wed.

His ability to spot a problem and solve it in an organized manner benefited his fraternity brothers who were in medical school with him, some of whom were having trouble in their classes. He managed to work into his packed schedule some intensive workshops on the basics which he presented in a more accessible and amusing format helping those who were struggling. His initiative saved a number of his classmates from dropping out and helped them become practicing physicians.

Dr. Olsen approached every situation with an organized and systematic approach, and that included giving his life to Jesus. When he married Joan, her parents were Christians and they began immediately trying to persuade the young couple to accept the truth of Christianity. Olsen, however, was scientifically minded and a world class skeptic. He did not believe that the Bible held real answers, or that there was much real proof of Christianity at all. His wise new in-laws gave up pestering him in exchange for a promise that he and Joan would attend church and study the Bible. Vig agreed he would go to church, while congratulating himself that he had not agreed to go often. He did have three questions that both he and Joan wanted answered:

1. Was there a God who had created the universe?
2. Did God reveal Himself to the human race through the Bible or other ways?
3. Was Jesus the son of God?[4]

He actually believed that it would be relatively easy to disprove Christianity, but he became intrigued by the consistency of the gospels, and then to his surprise, far from being easy to dispute, it was impossible. Familiar with scientific discovery that was often outdated in ten years, he was amazed to find scientific accuracy and consistency in the Bible.

He was further jarred by finding many facts that science had recently proved already recorded in the Bible at times when no one could have guessed they were true. The Bible said the earth was suspended on nothing, that it was not resting on a foundation, and according to Isaiah, the earth was round. The Bible spoke of the supernatural, and obviously something supernatural had happened to twelve very ordinary men to enable them to turn the world upside down. He came home one day to find Joan excited about discovering thirty-three different prophecies telling of the crucifixion. They both reasoned that God coming as a man was entirely logical if he wished to communicate with mankind. Their evidence was building, and these two objective researchers were becoming excited about the truth of their discovery.

He and his wife began to attend church, and at first no one suspected they were not devout believers, for they listened intently and asked questions about everything. God had lined up for them outstanding teachers, knowledgeable and loving, who were not alarmed when they discovered that the Olsens were seekers, not believers. In time and with incredible diligence on Joan and Vig's part, each became personally convinced that Christianity was real. They had become persuaded by the Great Creator Himself that He had created the universe and that His Son had died for their sins.

Their spirits were alive with hope and expectation.

After their conversions, they determined that as believers their logical next step would be to determine God's plans for their lives. When they honestly began to seek Him, they arrived at the conclusion that medical missions was an option they had to consider, although they weren't excited about it to begin with. They prepared a list with "for" on one side and "against" on the other and decided to write whatever came to their minds in the weeks ahead on either side of their list. On "against" they wrote of the need for doctors in America and the money to be made in America, but the "for" side continued to grow longer and longer by the day.

As they watched it grow, missions became more and more reasonable to the couple. When they added "Christ's example" and the fact that so few people were as qualified to go to a mission field as they were, they became convinced. With dread and excitement, they finally acknowledged that they were truly being called.

With God's plan in focus, they developed a three step plan of their own to proceed: receiving proper training themselves, choosing the right mission field where there was desperate need, and choosing a compatible mission board. Using these criteria, they waited for the Lord to direct them. When they thought about the thorough preparation part, Vig decided that he would have to do a second internship, this time in surgery. Internal medicine would not prepare him properly to open a hospital in a remote area, so he went back for five more years of hospital training. In those years, Joan gave birth to the final three of their four children, completing their family.

The Lord validated them as His servants with miraculous successes in very difficult surgeries.

After contacting twenty mission boards, they felt the closest alignment with the American Baptist World Evangelism Board, partly because they would need to raise their own support. They felt that the people who decided to support them would also pray for them. Realizing that they would need community to sustain them in what was ahead, they wanted close relationships back at home as well as on the field. Although they had no formal

Bible training, they took a number of correspondence courses, preparing through intense study to be thoroughly ready as God's ambassadors.

Finally, through a series of undeniable confirmations, they zeroed in on the country of East Pakistan, linking with others who also felt called to go with them, and receiving the blessing of the mission organization they had chosen. Vig wanted a team, a group of men and women who felt called to Pakistan, and on whom he could rely for emotional strength and wisdom, who would share the burden of the work, and who would become indispensable members of a community. He was a determined leader, but he knew his own limitations and his need for friends and allies.

Support in place at last and East Pakistan as their destination, the Olsens with their four blonde haired children in tow, departed for their new home. Arriving in Chittagong, a city of two million in the southern part of East Pakistan, they encountered a noisy and colorful scene. Masses of people were moving about on bikes, in wagons, in rickshaws, in carts, and there were mostly men; the few women they encountered were completely covered in the traditional burquas. The smells from the market filled the air, pleasant aromas of spice and produce, followed by a whiff of dried fish, along with the less pleasant smells of open drains and garbage in the streets. Cattle, goats, and dogs wandered about, mingled with the sounds of beggars crying for alms and sick people stretching forth their hands. Whatever they had imagined Pakistan would be like did not compare with the reality of the sights and smells and sounds, but their spirits were alive with hope and expectation.

Nothing came quickly or easily for the missionaries, as they set out to win the hearts of the people and the blessing of the government. Negotiating for the right piece of land took time and was difficult. Although they had been told before coming that the government would not oppose evangelism, the path to freely share the gospel was rockier than they could have imagined. Ultimately, they achieved every goal by turning to the wisdom of the scripture, especially verses in Proverbs; they learned to lay low, pray hard, and wait on perfect timing and God's favor before making their requests. Vig was determined and strong, but he knew that he would only succeed by following God's plan, so he was patient.

They began immediately to care for the sick, while they waited for the land and the hospital to be built. Vig called it a "careful and discreet" approach, taking his opportunities when they came remembering that "He that observes the wind shall not sow; and he that regards the clouds shall not reap." KJV He knew if he calculated his steps based on what his eyes saw, he would never move forward, but neither did he want to try and make things happen, so he determined to move out only when there was agreement among the missionaries in their spirits. The Lord validated them as His servants with miraculous successes in very difficult surgeries. As they saved the lives of person after person with medicine and skilled treatment, hearts were won over by their compassion. They became known as friends, not foreigners.

When the time came to finally build the hospital, once all the permits were in place, there was a huge amount of underbrush which needed to be cleared. Using American competitive ideas, Vig devised a plan. He challenged the Bengalis to a contest with the Tippera tribal people, promising bonuses to the ones who cleared the most. The plan worked; the land was cleared in record time.

On another occasion Vig prayed for the monsoon rains to stop so that a crucial survey of the land could be done. God caused the rain to stop, but only after a thirty mile jeep ride into the jungle with the skeptical survey team, while it rained without letting up, stopping only upon their arrival at their destination. Vig had confidence that God would back him because He had sent him, and yet he remained humble, fearing any presumption on his part that he might try and call faith.

There were problems to be sure. There were those who resented Christians being allowed to evangelize and who used their influence to try and stop the building, just as the opposition had done to Nehemiah. The missionaries fought against the mistrust of the people by praying for God's favor. God arranged for them to be in the right place at the right time to meet President Ayub, who would later become their strategic champion. Arriving as the only foreigners in the home of a new friend for a meal, Vig and Joan were delighted to find that the president was also invited. They were introduced to him briefly, and then they moved quietly aside, not wanting to presume upon his time. They were amazed when a messenger sought them out later to invite them to dine at the table with the president. Their new friendship was God's idea, and the words of Solomon came again to Vig:

> Do not exalt yourself in the king's presence, and
> do not claim a place among great men;

> It is better for him to say to you, "Come up here," than for him to humiliate you before a nobleman.

The missionaries demonstrated God's love to Muslims, Hindus, and Catholic priests equally, and God provided ways for them to receive favor from each group. They tirelessly treated cases of malaria, smallpox, black fever, and tuberculosis. Typhoid fever, cholera, dysentery, hookworm, round worm, and viral hepatitis were common enemies because of the polluted water and lack of sanitation. Infected wounds and tetanus thrived in the hot, humid climate. Vitamin deficiency and malnutrition plagued the people, and there were often complications in childbirth. All these diseases were in addition to the illnesses they might have treated in American patients.

Conversions were an ongoing part of their ministry, and they were welcome events, a cause for rejoicing, as was the ongoing training and discipleship of the converts. Some of the most effective discipleship took place in the context of real life.

Daniel, a local villager and recent convert, found himself in a scrap with the Muslim villagers who verbally attacked him for his conversion, causing him to retaliate by criticizing Islamic law and rules. A fight ensued that landed Daniel on a stretcher, choked and beaten. Dr. Olsen held court in his own living room, and when the charges were heard from both sides, he decided that each side had contributed to the outcome. Dr. Olsen agreed to deal with Daniel.

After Dr. Olsen carefully explained to Daniel eight different places in scripture where believers were cautioned to walk wisely and graciously, not maligning men, Daniel repented. Dr. Olsen pointed out that even the apostle Paul never blasphemed the goddess Diana. Daniel was touched by the passage that we should be "as wise as serpents and harmless as doves." KJV Peace was restored to the village, as the message of God's love triumphed.

After all the missionaries returned to stay and were back at work at General Memorial Hospital in the new country of Bangladesh, Dr. Olsen went from bed to bed greeting his patients who were Muslim, Hindu, Buddhist, and Christian, all recovering in peace in a place where no one was treated differently from the other because of his religious beliefs. He had often thought of other builders, Nehemiah and Solomon, who built for God, so once again they came to his mind. *Like Nehemiah,* he thought, *the "king granted me according to the good hand of my God upon me,"* and he knew the words of Solomon to be true: "The king's heart is in the hand of the Lord; He directs it like a watercourse wherever He pleases."

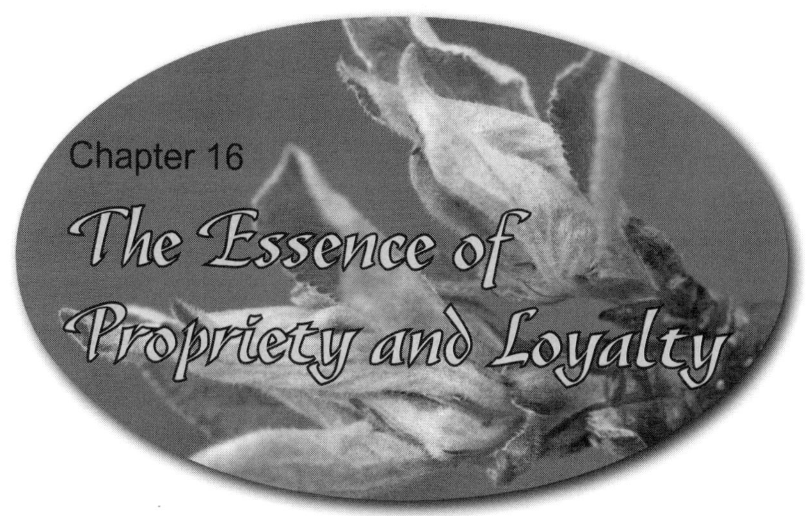

He sat quietly beside her, grateful for the comfort of her presence, as they listened to his mother's labored breathing. They had sent for him to come when she fell, and he had brushed them away, in his typical, calm, professional way, always insistent that duty came first. Instead the doctor came, diagnosed the broken hip, administered some sedatives and told her she would never walk again.

What had been so important that he could not have been with his aged mother when she faced the horror of never walking in her beloved garden again or savoring any other outdoor activity on her own? Serving a meal to his Lairdship? Pouring the wine at dinner? Answering the door? The housekeeper, Miss Stewart, had been with his mother, leaving her own duties to be at her side. He was moved by her compassionate gesture, yet it left him feeling even more personal regret and confusion over his own decision to attend to his duties as butler rather than attend to his mother's physical and emotional needs.

While he sat struggling with his guilt and remorse, thankful for this moment of reprieve from his duties, little Molly, who was usually the most vibrant and happy member of the household, burst into the room and fell in a disheveled heap at Miss Stewart's feet. Molly, the cook's daughter, had been allowed to serve in the household for the first time tonight, although she was barely thirteen, and something dreadful must have happened to her. She had lived here all of her life, practically growing up beneath the cook's feet on the kitchen floor, every member of the staff unabashedly doting on her and spoiling her. Now here she was, sobbing uncontrollably, her pretty young face twisted with pain and horror.

It was not appropriate for a man of his rank to question his employer, so he obstinately refused to intervene.

His heart beat wildly, for he feared he knew exactly what had happened. On two other occasions, Laird Godfrey had taken advantage of one of the chambermaids, but no one would have thought that his cruelty could have led him to this despicable act. He had obviously been insanely drunk, especially with the other noblemen filling the rooms for the annual hunt. As she related the Laird's heinous behavior with violent sobs, Maggie took her in her arms and rocked the child, kissing the top of her head and smoothing the locks of her auburn hair, although at the same time she was looking across at him with her demanding, blue eyes, filled with their own pain, questioning him silently as to what he would do.

As soon as they put the child to bed, Maggie spoke her mind. She believed they should tell one of the visiting lords, for an opportunity like this to have visitors in the castle when his Lairdship committed a crime like this one, might not come again. The lairds were known to execute justice among themselves. This kind of behavior had happened twice before at Lochly Hall, and if they did nothing, she was certain it would continue and they would have little recourse.

Maggie was fiercely adamant, "We must do something. I fear I cannot endure this any longer," and then she added most forcefully, "If you do not, I will leave here and I will never come back. I promise; I will leave here."

Her pleas and threats weighed heavily upon him all through the night for he loved her and the cook's daughter both. Images of his anguished mother, of wee Molly and of Maggie tormented him in turn as he tossed about trying to understand where his real duty lay. He did not want to have to deal with any of this, preferring to be left alone to ponder his mother's situation, but there was no time for that.

The morning was filled with the bustle of the hearty breakfast being prepared before the hunt, and his grief was secondary. When he awoke, he had resolved to speak of the matter to no one, so he arose and went about his duties as usual. Disappointed and hurt, Maggie Stewart would not look at him or speak to him, but he had determined not to dishonor his lairdship. It was not appropriate for a man of his rank to question his employer, so he obstinately refused to intervene. He would help Molly privately, but he would not betray his employer or embarrass him by involving anyone else in this matter.

The days that followed were ones he still recalled with pain. As he tried to recreate a feeling of calm within the castle walls, Maggie grew more and more distant from him. While he worked tirelessly putting things back in order, calming the fearful staff, and helping Molly find another position at a neighboring manor, he was forced to watch the cook say her tearful good-byes to her only daughter, while barely snatching a moment to process his own emotions. He found his solace in the fact that the castle seemed to be running smoothly once again, and that his Lairdship was avoiding his drink, a sure sign of his remorse, Duncan determined.

He had always taken his position here at the castle seriously, for he had practically inherited it. The two generations before him, his father and his grandfather, had served the lairds of this castle as butlers. His father had trained him personally in all manner of duties, as well as in the kind of polite deference that his job demanded. He had been taught also, by example. While the lairds that his ancestors had each served were men of character and high breeding, benevolent and kind, the present Laird Godfrey was not. There were times of peace and ease, but when he was drunk, they all feared what disaster his reckless improprieties would cause.

When Maggie resigned, just as she had said, he let her go in silence, telling himself that there was nothing he could do.

Duncan doubted his forebears could have endured his Lairdship, but he felt a certain pride that he was able to, even when Godfrey was harsh and abusive. On the occasions Laird Godfrey demeaned the staff, or was cruel to his own stable of fine horses, or gave in to his sordid passion or violence, Duncan was the one who felt he must restore order. He attempted to make things right by encouraging the servants to persevere, reminding them of the infrequency of these episodes. He reminded everyone of their duty to silence, lest the reputation of the Laird be tarnished. He felt the Laird was a good man and only on the occasion when his liquor mastered him was he ever harsh or abusive.

When Maggie resigned, just as she had said, he let her go in silence, telling himself that there was nothing he could do. He was left without her companionship at Lochly Hall. He had grown very fond of her in the five years they had worked together; convinced it was because they made a fine team. Each was impeccable in performing his or her duties, models of propriety and decorum.

The happiest days of his life had been with her at his side, not only because they were such an efficient team, confidently relying on each other's impressive skills, but also because he drew such comfort and pleasure from her company, a truth he denied to himself. For those five years they had overseen, conferred, hired, dismissed, trained, and executed every detail so that everything ran with precision. Her standards were as high as his, although he had to admit that she was on occasion, emotional in private, especially if she was tired or overwhelmed, and he never knew how to react on those occasions. Her emotions were alarming to him, but he could forgive her that slight infraction because she was so able in every other way. He, of course, was always private with his own emotions and never shared them with anyone. It was his custom to deny them any place, lest they interfere with his duties, so if they emerged in the slightest way, he shoved them down quickly and covered them, the way he would cover a blunder in the service of his Lairdship's dinner.

Why had he let her go? He knew she cared for him, because she had practically told him so. He cared deeply for her; although he was never able to admit it to himself or to her. He had never considered marriage for himself, always assuming that it would interfere with his work, so he might have been content to have her remain as his friend, the housekeeper. Although he had seen households briefly upset when staff married each other, it was fairly common.

No one would have minded really; in fact, his Lairdship probably would not have objected at all, but nothing in his nature or his life had equipped him to seize anything for himself, or to complain if it were taken away from him. Years of compliance and deference had made it easy for him to surrender his own desires or deny their existence all together. He had been so surprised by her passionate decision that he was ill prepared to act decisively to stop her. What did he have to offer her, anyway?

In truth, she had acted hastily, persuaded in her own mind that her decision to leave might provoke him to action or a declaration of some sort, but she had overestimated his ability to declare his feelings or move to stop her in any way. Once her passion had led her to make her decision to spite him, she felt compelled to follow through on it, a decision she would regret almost daily in the years ahead.

That had been twenty years ago. A singular event had occurred which had made all of these events fresh and alive again. She had written him a letter. In the letter, her very first communication in all these years, she stated that she had married, had a child, but her husband had recently died and she might be willing to return as housekeeper to Lochly Hall, since the cruel laird had also died. He was presently making the four hour journey to her village, by horseback, to meet with her, and he was nervously anticipating the reunion every inch of the way. He had rehearsed his speech in his mind a hundred times, for he was determined to insist that she return to her former position, but as his wife. She and Gilbert had only one child, a daughter, who was now married. At long last, he would make a declaration to her of his love. He could hardly believe that fortune had smiled on him in this way to grant him another chance.

He thought of how he had devoted his life to making others comfortable, and how little he had to show for any of it. He had no wife or child, no fortune, or even reputation to bring him comfort. The dust accumulated where it always had, and the silver grew tarnished with morbid regularity, an ever present reminder of his enduring lack of accomplishment. When his Lairdship had died in the riding accident - his mistreated and angry animal throwing him mercilessly from his back into a deep ravine - there was no thanks, no reward, no final accolade for Duncan and his loyalty. The castle was sold and he now served the new laird, a kinder man who seemed to appreciate him, but his best years were gone, buried with Laird Godfrey.

He had another chance to make things right, to reach out for his own happiness.

As he rode briskly through the Scottish countryside with its beautiful hills and serene lochs, he rejoiced over this opportunity.

He had another chance to make things right, to reach out for his own happiness.

Maggie Stewart was waiting at the inn where they had decided to meet. She hoped the age on her face wouldn't be judged too harshly, but Duncan didn't seem to notice at all. Her unhappy marriage had showed on her countenance until recently, but she had become more joyful anticipating this meeting. Duncan was immensely glad to see her, and she knew him well enough to tell, although he was too proper to reveal much. The one joy of Maggie's life that had sustained her was her twin sister who lived nearby. Her sister, Jean, was also newly widowed, but it was different for her, since Jean and her husband had a deeply intimate marriage.

Maggie wondered what she should do. She wanted to go "home" with Duncan, back to Lochly Hall. Leaving her sister to process widowhood alone would be emotionally hard, but it was doable. She would visit her sister periodically, and there were others nearby who could wisely help as needed. She determined that she would turn down the position, if that was all that was offered to her, but if Duncan were to give her a glimmer of hope that his intentions toward her were more than that of a housekeeper, she would return with him, but he must pass her "test" first. She could not endure the same torture of undeclared feelings and vain hope. She was too old for such foolishness.

"You look just the same," Duncan said. He meant it as the sincerest compliment.

"Older, to be sure, but thank you all the same," Maggie answered as she smiled her warm, accepting smile he remembered so well.

They spoke of their years together, and shared news of any of the staff that they had kept in touch with through the years. They laughed, drank their tea, and reminisced over old times, sinking into a common familiarity as easily as one would slip a foot into a comfortable, old shoe. They each said, in his own way, what delightful years those had been, for the most part, notwithstanding his Lairdship's indiscretions, which they carefully avoided mentioning. Surprisingly to Duncan, Maggie knew quite a bit about many of the staff who had departed, since he had lost touch with all those who had left. Finally, he felt he was able to broach the subject of her employment.

"I have spoken to the new Laird and have recommended you for the position. He is quite willing that you come."

"I am really sorry to tell you this," she said, "but I may need to reconsider accepting the position. My sister was just widowed the day after I wrote you, and I am not at all certain if I should leave her and return. I have been perplexed as to what to do." She waited for a reassuring word, a word of comfort, or the unlikely, desperate pleading that she return, matching the intense urgency reverberating in her own soul.

He knew he would regret this moment forever, and yet he was powerless to alter it all the same.

Duncan's heart lurched within his chest. What should he say? If he asked her to return as his wife, he would be depriving the sisters of their life time connection at a most critical juncture of their lives. Years of habit seized him, a familiar switch in his core, and he immediately became the dutiful butler, the undeserving lackey, the pitiful Duncan, who took the leftovers, ashamed to ask for more. He let his opportunity to say what he really felt slip away from him in an instant. Quickly, say something, anything to hide what you truly feel, he thought in panic.

"I quite understand. I wish you, of course, all the best," he said. Then after a moment, "I'm afraid I must make the trip back before dark." It had been his plan to stay the night at the inn, but he gave in to the familiar old compulsion to flee. "It was so good to see you again." He smiled. It was his most inscrutable smile, the one that covered the reality of his pain, and warned the recipient to move no closer. It was the very same smile she remembered when he had let her go the first time and wished her well.

As he said good-bye, tears streamed down her face. She would have gladly gone with him. All she wanted was his reassurance, but she had for the second and last time, overestimated his ability to give her freedom to receive happiness for herself when he had never been able to grant it to himself. He was a pitiful creature of the habits of a lifetime; staring into his empty tea cup. He knew he would regret this moment forever, and yet he was powerless to alter it all the same.

Duncan walked through the pouring rain toward the borrowed horse the new Laird had been kind enough to loan him for his journey, his shoulders slumped, looking almost dazed from the encounter. He didn't mind being soaked; in fact, he had never felt more perfectly agreeable weather in his whole life. The painful sting of the rain on his face was appropriately punishing, beating rhythmically against his skin. He deserved to be drenched and cold, he thought viciously, for he had just lost the one woman he had most admired and enjoyed in his whole life, one that would have made a perfect companion for his middle and golden years.

As he made his solitary way back home over the Scottish hills, past the lochs with their serene beauty, the fall beauty tormented him. It reminded him of the weekend that his mother had fallen when the other noblemen had come for the hunt. The burnished colors of the changing leaves, the crisp air, and the haunting memories of his choices collided upon him. It was the weekend his mother suffered the death of her dreams without her son at her side, and the weekend that his Lairdship raped the youngest of the chambermaids, Molly. It was the weekend that Maggie left him in her heart.

Now winding up the paths, returning home, the clarity of that night was painfully vivid. He could hardly see the road through the rain or the tears, but then he had little doubt that the horse would find its way. He was sure he would wind back into the highlands, somehow arriving at Lochly Hall, just like always. The new Laird would await his return, and he would continue to do the work he had always done. He would live out his days polishing silver, measuring the placement of the napkins with precision, pouring the drinks with a skillful turn of his wrist, returning to the safety of mindless compliance.

This moment of clarity would hopefully pass and he would be able to return to his work, reconciled with the past, able to go on. He would assure the ones he served of their importance by his compliance to their every wish. The essence of propriety and loyalty, his ears would remain tuned to the familiar sounds: the dropping of a tray even out of anyone's hearing but his own, the slightest spill during serving, or the muffled sneeze of a dusting chambermaid.

He went inside the castle, his clothes soaked from the rain, his appearance as limp and shriveled as his spirits. He quickly changed his clothes and checked to see if the new Laird needed anything, only to discover that he too had come in soaked from checking on the horses. With quiet efficiency, he removed the man's tall boots, and helped him soak his cold feet in warm water, with the same measure of decorum that he used when he poured a glass of wine, or measured with a ruler the precise places the silver should be nestled in the starched napkin on the massive dining room table.

"How did your meeting with the housekeeper go?" the Laird asked.

"Very well, sir. It seems she will be unable to accept the position after all," he said with measured calm, no tinge of discernable emotion. "Will there be anything else, sir?" Duncan said, badly wanting to retire.

"No, Duncan, I think not," his Lairdship answered, but he stared inquisitively at the butler for a few seconds, seeing past his bravado.

"Thank you, my Laird," Duncan had said, as he finished his final night duty and retired to his room, the extraordinary day ended at last. He sat in the comfortable solitude of his private room recalling the day's devastating events. He found his ancient discipline of focusing on others' needs was not serving him tonight as grief and self-loathing vied for supremacy, forcing him to see a truth he did not want to acknowledge.

Chapter 17
Their Souls Concerned Him Not

The year was 1523 in the small French town of Noyon, sixty miles north of Paris, where a plague was threatening the vitality of the community once again. Plagues had lessened in France, rarely reaching epidemic proportions as they once had, but still they occasionally hit a town, leaving families feeling helpless and fearful. Hygiene was being heralded as the key to keeping disease at bay, but even with that knowledge, plagues sometimes crept in, creating panic among the citizenry.

As the plague in the city worsened, Gerard Chauvin considered his options. He kept returning to his surest bet: sending his young son, Jean, away to Paris to ensure his safety from this insidious intruder. Jean was only fourteen, a little young perhaps, to be sent to the university, but he was an exceptional student and devoutly religious. His father had no doubt that Jean would prove diligent in his studies, nor did he have any fears that he would succumb to licentious behavior or the negative influence of older classmates. Even as a boy, Jean had an unwavering piety so strong that he often chided his peers for their unseemly behavior.

Gerard concluded that his son might as well start on his theological degree, safely away from the growing atmosphere of death in the community. After all, he was financially able to offer his son a fine education, as he was the lawyer and business administrator at the Noyon Cathedral. When his distingue pere told Jean what he had decided, the boy promised to be diligent in all of his studies and was ready to leave home as quickly as his father wished.

Although Jean was timid and rather weak in constitution, he loved to study. The thought of being among the most learned men at a university in Paris and dedicating himself to the relentless pursuit of knowledge suited his intellectual passion. "I will prepare myself to go, Father," Jean answered with pride that he had earned his father's trust with his impeccable behavior, while Gerard congratulated himself that he had raised such a dutiful son.

Men were awakening to sensual beauty, pursuing the arts with a passion, and using the arts as a stepping stone to God.

Gerard could not have known that he was sending his son from their provincial village and his pious Catholic upbringing into a city and university that were ablaze with reformed theology, ever growing Renaissance thought, and serious questions about the veracity of church practices and popular theology. He sent his son away to become a priest, and within a few years Jean Chauvin, soon to be known as John Calvin, would leave the Catholic Church, and France, to become an outspoken critic of Catholicism and a fierce Protestant reformer.

Jean arrived in Paris at a time when ideological change was sweeping through Europe, and he quickly became associated with many young men who were debating the issues of theology and who were being greatly influenced by the new waves of thought.

Within the first few years of his studies, his father began to have difficulties of his own with the board at the cathedral, and being sensitive to the winds of change, Gerard advised his son to pursue law rather than staying the course of the Catholic priesthood as he had first advised.

At nineteen, Jean switched from his pursuit of theology to law, which he studied until he was twenty three, but he never strayed far from theology, because it was his true passion. He had already made many close friends who were as deeply involved in the reform movement as he was himself, though he was not yet as vocal as some others.

It was the dawning of Renaissance humanism, where men were awakening to sensual beauty, pursuing the arts with a passion, and using the arts as a stepping stone to God. Architecture, painting, music, literature, and religious thought were changing and men were feeling a new freedom to pursue their passions and they were not seeing that as being in conflict with their pursuit of God as they had been taught in the Dark and Middle Ages.

These early humanists valued reason and the liberal arts, and they were returning to the classics, preferring to read them in the original Latin and Greek so as to savor their rich beauty and meaning. Although they were not as adamant about human worth and dignity as modern humanists, it was quite a change from the historic Christian virtues of humility, introspection, and passivity (or meekness), and measuring a man's success in terms of his spiritual attainment, not his worldly accomplishments.

The humanist reformers were embracing man's humanity, his gifts, his passions, his potential, and they were pursuing beauty in all forms. Literature and rhetoric were becoming extravagant and eloquent. Christians were learning to speak and write about Christianity in grandiose and scholarly ways.

New ideas spawned other new ideas. Jean Chauvin was a man for this season.

He was such an outstanding student at the university that his professors treated him more like one of them than a student. His professors sometimes let him teach their classes, so gifted was he in his studies and his presentation. In 1531 he received his Doctor of Laws degree at Orleans along with many accolades from his professors and friends. He would never pursue a law career or even stay in France long because he could not be silent about his Protestant ideas. His ideas were not just unwelcomed by the doctors at the Sorbonne – they found no champions among the nobility and the king of France himself was unflinchingly Catholic in his religion and politics.

The Catholic Church was fortified in the country, faithful to the pope, and it was not open to public tirades against its sacred infallibility. It was committed to being unforgiving to up-and-coming intellectuals who felt compelled to give speeches or write pamphlets about its shortcomings. Not only did Jean have many friends who made it dangerous for him to stay, he was deeply involved in the movement himself. By the time he was in his mid twenties, he had gone through a powerful conversion experience and proceeded to write his definitive work on theology, Institutes of the Christian Religion which became an instant best seller.

He wrote it to defend the position of the French Huguenots, but in it he created a very readable and scholarly presentation of Christian doctrine outlining many of the basic principles he held throughout his life and that Christianity holds today.

Jean's life was in danger in France, and for several years he lived outside the country intermittently, but finally he left for good. He had hoped to go to Strasbourg, Austria, but a new outbreak of war prevented him, and he went instead to Geneva, Switzerland, where devout Protestants, already familiar with his work, convinced him to remain. More accurately, they insisted, telling him that God would curse him if he did not stay and help them. Fearing he might miss God's will, John Calvin, stayed, almost the entirety of his remaining life.

He was impossible to reason with once his mind's trap had clanged shut.

The citizens of Geneva spoke French, and while most of Switzerland was more culturally linked to the reformation sweeping Germany at the time, Geneva was not. It suited them to have Calvin leading and building their reformed church. They had overthrown their governmental rulers, the House of Savoy, and were determined to make Geneva into a Protestant city, which it officially did become in 1535.

John Calvin was not a person of natural courage, nor did he relish confrontation. It was his sense of rightness that enabled him to never back down from a fight. Once he had arrived at "truth," no man could persuade him otherwise, and he was impossible to reason with once his mind's trap had clanged shut. He relished the idea of reforming a city based on biblical principles. He studied the scriptures and sought to be as literal as possible in every structure he put into place, both socially and in the church.

At the same time, Calvin blasted the pope with Luther's kind of fortitude using publications, letters and the pulpit. He called him "spurious" and his office "a sink pool of pollution" and the Catholic Church "counterfeit Christianity." It was Calvin's goal to return to the faith of the Bible rather than the "frightful form of religion" called Catholicism. When he combated the Catholic Church, he believed he was battling the embodiment of the anti-Christ, not unlike most reformers who were fed up with abuse in the church and who were clamoring for it to acknowledge its sin.

Calvin had been influenced by the Swiss reformer, Zwingli, a student of Erasmus, the Dutch humanist reformer. Essentially, their core teaching was this: anything that was not explicitly quoted in scripture should be rejected, and anything that was contained in scripture must be followed without compromise. Calvin developed his theology taking Zwinglianism farther than even Luther did. He envisioned a society based on biblical structure, one where men used the scripture to pattern everything about their lives.

From the pinnacle of self-legitimizing correctness, Calvin built a fortress that none could penetrate.

Calvin developed a new method of exegesis as a biblicist. Before Calvin's method, men studied ancient commentaries, earlier theologians' thoughts and opinions, and sought to transfer knowledge of God down through a living chain from the past. Calvin insisted that if theologians wanted a literal interpretation of scripture, it could not be arrived at except by study of the original. So, he studied the words, the sense of the words, their Greek and Hebrew meanings, their meanings in context of the time and events of their writing, their meanings in the sentence, and in the passage - in other words, he left no stone unturned in his attempt to be accurate. He would entertain no truth that could not be documented from scripture.

He created the method of study that is still honored and practiced throughout many Bible seminaries in the world. He reasoned that if he were to be a man of the Word and live by the scriptures, he must study them night and day, pulling from their pages every minute bit of truth he could find. Being logical to the core, he was able to generalize with such sound judgment, with such consistency, and with such an attention to detail, that he astounded men who listened to him or read his writings.

There was no refuting Calvin, for no man was more scholarly or surer he was right in the entire world. Those who met Calvin after they had read his works were often surprised by a man who looked effeminate and weak, but who could obviously argue and defend doctrine with eloquence and dogmatic certainty.

There was also no way of arguing successfully against his piety, because it only proved to Calvin several things about the person opposing him. The person was misguided, ill informed, disrespectful of authority, and lastly, filled with the kind of idolatry which always blinded the minds of the less pious. From the pinnacle of self-legitimizing correctness, Calvin built a fortress that none could penetrate.

As has always happened to a man who believes that he stands and can examine the standing of others, he was not far from falling. Where Calvin would fall was in his lack of comprehension of the love of God, that love which is vast and deep and wide, which is incomprehensible and unfathomable, from which nothing can separate us and no man, not one, was intended to fear or run away from.

And as man is wont to do when he embraces holiness without love, Calvin inadvertently bowed to the law once again, and not to the spirit of the law. The law was meant to enable us to see our need and brokenness. It was never meant to become an achievable mark by which we measure our success as Christian believers.

In the process of being accurate, he failed to understand the intent of the Spirit in writing the scripture. He only lived by the letter of the Word of God. Sadly, what Calvin missed was the all encompassing love of God that Jesus had come to show the world.

Jesus Himself had not come to interpret scripture, establish laws, and put the twelve in offices to enforce them. If He had done that, He would have helped stone the woman caught in sin, for that would have been legally permissible to keep the "moral code" in place.

While Calvin's understanding of many things was astounding in its correctness, he seemed to disregard the life of Jesus who gravitated to sinners, healed their brokenness, and never once acted as though He came for a select few.

Although Calvin considered himself exact and irrefutable in his interpretation of scripture, often he missed the essence and the heart of God's message. His writing is scholarly and correct; his reasoning largely unimpeachable, but in his life he was a severe and irritable man who had few close friends. He was truthful and steadfast to his convictions, but his truthfulness didn't attract men to Jesus. Instead it repelled them from the stench of the merciless law.

Calvin set about to organize Geneva - both church government and the social organization of the city - based on biblical principles, the first reformer of his time to be so ambitious. He categorized church offices into pastors, teachers, elders, and deacons. He developed a catechism in order to teach doctrine to church members, and also developed a moral code for the citizens of the city.

Initially, the townspeople were convinced they had traded one pope for another, and were far from enthusiastic about his reforms and the new watchdog over their morality. When they fought back in an early toe to toe conflict with their new pastor, he disciplined the entire church by refusing them Communion when they arrived at church on Sunday. He did not believe in permissive fathering that bowed to the capricious whims of the local community; strong discipline was needed to emphasize transgression that would not be tolerated.

Calvin was not arbitrary or impulsive, for he did nothing without scriptural permission, but the city government resisted their overbearing pastor and rose up and threw him out. Utterly unremorseful for his part in the fiasco, Calvin promptly shook the dust from his feet and moved on to Strasbourg where he remained from 1538 until 1541. At that time Geneva became either repentant or jealous of Strasbourg's notoriety with Calvin at its helm, so they begged him to return to them. Although he was torn and preferred Strasbourg, he went back to Geneva because he believed that duty demanded his return. He went back, but not before securing permission to do things his way.

He returned with a wife, Idelette de Bure, a widow with a son and a daughter, whom he had married in Austria. Part of his reasoning he gave for marrying her was to demonstrate his doctrinal belief that clergy should marry and not remain celibate. Calvin and Idelette had only one child, but the child would live only two weeks. Their marriage would last for ten years before Idelette would also die. Calvin spoke well of her, saying, "She was a helper to me in my ministry, never opposing me, and never bothering me with her children. She was great in spirit."

Apparently the "Father of Geneva" had very little time to father his step children, as he was driven by duty and work. When she died, although he mourned her death, he was far too dedicated to his duties to take any time off to grieve. He considered her death, in Paul's words, "For our light and momentary troubles are achieving for us an eternal glory that far outweighs them all." Once again, the Word of God sustained him and excused him from duties that love might have required of him.

There was nothing about Calvin's message that would have given hope to the wicked.

No mention is made of his children dealing with their own grief at the loss of their mother, but it is not likely that Calvin and the children were able to find comfort in each other's arms through the tragedy. The children had probably learned not to bother him while he was at work, and he had probably never found solace in a child's love, or even a father's. If he were distant and aloof, they knew what an important man he was and how important his work was to God and to others.

His duties did not consist of giving and receiving love, but of preaching one whole week out of every two weeks, lecturing three times a week, presiding over the meetings of the Presbytery, and expounding on the scriptures to the congregation. He wrote seemingly endless commentaries outlining his views and interpretation of scripture, and he answered letters from proponents of his beliefs and from opponents who wrote to him from all over Europe. When he died, there were an estimated 4,000 letters he had written.

It is said that the good people of Geneva sought him out as a friend, but if the wicked encountered him on the street, they ran in terror. If the same thing had happened to Jesus, the Pharisees could have become his disciples and he would have struck terror in the heart of Mary Magdalene and Zacchaeus. What could have blinded the eyes of such a brilliant scholar to the message of love which Jesus preached? The answer lies in one doctrine in particular.

There was nothing about Calvin's message that would have given hope to the wicked, or spoken comfort to sinners, or caused the fatherless to long for their heavenly Father, for Calvin's study of scripture had led him to believe in the doctrine of predestination. He was convinced that God predetermined who would be saved and be given eternal life, although these "elect" were without merit. Conversely, God also determined who would be punished and sent to hell, a judgment everyone deserved and some received by God's election.

This one belief system permeated his entire ministry, for if one is doomed to hell, and God has not seen fit to save him or pluck him out of his fiery reward, then what could mortal man do for the poor soul? He was completely satisfied that sinners would reap what they had sown, so their souls concerned him not. Their moral behavior was a concern, however, because they helped define the climate of the city, so they had to adhere to certain behaviors or be punished.

Why a sinner would have wanted to remain in Geneva curtailed from worldly pleasures, despised by the saints, and doomed to hell is a mystery of the deepest sort.

The righteous, on the other hand, were of great concern to him, the "elect" as he called them from scripture. It was not enough to interpret scripture and admonish the sheep to obey; he guarded over their lives like a dutiful father, meting out punishment for any bad behavior which was reported to the Consistory, a council that he had established for such purposes.

One might wonder, if God was the sovereign God who decided who would be saved, could He not also be the sovereign source of righteousness after salvation? Would He not be faithful to complete what He had started in a believer's life, convicting him and sharing with him His own blameless life, so that he might be presentable on the last day? Was salvation a free gift, but righteousness only achieved by hard work?

Calvin demonstrated in an exemplary way his own understanding of Father God as a stern judge who watched man from His lofty perch, counting his sins against him, and faithfully disciplining him so that his behavior might eventually become acceptable. God's expectations for the elect was sinless perfection and so they must be forever striving for holiness where they could enjoy His fellowship, love, and favor reserved for those who attained His standard.

As the bar moved higher and higher, the obedient grew more and more proud (or more secretive), the "chosen" became fewer and more tight knit, and they judged others and themselves constantly to find out where they stood on the measuring stick of obedience to the law and in competition with the brethren.

On the other hand, many of Calvin's doctrines have blessed the church immensely. Calvin developed the doctrine of penal substitution - Jesus being the substitute for man's sins, paying in full the price for a believer's sins. It became a prominent church doctrine that has liberated Christians through the ages. Even then, it was only good news for the elect, but entirely unattainable for the damned. No one was entitled to God's love except the elect, because there were many God couldn't love, some from whom He had already turned His face.

Naturally, the elect loved the elect and they shunned the sinner.

Naturally, the elect loved the elect and they shunned the sinner. It was perhaps a warm and sincere love the elect shared, but it was at least mutual respect and oversight, for it could not come near unconditional love which must first be received from God in order to be "shed abroad."

Calvin discipled a few select men, and to the rest of Geneva, he confirmed their worst fears: that they were unlovable, unacceptable, and doomed to hell. No wonder they ran in terror. He portrayed God as a Father whose offspring had utterly disappointed Him, ones He had determined before creation would fail, so He turned His back on them and left them fatherless. It was the God he had found through his study of scripture and the one he had experienced in his own life. He could not comprehend the sinner's plight, and by God's grace, he didn't have to. There was no place of refuge for the broken or the wounded or for those whose life's cruelties had mocked and abandoned. They were but players on the stage of life, pitiful characters, cast in losing roles, waiting to be booed from the stage.

The ministers of Geneva maintained that Calvin had a warm and nurturing heart, and for them it was undoubtedly true. He was a true friend to those with whom he "voluntarily associated." His theory was that we should choose our associations based on acceptable and harmonious values and beliefs, a way of thinking that would spread throughout the church and throughout Europe in the years to come. He "came out from among" the sinners, as they were vile and wicked company, a trap and a snare for true believers. In his words, "God preordained, for his own glory and the display of his mercy and justice, a part of the human race, without attributing any merit of their own, to eternal salvation, and another part, in just punishment of their sin, to eternal damnation."

Calvin held essentially the same theology for his whole life, never seeing any need to alter it, for he was as certain of its correctness as he was his own salvation. While other reformers sometimes changed their opinions about certain scriptures and doctrines, he held tightly to his own.

The more he studied and wrote for religious liberty and tolerance, the smaller his own world became. Religious liberty meant the right of free worship, but free worship, to Calvin, meant a form of Protestantism that abided by strict rules of the faith, worked hard to please God, earned His love, and excluded the masses. It did not mean freedom for the individual believer to walk in the conviction and life of the Holy Spirit, being accountable to God, while working out his salvation by receiving the righteousness of Christ.

Calvin took his divinely ordained authority, and established a Consistory which was an ecclesiastical court made of elders and pastors whose job it was to maintain order among the church members and its officials. If offenses came, they might be cultural behaviors such as wild dancing or the singing of bawdy songs, or grave heresies or blasphemy. Typically, the punishment for minor offenses was to attend sermons or classes. The maximum degree of punishment for any offense was excommunication itself, which was reversible if the sinner repented.

As people were being persecuted throughout Europe for following the reform teaching, multitudes poured into Geneva seeking asylum. Those who were like-minded were offered asylum and treated well, whatever stream of reformation that they came from. Usually, though, they weren't in Geneva long before they were Calvinists through and through, for the exiles made some of his strongest followers.

Calvin chose many of his pastors from the ranks of the French immigrants. When some of the citizens of Geneva became offended at this practice one of the local Swiss complained. Calvin had the man disciplined by walking through town wearing a hair shirt ending at the town square where he had to beg for mercy.

There was no way Calvin could allow the questioning of God's authority to go unpunished.

Only once did Calvin find it necessary to seek the death penalty for a heretic, a man named Michael Servetus, a Spanish physician and theologian. Servetus had presented a publication in 1531 denouncing the Trinity. His pamphlet was largely disregarded since the Trinity was the one doctrine that Christians and Catholics agreed on, but Calvin was inflamed at his audacity.

Although Spain and France had both sentenced him to death for blasphemy, he escaped into Switzerland and showed up at Calvin's Sunday church service. Why had he come? He knew Calvin slightly through correspondence, so perhaps he was seeking asylum in Geneva as others had done, but Calvin welcomed only his own kind, not just any religious lunatic who showed up. Maybe because Servetus had been in touch with Calvin before, he expected friendship; whatever he expected is moot, because Calvin had him arrested and wrote out heresy charges against him.

Servetus was burned at the stake, although Calvin did plead for a more humane punishment of beheading. Such executions were common throughout Europe during the reformation when believers rose up against each other, each fighting so that "true doctrine" could be established.

At the end of his life, Calvin's one regret was losing his temper on occasion. He did not regret the execution of Servetus, as the removal of heresy and maintenance of the purity of faith in Geneva were the primary focus of his life. Calvin believed that the apostles themselves, had they had a Christian government supporting them, (which in his eyes would have benefited them tremendously) would have punished blasphemy with the same civil authority he soberly executed when necessary.

At only fifty-five, Calvin's health failed him badly. He had migraines, hemorrhages in his lungs, gout, and kidney stones, none of which deterred him from teaching. He was known to be both carried to the pulpit and to lecture from his bed. For the last ten years of his life, he ate one meal a day at his doctor's suggestion, a glass of wine and an egg at noon. If friends advised him to rest from his labors, they received the frosty response, "What! Would you have me be idle when the Lord comes?" The "Puritan work ethic" has its roots in Calvinism. It is a concept that Calvin birthed that God requires that we be hard about our labors or be found as "lazy servants."

When he died in Geneva on May 27, 1564, the Swiss ministers gathered around his bed and wept at their loss. They had lost their father who had taught them and then guarded over their steps and their souls, a watchful eye enforcing purity in Geneva, guarding the church from heretical points of view, feeling the weightiness of presenting the elect he shepherded, blameless before the Lord. As Calvin entered into the gates of heaven, one would hope that Jesus met him at the gate, covered him with a mantle of His unconditional love, wrapped him in His warmest embrace to remove the chill from his bent, emaciated shoulders, then took his hand to usher him into the Father's presence, the gentle and loving Father that Calvin had never encountered though He is seen in all the pages of scripture.

Chapter 18
Immeasurable Grandeur

Job held the sleeping child tenderly to his chest, rocking her back and forth, as he kept an unconscious rhythm with the distant music drifting through the air from the celebration. The late hour had made the child fretful, so he had walked outside with her into the cool night where she had fallen asleep on his shoulder. When he felt her little body grow limp and heavy, he knew she had quit fighting sleep. He sat down and cradled her in his arms, as he continued to rock her and contemplate what God had done for him. *Four generations, and every one more precious than the last,* he thought to himself, for as he aged and had less to give out of his own strength, he found that love was easier, flowing freely without so many conditions or expectations, especially the ones he put on himself.

He had worked hard to love his oldest set of children - the ones he had lost - by providing for them, sacrificing on their behalf, teaching them to obey, and repenting for them when they didn't. Now he trusted God more easily with the lives and the well being of these little ones, and sometimes, like right at this moment, he felt the heart of God surge through him. He loved this little girl for no reason other than she was his offspring and he was touched by her vulnerability and her utter dependence on him. She was vulnerable in a way that he too was vulnerable, and he had come to know that only the God of the Universe could really protect either of them.

At that moment, she opened one sleepy eye to determine who was holding her, and when she saw her great grandpa, she gave him a half smile, and snuggled closer to him, content and assured that all was well. His heart marveled that seeing his face had comforted her, and it caused him to thank God for the incredible gift of family and the blessed tool it was to teach a man what he needed to know about the Father's love, about giving and receiving, joy and grief, the depths and the heights of the most precious thing on earth.

There had been a time when he worked very hard to achieve success, when he labored responsibly to secure blessings, because in a secret place in his heart, though he would have denied it, he felt he more or less deserved what he received. He had counted his blessings, tried to control them, and had doled them out according to his own good judgment. He had been good at the system he understood: an achiever, an example of obedience, a son of whom his Father should be proud.

Then God allowed everything that Job understood to be crushed. When Job recognized that the ability he had always prided himself on - to see the big picture and his sizable competence to manage the affairs of life - were trivial in comparison to God's, he was never the same again. It is one thing to seek to know and please God through sacrifice and obedience, and quite another to meet the Creator Himself face to face. Job now knew that God had not been capricious in his testing, for it had transformed him.

At one time he had sought to insure his children's happiness and security. Because he was only a man with good intentions, he had failed. He simply was not big enough to be god to his children, no matter how much he wanted to. Back in the day, he had poured all of his emotional energy into his business. Now his spirit sang in harmony with his generations, and he was profoundly grateful that he had lived long enough for life to take on the purpose it had. He had come to peace with being a patriarch. He had secured blessings that trickled down on the succeeding generations like a warm summer rain, and it delighted him to watch it. The acquisition of possessions had once motivated him, but now, they seemed to flow effortlessly, from his children to their children and the succeeding generation. It brought him greater fulfillment to see the impact of blessings that flowed from God, through him, to others. "If I should die tonight, my legacy will be a lasting one," Job whispered to the beloved child who continued to sleep in unencumbered bliss.

One of his hands was trained in frugality, while the other hand was open and ready to give.

Job had once "owned" everything in his possession, and losing it had caused him to confront and question God. What a foolish man he had been to try and confront God, not that he wasn't a masterful negotiator, for Job had remarkable business sense. He seemed to know instinctively when to buy and when to sell. He was talented at every aspect of business: manual labor, design, assessing the market, predicting rising and falling prices, and he could make a deal with anyone, usually buying below the market value, while leaving the customer feeling satisfied and happy.

Job kept his friends, usually for life, and although they spoke of him as a shrewd businessman who cut a deal leaving them a little short, they liked him and they liked doing business with him. "No one squeezes the last drop from the grape like Job," his friend, Bildad, had once joked, but truthfully, his friends were proud to know a man whom others respected for driving such a hard bargain. They liked to see him coming, because he was usually jovial and engaging, unless he was losing in a business deal, which always troubled him.

Job had a purpose in watching his losses and gains carefully, because the more he had, the more he could give away. One of his hands was trained in frugality, while the other hand was open and ready to give when it seemed like a good investment in a life or a cause. He gave like he bargained, cautiously and carefully, bringing all of his sound judgment to the table and giving, usually, where he saw the greatest potential harvest. A beggar by the gate didn't move him, if the beggar were able bodied. He had rather give to a young man, full of promise, who lacked capital to start a trade. Even giving was done with his powerful sense of responsibility and accountability to God as a steward.

Job had learned finesse over time. He had been a scrapper early on, fighting for what was his, but he quickly discovered an innate penchant for negotiating. Realizing that each friend or acquaintance could open the door to one hundred other people, he tried hard not to lose a single relationship from his vast network. He preferred to maneuver carefully around his opponents and hang on to his friends. He liked to hold his options open until the last minute, so getting a firm commitment from him was nearly impossible, because he never wanted to be held to something he had said earlier if the market had changed or his vision had shifted. It was a trait that caused angst to those men who required words to assure themselves that contracts wouldn't be broken, but Job preferred never to speak too quickly or too finally on any subject.

"Job has an eye for the past, the present, and the future," people would admit with admiration. He saw limitless possibilities and endless opportunity. "I need more land to expand my crops or I need more sheep," he would say, not impulsively, but as though he was prompted by an inner voice moving him in the right direction with the proper momentum. He envisioned what should come next: barns, roads, or herds, and he worked hard to stay in rhythm with time, demands, and his own sense of priorities. He usually put too many irons in the fire, but even then he managed to balance them indefinitely, using his natural perseverance and sheer determination, working long productive hours, foregoing sleep or whatever else needed to be sacrificed, in order to make his projects successful.

The day that Job's life became a tragedy and his name a byword for suffering had been more than one hundred years earlier, as hard as that was to imagine. It had begun in an uneventful way. On that particular morning, Job was up at his usual early hour, micromanaging the servants by giving them their instructions for the day. "We will need to take the sheep further up the mountain for better grass and fresher water," he said. Although the servants were well aware of the change of seasons and knew when to transfer pastures, they nodded agreeably. "You will also need to see to the feast for tonight." They had been in preparation for days, but they understood his hands-on management style and respected it.

As soon as he outlined the day, he made his way to an altar where he regularly sacrificed on behalf of his children. He feared they might inadvertently sin, and he regarded their relationships and right standing with God as one more thing he watched carefully over. He knew what God required; maybe they would not take things as seriously as was necessary and their neglect might have disastrous results, so Job preferred not to take the chance. His children took for granted their father's spiritual protection with the same nonchalance they accepted the fruits of his financial responsibility.

Job regarded all irresponsibility as foolishness of the most serious kind, a precursor to disaster and ruin. For anything to run with highest efficiency, he felt he needed a significant amount of control. There was a right and profitable way to do anything, and he cared about both. He expected people who worked for him to share his work ethic and be frugal in their use of time and resources, and he was vexed by laziness and sloppiness. How one managed his financial affairs spoke volumes to Job, and his own bottom line of profit always told him how it was going from day to day and year to year.

Job took God's laws seriously and he counted on His total protection in return.

That very day, with no warning or cause, four messengers came, one after the other, each with more shocking news than the last to tell him. The first messenger ran up breathlessly, declaring that the Sabeans had attacked, carrying off his oxen and donkeys and killing his servants. As Job tried to grasp what this staggering loss of a strategic farming resource would mean to his financial empire, another messenger appeared informing him that a fire had fallen from heaven and burned up his sheep and his servants. These were the same servants he had just spoken with, valued friends, almost like family. He was stunned, stricken to his heart, when he saw a third messenger approaching.

Here comes another messenger. Maybe he will say the last one was mistaken. Job waited expectantly, still slightly optimistic that all of this was a mistake of staggering proportions. The third blow was crushing.

"The Chaldeans have stolen my camels and killed my servants?" There went his key resource for all the trade routes his men worked. The pummeling blows were coming so quickly and were so unexpected that Job wondered if this could be supernatural, but how could it be? He had not sinned against God.

As he was reeling from shock and dismay, he saw a fourth messenger approaching, distraught and trembling, bringing him the worst possible news. The messenger related how his children had been killed by a mighty wind that crushed the house where they were feasting, and all of his ten children were dead.

With each piece of news, Job felt less in control, but with the horrendous finale, he lost control of everything, including himself, and he sank to the ground a weeping, broken man.

Job took God's laws seriously and he counted on His total protection in return. *Impossible,* he thought. *How can this be?* He was trying to piece together shattered thoughts, groping for a rational explanation for what was happening to him, and when he could find none, he cried out in misery, feeling his mind grasping for something beyond the reality that he had always held to be sacred and infallible: that God kept his side of the covenant when we kept ours. If that wasn't true, then what hope did man have?

Reaching deeply, he forced himself for a moment to overrule his emotions of outrage and anguish.

> Naked I came from my mother's womb, and naked I will depart. The Lord gave and the Lord has taken away; may the name of the Lord be praised.

He heard himself declare words of faith that he knew were absolutely correct, but where was the justice in them? There had to be a logical explanation.

Job had experienced setbacks before. There was the time he bought the livestock and some of the herd had been diseased, spreading it through the rest of his livestock, resulting in a seriously, unexpected loss. He had known years when the rains had been too heavy, and then the years when the rains were too few. But even then, the slightest setback troubled him, for Job always equated success and prosperity with God's blessing.

There was nothing in Job's makeup or in his concept of God that prepared him for reversal. He was not the kind of man who braced himself for ill winds and disappointment, who half expected to lose a crop every now and then. No, disappointment always took him by surprise, ambushed him like a thief in the night and intruded on his sense of well being. He would usually shut down emotionally for a few hours or weeks trying to process setback, because it struck deep into his heart, shaking him and leaving him slightly traumatized, disturbing his reality with a twisted cruelty as it taunted his concept of the way things should be. Life was controllable. You served God and He cared for you.

So Job tried to reason, for above all else Job was a rational man, but he was having immense difficulty, because unbearable grief was flooding his thoughts. Nothing he thought was comforting, and his mind continually screamed, *I have lost everything.* To a man who bemoaned the slightest loss, who sought explanations for it and solutions and remedies to fix it, and who equated peace and contentment with the absence of loss, this was shattering. Whatever control he had ever thought he had through upholding his part of the bargain was gone. He felt mocked by his losses and abandoned by his God. Logic failed him, and even his trusted style of preserving through a crisis until increase showed up again failed to encourage him. This was no slight decline, no slump; it was complete and utter loss, and he didn't have a single notion of how to consider rebuilding, for all of his options were gone.

He more or less waited for their cards to be placed on the table in front of him, while he held his tightly to his chest.

To Job there were always rules of engagement and social contracts, and he had been careful to honor the ones that he believed pleased God. He had fought hard all of his life to get where he was, but in the process he had obeyed God, given to the poor, and been an exemplary steward of God's blessings. He despised being taken advantage of, and he never walked away from a fight when a man wanted to take what belonged to him. Job much preferred negotiation to confrontation, but if one took what was rightfully his, he had better prepare for war of some kind. Now God had taken everything.

Day after day he grieved and tried to find some logic to steady his mind which skipped unbridled from tragedy to tragedy in a horrible and uncontrollable pattern, despite his best efforts to settle it in peace. Weary and distraught, he passed into the blessed unconsciousness of sleep, only to dream of a wind on the horizon coming toward him, ready to destroy everything in its path. He awoke in panic, and in pain.

Hideous, oozing boils now covered his body, and he was tortured no matter what direction he moved. He tried to rise, but he was overcome with tormenting, relentless pain. What little grip he had on his sanity, was shaken with an even greater instability. *Why am I being punished?* Job thought. An even more bitter thought rushed suddenly to his mind: *I don't deserve this.*

As he sat in physical and mental anguish, he realized that his whole body was tense, as though he was now bracing himself for further disaster, and that while he had once expected only blessings to come his way, he now expected sudden tragedy to overtake him at any moment. He felt totally at the mercy of God, and he wasn't sure what this unpredictable deity might do next, or even if He were good.

Job usually stayed in control by a masterful strategy, waiting and listening. If he listened carefully and long, men would usually reveal what they wanted. Once he understood what they wanted and what they needed, he could customize his negotiations to their personalities and desires. He more or less waited for their cards to be placed on the table in front of him, while he held his tightly to his chest. He could wait and see what God said about this, or he could curse God and die. It seemed far more logical to wait. A lesser man might have turned from God, but the stubbornness and perseverance that had brought him thus far in life, enabled him to hang on and wait - besides he never folded when he thought he could win. He had very few cards left to play, but what he really wanted was to see what was in God's hand.

When his friends walked into the courtyard and saw him, they were horrified, for Job was the most admired and competent man that any of them knew. He was always a well groomed, imposing figure, but when they saw him, they each secretly wished they could retreat, so appalling was his condition. There was a faint putrid smell, and the boils on his face and his puffy, red eyes made his face look like a hideous pagan mask. He looked no different than a pitiful outcast sitting by the city gate begging for alms. He glanced up, nodded, and looked back down again, and they saw in his eyes an emotional pain far greater than any physical one. They were ashamed of their revulsion and did their best to hide it; after all, this man was their friend, one they used to envy.

He did not want to talk and speculate on his condition. *They can stay if they don't speak,* Job thought to himself, as he was in no mood for conversation of any kind. And so they all sat together, each lost in his own troubled and turbulent thoughts. Job saw his beloved children running and playing: one by one they came; unbidden memories flooding his mind like a giant panorama, they were children and then adults, all flowing together with bright colors and beautiful melodies until the colors became darker and darker and despair consumed him.

These men sat soberly for seven days without speaking, feeling sympathy and compassion for their friend, sincerely touched by his misery. What could they say to comfort him? What could they do to help? One thing they knew for certain: tragedy like this could not fall without sin. Time and again their minds would wander back to their fundamental understanding of God's ways: a man is cursed if he does not obey. What had Job done? They must help him see, so he could walk in the favor of God once more.

Finally, it was Job who broke the silence, as his misery and self-pity tumbled hotly from his lips in the presence of his closest friends, but his tirade of anger only frightened them. Because they had never suffered like he was suffering, they were horrified at his pain and entered into debate with him regarding a level of misery they knew nothing about. Their words were correct, but they were hollow and lifeless to Job. These friends had never won an argument with Job before, but now they persisted against his legendary stubbornness believing it was imperative that he hear them just this once.

He had never moved from his staunch position that God was treating him badly even though he was innocent.

In the end, Job had the last word and they withdrew into silence, noting that he had never moved from his staunch position that God was treating him badly even though he was innocent.

"I will sign a defense," Job said. He had become angry enough at the unfairness of his dilemma, that he finished by demanding an audience with God Himself, issuing a subpoena to the Judge. He would show every single one of them just who was right.

Job was certain that he had not brought this tragedy upon himself. If God would give him an opportunity to speak, he felt certain he could clear this up, because justice was on his side. "I have not lusted, denied the poor, ignored the fatherless, or turned even a traveler away." What could God possibly accuse him of or have against him to cause him to endure this kind of misery? Nothing.

Suddenly, the voice of God came and silenced the voices of the men. Job now had his day in court, but in an instant Job realized that God was not appearing in his court, he was in God's.

"Would you condemn me to justify yourself, Job?"

"Would you discredit my justice?" God asked.

Had Job really planned to put God on trial? God began to question Job, not about Job's understanding of His righteousness, because both God and Job knew that was not the place Job's understanding was lacking. What man ever came into a courtroom and put the judge on trial? Question after question, Job felt his bravado fade and his case dissipate, until he felt like a small child who had questioned his parents' wisdom about his bedtime or demanded recompense from them for some measly chore he had performed.

Had his efforts to obey God's laws made him an equal to the one who was Justice, whose very being was Truth itself? All of his righteousness was an effort to please God by obeying his laws. God was Righteousness. What had he ever given away that had not been given to him from God? His deeds were so small, nothing more than sharing blessings that had come from the hand of this majestic, benevolent King who could use earth as His footstool. Job tried to back out of the conversation. He felt humiliated beyond measure.

"Surely, I spoke of things I did not understand, things too wonderful for me to know." Job said.

He was not God's peer, nor had God broken a contract with him. How could a man hold God accountable? What did God owe any man? Job was truly sorry he had ever entered this debate, but he could not hide from His voice and His presence, and as he listened he realized that humiliating him was not God's intent at all.

As God spoke, Job began to imagine very graphic images of the things God described. He saw God the Builder as He measured out the foundations of the world and suspended them into space, defying all the laws of architecture that man would ever pride himself in comprehending. He saw Him limit and tame the seas, and he saw the expanse of the ocean and waves that were as high as mountains with white caps hitting into cliffs and shores, enraged by the wind. He thought he felt the ocean spray on his face as close and real as God's breath, and it was terrifying enough in its raw, brutal power that Job shuddered. Every word that God spoke to him about who He was seemed to push him farther and farther into the light and the vastness, the boundless creativity, the colossal mind, the immeasurable grandeur, the limitless power.

Unbelievably, peace was coming to him for the first time in weeks.

God spoke of his storehouses of snow and hail, and Job shivered, although he had never seen snow or hail, not even once. He was taken places and shown things so far beyond his imagination that his mind was not able to process what he was seeing and hearing, yet he was certain that God was neither boasting about Himself nor mocking him.

In the midst of God showing him His wonders, Job began to feel an odd and unlikely sensation. Unbelievably, peace was coming to him for the first time in weeks. God's voice and His magnitude had steadied him and conquered his fears. He never felt so out of control or so safe. Finally, Job had raised his eyes and seen the vastness of the God of the universe, and looked away from his own sense of loss and grief, and his own righteousness, and in that moment, he comprehended something about his God that he had never known. He was a God who wanted to be known for all His grandeur, not just His blessings and judgments. Despite all that had happened to him, his heart entered an entirely new rest.

In the years to follow, God demonstrated to his servant, Job, once again His grace and favor by completely restoring, and even increasing, all that he had lost. He was given twice as much prosperity, ten more sons and daughters, and he was allowed to live one hundred and forty more years enjoying the blessings of God, but Job was a different man than he had been before.

Job still obeyed God carefully, but he arose each day with a desire to see the vastness of God's creativity expressed in Job's own world. He no longer basked in the false security of his social contract with God, exchanging obedience for blessing. Rather, Job learned to walk with awe over the endless facets of God expressing Himself in Job's world of farming, trading, investing and governing.

His greatest compassion was toward men who misunderstood the ways of God, seeing Him as Judge, for he knew what an easy trap that was. He never felt entitled to blessing again, only grateful for the ones he received, and yet at the same time, he was more generous than he had ever been, relying on God's provision rather than on his own strength and abilities, or even his own obedience. He gave his sons a rich inheritance, and although daughters never received an inheritance in his culture, his three daughters did.

Much more importantly though, every morning that Job awoke, he was filled with an expectancy that the day would be glorious, a day of discovery. Every day was a new search and a new experience and he saw God in all of it. God was in the simplest thing, like the trust of this child, and in the most complex matters of the universe. He had taught his generations to worship, not with careful sacrifices in order to negotiate protection, but with reverence and awe and celebration of the boundless goodness of the God of rich complexity, the God of all creation, who cared about the minute details of men and women and children, and who planned good for their lives and comfort for their sorrow. He was a God who watered the desert even when no man had ever lived upon it because He cared for all of His creation.

"Our God is amazing, little one, full of surprises," he whispered to the sleeping child, and she snuggled closer wrapping her little hand around his.

Nehemiah's eyes scrolled down the list as he checked the quantities of wine he had ordered against the number of clay jars which had been delivered to the palace. When he was done, he nodded to the young men waiting patiently at the gate. Then he motioned to a threatening looking guard who briskly stepped aside when he received Nehemiah's signal. Nehemiah did not have to perform this particular duty himself, but he liked to occasionally. Every now and then he monitored the daily deliveries, because he felt it insured that all those who brought goods to the palace knew that at any moment Nehemiah could be checking their lists and counting their products instead of the usual person. This prevented any sloppiness or cheating that might creep in if the merchants assumed more lenient men would be watching them.

Generally, he was greeting noblemen and foreign dignitaries, always with ease, granting or denying them access to the king with enough authority and commanding presence that few dared to argue with his decisions. His was a familiar face in court. He was known for his loyalty to the king, his ability to organize and carry out a multitude of tasks at once, as well as for his explosive manner that was part sincere outrage at incompetence and part dramatic effect meant to instill fear and to produce an instantaneous attitude adjustment.

He was envied by many for his place of prominence in Babylon. After all, his people had come to Persia as prisoners of war from Judah, and now he held the prestigious office of cup bearer to the king. Today that would be equivalent to the chief of staff to the president. He was well compensated for a job that others envied, wielding power with decisive and deliberate precision. He enjoyed being the person others came to for final answers throughout the day. Nehemiah was the kind of man who would have probably taken over any project he was involved in. Although others envied his power and the perks of his office, few would have taken the job if it had been offered to them, because it was demanding and risky to be the person who was most responsible for the well being of the king.

Although they had been captured and relocated to Babylon, Nehemiah's parents had trained him to love the God of Israel and to honor his fellow man. Mosaic Law commanded that he not steal from his neighbor or covet his possessions, and his adherence to God's teachings had made him a trustworthy man of integrity. His father, Hacaliah, had told him many times, "Son, learn the ways of God. Obey His laws. Maybe He will relent and have pity on us and let us return to the land of our fathers. Do not make the mistakes of our forefathers who were careless about God's laws, mocking Him and taking advantage of His mercy." Nehemiah had heard God's laws explained with such intensity and with such emphasis on the consequences of disobedience that he had no desire to repeat Israel's history in his own life.

Nehemiah had found favor with King Artaxerxes, an astute leader, who prided himself on his ability to judge human nature. He truly possessed a talent for discerning a man's character, noting and interpreting the smallest detail about a man and his behavior. This skill had grown more remarkable over time, strengthened through necessity. He had made the observation of men not only a past time of his, but also a calculated means of protecting himself and his kingdom. When he made the foreigner, Nehemiah, his cup bearer, he knew exactly what he was doing by placing him in charge, and time had proved his wisdom because Nehemiah was perfect for the job. Although Nehemiah moved hurriedly from task to task, almost like a force of nature, he was energized by the magnitude of the task: the greater the task, the more driven and happy he seemed. Artaxerxes trusted him completely.

Nehemiah could be stern and commanding, barking at those around him to complete their tasks quickly, but he was also capable, in his leadership style, of drawing out the best in those who worked for him, even if they didn't like him. His goal was always the king's pleasure, not the approval of his peers and underlings. Consequently the king never had to worry that any detail would escape him or that he would allow the king to be embarrassed on occasions of state. Whatever the king wanted and however Nehemiah determined to make it happen, the king was to have his way, and quickly. That was Nehemiah's chief goal, and he didn't care how many enemies he made among the people he used to accomplish his work. Nehemiah assumed, often wrongly, that others were as focused on the end product as he, and he was occasionally taken aback when he heard that someone had complained about his lack of compassion or kindness.

Nehemiah looked around him at the efficiency he had helped create and felt a well deserved sense of accomplishment. He knew that even though he was in a foreign land, he was very fortunate to have achieved one of the greatest positions in the court - the highest to which a foreigner such as himself could rise. He could have been stuck doing some task for which he had no talent or interest instead of using the abilities that God had given him. He had risen to this position easily, because ever since he had been noticed by the first steward he had served, men had stepped aside for Nehemiah to engineer and execute tasks in his authoritative manner. No task was too small to do quickly and efficiently, and no task was so big that it intimidated him. He was naturally more challenged by the bigger tasks, but even a small one could be invigorating if he concentrated on making it bigger and better. Every time he saw a segment of the palace that was running with minimum efficiency, he found a way to bring it under his control and reorganize it. He had done that until almost everything was now his domain, but few complained that Nehemiah thought he could manage the work better than the rest of them; most people agreed that he could.

His style was decidedly aggressive, complete with a dramatic temper.

Of course there were some who resented his far reaching arm, but everyone knew the favor he had with the king, so anyone who felt provoked by Nehemiah's control kept his opinions to himself. Those closest to him in command respected him and accepted his leadership style without comment because he got things done, which made them all look good. His style was decidedly aggressive, complete with a dramatic temper, but most people admired Nehemiah, or at least respected him, appreciating the end product. Nehemiah remained oblivious to most opinions about him, for he was far more concerned with his task than with making friends among the staff. He worked long days, and retired when he was satisfied that everything was under control. He fell asleep planning the next day and thinking of more efficient ways of doing the tasks at hand.

Men very rarely appeared in front of Nehemiah who had come from the land of his fathers. For many years there had been a trickle of refugees returning to Israel, and news of the resettlement project occasionally came back to those remaining in Babylon, but on this day, he found men standing before him who had actually just arrived from Judah. He swiftly seized the opportunity to ask them how the people of Judah were doing, but he was not prepared for their answer or his own reaction.

"Those who survived the exile and are back in the province are in great trouble and disgrace. The wall of Jerusalem is broken down and its gates have been burned with fire."

Nehemiah had hoped for better news, for he knew about the resettlement, and he had been told that there were attempts to rebuild the wall surrounding the city, since an unwalled city was an open invitation to thieves or invaders. It was not a place where they could live with any degree of peace or safety. It was also an affront to his pride as a Jew, and he still had pride at being one of

God's chosen people, despite everything that had happened. The only true and living God had chosen his people, and while they had deserved the 70 years in exile, having the main city wall still in shambles one hundred years later, signified more to Nehemiah than a judgment. It seemed to him like a breach with their God, a monument of shame, and an enduring state of disconnectedness. It made them and their God an ongoing laughing stock to the nations around them.

Nehemiah was surprised at how intense his emotions were as he sat down and began to weep in an uncharacteristic display of emotion. Something had been awakened within him that he never knew was there. All he could think was that someone needed to take charge and see that the city was safe again. For days he grieved, fasted, and prayed; he could not imagine why he should feel such a depth of pain, why this burden had landed so solidly upon his shoulders. The weight of Israel's sin and the shame of what it had wrought almost crushed him.

Finally, he prayed. "Please forgive me for my sins and my forefathers' sins. We have acted most wickedly and have deserved your judgment. We have not obeyed your commands given us through Moses. You said you would scatter us if we disobeyed, and you have done that, rightfully so. But you also said you would gather us as exiles and return us to our land. Please grant me favor with the king, for I am going to ask his permission to return to assess the damage and see what can be done."

Nehemiah would certainly need divine favor, because it was impossible to predict the reaction of the king. If he were denied, he would never be able to mention the matter again. Since Nehemiah had heard the news, he had become obsessed with a plan, a preposterous plan to rebuild the wall. He knew that if he got to Jerusalem he could make it happen, but it would take the right words, the right favor, and the right timing to get the king's backing. Vision, will, and determination were always on Nehemiah's side, so he focused every part of his being on this task that he wanted to do. He had performed well at his job and he had enjoyed success, but now he felt a deep passion burning inside of him. He was alive with a new destiny and purpose. He knew he had the skills and the heart for the task, and if God would grant him favor with the king, nothing would be able to stop him.

> *Vision, will, and determination were always on Nehemiah's side.*

It was a risk to show his sadness to the king. He never had considered doing such a thing before; actually, it was not permitted. It was his task to make sure the king was happy and pleased, not the other way around. Yet if he allowed himself to pretend that all was well with him, it could be a costly lie, haunting him for the rest of his life. To give the king a chance - better, to give his God a chance - to touch the heart of the king, was a risk he had to take. He knew the king was observant, so he purposed not to mask his feelings. He would be honest about what was troubling him, if the king asked.

"Why does your face look so sad when you are not ill? This can be nothing but sadness of heart," observed the king who never let the furrow of a man's brow or his slightest agitation go unnoticed.

Here is my chance, Nehemiah thought. *God, help me!*

"May the King live forever. Why should my face not look sad

when the city where my fathers are buried lies in ruins, and its gates have been destroyed by fire?"

"What does any of this have to do with me?" asked Artaxerxes.

"I want to return to the city and rebuild the wall. I want your permission."

Nehemiah held his breath. The king looked at the queen and back to Nehemiah, studying his countenance and noting the determination and the fire in his eyes. What had come over his cup bearer? Should he really grant permission to a Jew to return to his homeland to secure the city by building the wall and setting in the city gates? What kind of precedent would it set? Nehemiah was a favorite of both the king and queen. They never doubted his loyalty to them and often congratulated themselves on their good fortune in having him. As the king took mental inventory of very good reasons to grant him permission as well as to deny it, he realized that Nehemiah was passionate about returning, more passionate than he had ever observed him to be. He could not deny this man's request when it obviously meant so much to him. Nehemiah had earned this privilege, and he would grant it to him.

"How long will your journey take and when will you return?" the king asked.

Nehemiah realized that he just received permission from the king. He knew he would need letters for the governors of the Trans-Euphrates so they would know he had permission for his undertaking, plus rights to cut timber from the forests, so while the king was agreeable, Nehemiah asked for everything he needed. Once he saw the door of favor open, he stepped through it, confidently, without hesitation. It was clear that God was on his side.

He was given the letters he had requested, as well as a number of officials and cavalry men to accompany him on his journey to the city of Jerusalem. After making meticulous arrangements for his staff to run the palace in his absence, his entourage left for Jerusalem.

He told no one in his team what he intended to do. Nehemiah was the kind of leader who men could follow without second guessing him or feeling that he expected them to be interjecting their ideas at odd times so he could use them to calculate his plans. He didn't need input; he needed cooperation and loyalty, and those things most men found easy to surrender to him. Anyone who couldn't follow this kind of leadership, or who was too proud of his own cleverness, or who chaffed at submission, usually stayed far away from Nehemiah.

He had learned that many men called things "impossible" that he would simply relish as a good challenge.

When they finally arrived in Jerusalem, he waited until night fell before he set out privately to survey the broken wall. Even then, Nehemiah didn't want input or agreement for that matter, so it was entirely understandable that he surveyed the wreckage alone. He had come to repair the wall, and that is what he would do, needing only to assess the damage and calculate the time and the materials that would be necessary to do the job. Because

Nehemiah never trusted hearsay, he had to see it for himself. He had learned that many men called things "impossible" that he would simply relish as a good challenge.

Once he made his plan and announced it, people poured in from all over the region to help, inspired by his courage and leadership, and the novelty of a Babylonian born Jew coming from the king with authority to rebuild. The returning exiles were desperate for strong, integrous leadership. The Levite, Ezra, had been with them, ready to point out their breach with God and to help them repent, but Nehemiah was completely different. Here was a man who understood the physical dilemma, who wanted to rebuild and protect, and who inspired others with his leadership. His unexpected presence was thrilling and commanding, a God send, and there was also the matter of his being here on the king's business which had impressed all of them.

There were ongoing disputes among the returning exiles that badly needed to be settled. Up until now, there was no one in government to protect their property and interests. In fact, the noblemen who had returned were part of the problem, not the solution, as they were taking unfair advantage of their poorer brothers, charging them high interest on the farm mortgages and even taking some of their daughters as slaves when they couldn't pay back what they had borrowed. Others were going hungry for lack of grain. Hopefully, Nehemiah, they thought would surely tend to these matters right away.

"I spoke to him, and he seems only concerned about the wall. Does he not care about our suffering and our mistreatment?" a shabbily dressed man whispered bitterly to his wife and spat on the ground in anger, walking away from Nehemiah with his head bent down and his shoulders hunched in disappointment. It appeared that the visionary was single minded in his focus, and right now, that focus was rebuilding the wall. Others came and went, seeking counsel or intervention, but Nehemiah brushed them aside or suggested they too join the work on the wall.

Soon more laborers appeared and the organized pandemonium of work began, the laborious task of clearing away rubble, recovering useable bricks, and making new bricks of straw and clay, drying them, and setting them in place. Working side by side were noblemen, priests, women, artisans, farmers, laborers, and young people. These weren't skilled stone cutters and masons, but what each lacked in skill, he made up for with passion and endurance, for each was a Jew who saw deep meaning in the wall.

To some it represented the restoration of the blessing of God. To others it meant protection, and to others, national pride. To many, it was the rebirth of their nation that they had dreamed of, and the end of their disjointed existences, living as they had as isolated aliens within their own borders. Nehemiah was pleased with this rather diverse and untrained army of workers, for he much preferred commitment in heart and commitment to his leadership than skilled laborers who were half-hearted. This was a super human task and his formidable determination, iron will, and far reaching vision ignited theirs, producing the delightful hum of productivity everywhere. Nehemiah stopped briefly to capture the beauty of the synchronization of the people at their noble task. He spent hours listing the workers' names, their accomplishments on the wall, their trades, and the places from which they had come to join the project. He loved organized lists and details, and to him, these were details worth noting, worth honoring and remembering.

In the midst of the work, Nehemiah had to face the challenge of Sanballat and a group of Samaritans who lived nearby. These men had no interest in seeing the walls rebuilt since it would cause more Jews to return, and the old rivalry between them led them to attempt to discourage the builders. Nehemiah was not threatened by their tactics; in fact, he inwardly scoffed at their puny efforts to stop the work. He had faced far more threatening foes in the royal court, men who were truly skilled at political intrigue. He could easily ignore these Samaritan ruffians whom he assessed to be mostly empty wind, but for precaution's sake, he instructed his people to work while carrying their weapons. They would fight if necessary, but they would not stop the work.

He was alive with strength and joy, duty and desire, passion and purpose.

Nehemiah easily brushed aside Sanballat and kept his focus on the wall, and with equal ease ignored the injustice in the land. Maybe later he would take time to resolve civil issues and nurture the people, but not now. At the moment, problems not related to the wall were like worrisome gnats, aggravating but not deadly. The only thing that had to be done, and done quickly, was the completion of this wall.

At least that was his mindset.

Much to his dismay, the outcry of the people grew so loud that he finally had to reluctantly stop construction for a day and deal with the noblemen who were abusing the middle class. Nehemiah was obviously angry at their behavior and even more angry that he had to stop his project and address the issue: "What you are doing is not right!" Nehemiah bellowed to the noblemen he had assembled who were now quaking before him. "Shouldn't you walk in the fear of God to avoid the reproach of our Gentile enemies?"

Nehemiah was very good at confrontation and people usually decided to rethink their positions once he had made his abundantly clear. He insisted that they give back to the farmers the fields, orchards, vineyards they had foreclosed on, and stop the practice of usury. Remarkably, they did so, as though they had been waiting for someone to make them do what they knew all along was right.

After that brief time out for social justice, Nehemiah saw to it that the laborers worked relentlessly. They slept in their clothes; they worked with their weapons; they worked from first light until the stars appeared, ignoring threats and taunts and overcoming personal fear and fatigue. "Your strength is the joy of the Lord," Nehemiah would shout when the sun beat down upon them and they were exhausted. For the first time in his life, Nehemiah knew the truth of what he said. He was alive with strength and joy, duty and desire, passion and purpose. From his spirit came the deepest desire to accomplish this task, born of a certainty that the passion that was driving him was God's and he was doing what he was meant to do. He had always been dutiful, but he had never before found something that he had felt so passionate about. The combination of his sense of duty and this desire had brought him into a place of true freedom for the first time in his life.

His strong spirit and his commanding voice called to the spirits of those who worked on the wall so that a supernatural joy and strength sustained them too, for they were discovering the incredible joy Nehemiah described. The task was the wall, for the wall gave them back Jerusalem. It declared the Lord's favor on them again, and it struck terror in the hearts of their enemies that such a thing could be done. They worked like madmen and women driven by their own need, God's strength, and this loud and demanding visionary who unleashed their own passion and drive. Day after joyously exhausting day, he drove them toward the goal of a completed wall.

King Artaxerxes thought he understood what Nehemiah wanted and needed in life, but there was another King who knew him even better, the One who had designed him and orchestrated this grand project for him where duty and desire met and where he could break through to a place of the sweetest freedom. This King knew just what Nehemiah needed to accomplish in order to ignite his passion and fulfill his sense of duty.

Here, the grim and formidable Nehemiah discovered how much joy there was when a man reconciles the passion in his heart, his own desires, and the duty he feels called to perform. He could never live again just to accomplish, to build, to stretch his powerful hand out in duty without passion, for he had discovered that when his own desires and passions were aligned with God's, he would be able to find strength and meaning and joy which far transcended mere power and privilege.

From that moment on, he wanted it all.

As Barbara Ann Spooner slipped her feet into her satin wedding slippers on a cool May morning in 1797, she smiled back at her happy reflection in the mirror. This was the day she was marrying the honorable Mr. William Wilberforce, a man in his late thirties who was already a distinguished member of the British Parliament. Although she had known him only six weeks, and was barely twenty, they were both convinced that their marriage was a good idea.

She and William were ignoring the advice of all their friends and marrying quickly. Their haste had caused a little stir, but William never minded "stirs" and she found she was enjoying the spontaneity herself. He had been introduced to her as the "wittiest man in all of England," and she had discovered quickly that he was delightfully light hearted and charming, possessing a personality that would have never given him away as the foremost crusader for the abolition of slavery in England. She was certain she could help him in his work, for she was an admirer of his cause, as well as a perfect balance to his more impulsive nature.

William Wilberforce was known to be a force to be reckoned with. He had achieved this reputation not because of his stature, for he was small of stature, or his constitution, for it too was weak; most would have agreed he had earned it by his display of dogged determination when he knew he was right. William was not the kind of reformer who thought truth should prevail despite laws or institutions, for he was a loyal subject of the British crown, one who respected government and law and sought only to oppose it if it were wrong. He believed that government and its people could change and would change if laws were continually challenged by morality and by the determination of Christians who fought for right.

The average Englishman preferred to dismiss its harsh realities.

Elected to the English parliament as a Tory at the age of 21, he would become the most persuasive voice in government denouncing the practice of slavery, an institution which, when he began, had almost unanimous public sanction and profound economic roots. It was an institution that most of the English chose not to ponder too deeply, since most people were not closely connected to it and could ignore its moral implications. The average Englishman preferred to dismiss its harsh realities. Some broadly assumed that the Africans, who were sold, were well cared for as much of the propaganda suggested. Others, who were more realistic, dealt with it by deciding that the slaves were something less than suffering human beings.

Wilberforce was considered to be a madman by many when he adopted this particular cause, but his Christian beliefs drew him into the midst of the debate, although prudence and concern about his political career should have dissuaded him. England was the foremost shipping nation in the world, sending out thousands of ships every year, many loaded with slaves; in fact, he estimated that 100,000 slaves per year were being transported by the primary slave trading nations. The slave trade lasted for four centuries in which somewhere between nine and twelve million African slaves were sold all over the world, but half of them were sold in one century alone: the 18th, the century in which Wilberforce began his fight.

Obviously, slavery was a huge enterprise with many ramifications, a fact which gave credence to some very compelling pragmatic arguments that countered idealism. Were England to abruptly end the slave trade, it would undoubtedly wreak havoc on the sugar and coffee plantations in the West Indies, not only English owned, but also owned by the Dutch and French who depended on English ships. The English people also relied on the goods supplied by the West Indies, coffee and sugar, which were part of the comforts of the culture. Beyond profit and pleasantries, there was also the fear that England would diminish her place as a world power by letting France or the United States leap ahead in shipping, neither of which was politically palatable.

Most people felt that slavery was an unfortunate evil, but its place in the world system had been established long before their time in history. Some argued that even Jesus didn't advocate freeing slaves, teaching instead that they should submit to their masters. When Wilberforce became convinced enough to take his argument to the floor of the House of Commons, he raised his commanding voice and his eloquent tongue to challenge a nation. He was not seeking to make friends or enemies; he was fighting for a just cause that he honestly believed in. He was convinced from the beginning that because he was on the side of justice, he would win in the end. His opponents seemed to include every practical man from aristocrat to commoner, most politicians, and sadly, even some of the clergy of the day.

There was however, a growing number of abolitionists looking for a spokesperson in Parliament who would devise a way to rid England of what they had come to know was a hideous crime against humanity. Quakers and Evangelicals were both joining the fight. All agreed that the first step was to raise the social awareness of the problem. When respectable men approached Wilberforce and asked him to be the spokesperson in Parliament, he prayerfully considered the cost, and decided there was no way he could escape using his position for the highest good of the most desperate people.

Had he been a man given to personal ambition, he would have refused, because it was far more likely that he would lose his good name than convince his opponents to agree with him. He walked into the battle well aware of the personal sacrifice and the low opinion many would have of him, but it was not himself he was thinking of.

What had persuaded a young man, a Cambridge man, from a wealthy merchant family to become a champion of slaves? It may have begun when Wilberforce became acquainted with John

Newton when he was only nine years old and he lived for a time with an aunt and uncle after his father's death. This part of his family was Methodist and friends of John Newton, the slave trader turned evangelical Christian. William was influenced by Newton's religious views, as well as those of his aunt and uncle.

His mother, however, began to fear his total indoctrination, and removed him from their home. Her strategy seemed to have worked. As a young man at Cambridge, he was far from a serious reformer. He used his wealth to party, and was no different than most other affluent young men around him who felt they had an inordinate amount of time to pursue something worthy, and so they wasted much of their time with frivolity. He hung out with the socially elite, including the future prime minister, William Pitt.

His laughter was as contagious as his sunny disposition.

He later felt remorse over the time he had wasted when he experienced a deep conversion in 1786, an event that altered his world view entirely. He sincerely regretted his University years so much that although he was social by nature, he confined himself to solitude and became an avid Bible student. In fact, he spent eleven years, in an enforced time of study, spending long days catching up on his knowledge of God. He did not significantly emerge into the culture again until he met Barbara Spooner.

Although Wilberforce agreed with Calvin on much of his doctrine, there was a striking difference between them on one key issue. No Calvinist was considered to be very joyful, and William Wilberforce was known to be the most joyful and happy man in

England. His laughter was as contagious as his sunny disposition and he possessed such a beautiful singing voice that the Prince of Wales said he would go anywhere to hear him sing. When he was elected to the House of Commons at 21, he was known primarily as a light hearted young man, but over the next fifty years, his character grew to great depth and he used his oratory skills, his beautiful voice, his enthusiasm, and his profound commitment to live out a Christian conscience with deeds, not just words, to bring about historic change.

He was not alone in this focus. The new Evangelicals were influencing the country with their call to model authentic Christianity, and in their quest for moral reformation, they had determined to include the abhorrent slave trade. Wilberforce became an evangelical despite his family's warnings, and he was befriended by Quakers and others who were already actively crying out against injustice before he embraced the cause. It was his conscience and his convictions that drove him to appeal to the highest Christian standards for himself and his fellow countrymen. He was confident that once England understood the truth, she could be challenged to change her laws and her culture, regardless of the cost.

He valued their opinions immensely and leaned upon their strength.

Wilberforce never thought the grim persona of a dutiful Christian changed society. To him, the basic conditions of men mattered, and he saw his calling as alleviating suffering and bringing joy to mankind. Although he had high ranking friends, he cared deeply about the plight of the poor. Never seeking to divide the social classes, but to bridge them, he challenged the honor of the rich to come to the aid of the poor, and he treated the poor with the kind of respect he knew Jesus exhibited.

God saw to it that men of character and influence were there to advise Wilberforce in strategic times, and these were men, such as John Newton, whom Wilberforce gladly listened to. After William's radical conversion, he considered leaving Parliament and becoming a clergyman, but he was persuaded by the old man to stay right where he was. Newton felt certain that William was in the right place to be used most effectively, arguing "God put you there and you must stay where you have the most influence." His was the loudest and clearest voice, ringing in one of the most strategic places, battling with truth and passion, but those men and women who surrounded him and supported him, waged their own campaigns against evil and were essential to his victory, as he well knew.

Had William been more of a maverick or a loner, he might not have heeded his friends or finished the task, but he always engaged with a small group of men and women who served as his sounding board. Their agreement and approval of his plans was essential to his peace. He became a hero to many of the English who despised the slave trade while to the leaders of the shipping industry and many of his peers, he was their personal arch enemy. Despite being a legendary public figure pulled in many directions, he was able to live without being compromised by the love or hate of either group.

His small group of confidantes, however, was a different story, for he valued their opinions immensely and leaned upon their strength. This group, called the Clapham Sect, named for the London house in which they assembled, would fight the battle continually, drawing support and resolve from each other. Members of the sect included Hannah More, Granville Sharp and Henry Thornton, leading campaigners and philanthropists of the day who threw their personal energy and money into the battle.

This group shared a common commitment to Jesus Christ, to each other and to the cause for which they labored, but they were an unusually inclusive group for the time in which they lived. Wilberforce was a Wesleyan; his closest friend, Thornton, a Calvinist, and Thomas Clarkson was a Quaker pastor. They made family and community life a strong priority, and they took a very long view of the cause for which they labored. At the end of his life, Wilberforce had 400 letters in his possession from his friends, letters of remarkable insight and encouragement, showing the integral part which they played in his victory.

Charm and personality would have never sustained him during this long, arduous battle, although he had both, for he was pushed beyond his own gifts and determination when his health failed. He suffered from ulcerated colitis, curvature of the spine, and throughout much of his life had to rely on opium tablets - a common prescription of the day - to control the pain.

His own resolve would weaken at times when his health failed and defeat was looming, but his friends and the grace of God surrounded him and sustained him. John Wesley's early warning rang in his ears: "Unless God raised you up for this very thing, you will be worn out by the opposition of men and devils. But if God be for you, who can be against you?" And though devils and men tried to wear him out in every conceivable way, God proved faithful. Fortunately, Wilberforce never relied on his personal strength to win the war, but he did believe that if he remained faithful to his part, victory through God was possible.

Resolve, however, was not enough. It took strategy and the Clapham Sect knew that the first step was to draw the attention of people to all facets of the issue. Conversations about the cruelty of the slave trade were rare and would have remained so if William and his associates had not made them an increasing part of their own conversations.

The Anglican preacher, Thomas Clarkson, wrote a graphic and appalling pamphlet against slavery after carefully researching testimonies from freed slaves, the conditions of the ships, and statistics he was able to piece together. It was horrifying to those who read it, and helped supply the tangible evidence necessary to wage a campaign of literature against slavery. Clarkson vividly described the cramped quarters, the ghastly conditions, and the statistical evidence of the huge percentage of slaves who lost their lives in transport, in horrific detail; only the utterly heartless would not have been moved.

A nation never changes its mind unless individuals have.

Clarkson remained a strident voice against slavery throughout his life, a close friend to William, as they courageously waged a campaign of public opinion. With Clarkson's pamphlet and the touching autobiography of the former slave, Olaudah Equiano, they circulated information that began to affect the thoughts of a nation. It was the first public media campaign of its kind, and gradually a nation became morally outraged at the practice of slavery. The reformers understood that to outlaw the practice without the nation changing its mind would be a shallow and precarious victory, so they wanted to be certain that England despised the practice. Their core strategy was to destroy its legitimacy on every front available to them.

Josiah Wedgewood, the famous originator of Wedgewood china, used his prominence and skill to create a medallion with the picture of a slave in shackles and the words: "AM I NOT A MAN AND A BROTHER?" The medallion was widely sold and proudly worn throughout the country. The brotherhood of man in relation to slavery became the most compelling and convicting argument the abolitionists had. Private citizens began waging personal boycotts, refusing to use sugar for their tea if it came from slave plantations. Some stopped buying sugar entirely demonstrating their willingness to be deprived rather than encouraged such an abomination. Such action was vital to counter the argument that abolishing slavery would irreparably damage trade.

Once people began to recognize and consider the brutality of what these unfortunate Africans were suffering to put gold in the pockets of a few, the nation began to change its collective mind. Endorsing the degradation of slavery was too high a price to pay to provide a few luxuries that could be foregone or could be purchased from free men. Of course, a nation never changes its mind unless individuals have, one by one, and Wilberforce never quit influencing the man who stood right in front of him, not by accusing, but by assuming as much personal guilt for the problem as he expected any one else to bear, a humble attitude that made his words palatable. Wilberforce never rose to accuse the traders or the profiteers, but he appealed to the moral conscience of a nation to open its eyes and see the blood that was on all of their hands, including his own.

The abolition of slaves was not his only platform, for at one time he served on some 70 committees or boards in England seeking to right social ills. His passions as a social entrepreneur ranged from the Bible Society, the Society for the Prevention of Cruelty to Animals, the Society for the Betterment of Conditions for the Poor, to the Sunday School Society. He used every contact he had in order to further the cause of abolition.

William was a "doer," and he never had the time for half of the ideas he envisioned. He lived to do good with a simple and generous grace, even choosing to give away one fourth of his income to the poor. He was a man who practiced what he preached, and nothing about his message was deceitful or manipulative. He didn't ask anyone to live by a standard he did not seek to live personally in his own life, nor did he attack or belittle, but he appealed to the highest spiritual place he believed that God had empowered man to live.

William was not an entirely serious man, passionate only for his cause. In the midst of his struggles, he always made time for his favorite people: children. Statesmen who were in deep conversations with him sometimes reported being interrupted by children's voices asking, "Mr. Wilberforce, can you come out and play?" Often he would leave serious talks with dignitaries to romp in the yard with his own children or ones from the neighborhood. Although his behavior was unusual for polite society where children didn't ordinarily interrupt the adults to find a playmate among them, he was known for playing marbles, Blind Man's Bluff, and running races with the children at odd times, reveling in their genuine acceptance and gaiety. He was always so spontaneous and childlike himself, that he was willing to enter into play at the children's level, apparently coveting their easy and unconditional approval.

A friend described his home as "pell mell, topsy-turvy, and chaotic" with Mr. Wilberforce frisking about as though he had "quicksilver in his veins." It was said his presence was "fatal to dullness" and his "mirth was irresistible." He hated religion that was filled with prohibitions, but preferred a Christianity that was filled with privilege and hope, one that caused those who were suspicious of joyless religion to be compelled to consider his. The children in his life, both his own and the children with whom he came into contact filled his bucket with joy again and again, for he loved to hear their laughter and engage in their spontaneity and joy.

Gradually, England changed its mind about slavery, although many things still served to delay the decision to stop the trade. An untimely war with the French came and went, and even personal allies who were supposedly in William's camp continued to postpone or compromise the decision in Parliament. Once he was hindered by news of a frightening slave rebellion in Dominica that caused a wave of shock in England. The critical vote seemed within grasp so many times, only to be delayed.

Few issues have been championed so long and faithfully by a single individual in a political arena. His ability to bounce back after defeat was always encouraging to his followers and frightful to his adversaries, for they knew such persistence would probably win in the end. Session after session, year after year, the arguments continued on the floor of the House of Commons.

There were years when in every single session, Wilberforce argued against the slave trade. He was not arguing some lofty truth or elusive principle: he was fighting courageously for the men and women themselves who were losing their lives in daily squalor and brutality without dignity or anyone to defend them. He became "their" voice and "they" haunted his soul while God renewed his spirit; he dreamed about them in the night and argued for them in the day.

William defied public opinion and endured the enmity of men to see the cause through to the end and become a national hero. He was a rudder, one of a courageous group, who took on the conscience of a nation and believing he could see the ship turn, stormed the hallowed halls of Parliament with consistent logic, appeals to liberty, and calls for true Christian justice for eighteen years until he saw the trade abolished.

When the law passed in February 1807, it brought to him tremendous moral authority in England, more than most Englishmen have ever experienced; however, it also caused him to have to endure threats upon his life and experience public outrage against him in the years that followed, as all of his words and deeds were held up to public scrutiny. It was not a place that he had sought or desired to be, and he lamented the price of fame.

He had run a marathon, not a sprint.

A vocal opponent once decried him for pretending to care about African slaves but doing nothing for England's wretched poor. The cry was false, but heroes are often called hypocrites when they challenge controversial ideas, and all of subsequent actions become fair game for a predator's criticism, if that will serve to diminish their influence.

He had never sought popularity, and when he seemed about to lose it, he only bemoaned ever having had it thrust upon him. He also endured sadness within his own family; his wife became depressed and despondent, and his daughter, Barbara, died at 32, of tuberculosis. Of his four sons, the eldest rejected Christianity for a season, and although he returned to the faith, he and two of his brothers ultimately rejected the evangelical message their father had loved so passionately and embraced throughout his life and returned to the Anglican "high church" which disappointed him.

Even with the decision in 1807, when the country began to sincerely try to bail herself out of the trade, it would take another twenty-five years to stop all of England's participation in the trade and to emancipate her slaves. Sadly, an appallingly large number of slaves continued to be transported in those years.

God had appointed a time for William Wilberforce that coincided with ridding England of slavery and he lived to see his work completed, twenty five years later, in 1833, three days before his death. At that time, England not only abolished slavery, but she dug into her own pockets for twenty million pounds in order to compensate slave owners for their losses. William was immensely gratified to see his country not only choose to right a wrong, but to do it with such honor.

It had been forty-four years since he had stood in Parliament to give his famous speech of 1789, recognized as one of the finest speeches in history, but in the end it was not the words of a riveting speech by a fine orator, but perseverance that won, and the notion that a nation would eventually acknowledge its guilt and change its mind never left him. He had run a marathon, not a sprint, and he had been right about men doing the right thing if they were hard pressed by the truth. In that early speech, he said:

> When I consider the magnitude of the subject which I am to bring before the House - a subject in which the interests, not of this country, nor of Europe alone, but of the whole world, and the posterity, are involved, and when I think at the same time on the weakness of the advocate who has undertaken this great cause - when these reflections press upon my mind, it is impossible for me not to feel both terrified and concerned at my own inadequacy to such a task. But when I reflect, however, on the encouragement which I have had, through the whole course of a long and laborious examination of this question, and how much candour I have experienced and how conviction has increased within my own mind in proportion as I have advanced in my labours - when I reflect, especially, that however averse any gentleman may now be, yet we shall be of one opinion in the end; - when I turn myself to these thoughts, I take courage - I determine to forget all my other fears, and I march forward with a firmer step in the full assurance that my cause will bear me out, and that I shall be able to justify upon the clearest principles, every resolution in my hand,

> the avowed end of which is, the total abolition of the slave trade.

Confident that in the end England would be of one opinion about slavery; he had not abandoned hope until it became a reality, and he had won this great victory through a war of words and opinions, without bloodshed. He was buried in Westminster Abbey near his old friend, William Pitt. His monument declares that he "outlived all enmity" to die a popular and beloved statesman, a testimony to his fair regard of all men, whether members of Parliament or African slaves. It took many years for enough men to be convinced to turn the tide, but he never threw up his hands and quit, nor turned to a project that was less difficult and less frustrating, one where he might have rested on his popularity and resident joy, or used his influence in a less controversial cause. He lived through what the apostle Paul described as being "pressed on every side, but not crushed; perplexed, but not in despair" achieving his greatest triumph by letting his task carry him into a grace that Paul had also understood. It was in that supernatural place that God did the impossible through men who stayed the course and finished the race.

Perhaps there is no more touching tribute to his life's work than the slave song sung in Barbados by freed African slaves, men and women who sang of his heroic work and owed him an almost inconceivable debt of gratitude:

> Oh, me good friend, Mr. Wilberforce, make we free!
> God Almighty, thank ye! God Almighty, thank ye!
> God Almighty, make we free.

I'm nobody! Who are you?
Are you nobody, too?
Then there's a pair of us - don't tell!
They'd banish us, you know.

How dreary to be somebody!
How public like a frog
To tell your name the livelong day
To an admiring bog!

Emily Dickinson

Hurry up! Miss Emily's made bread," the freckled-face youngster shouted into the air aiming toward several different groups of children playing outside in the neighborhood. Dropping whatever they were doing, ten children ran with him, reporting breathlessly to the summons beneath her window.

When they had assembled, they counted their number and tore the three loaves into equal parts. At home, they were never allowed to greedily tear bread apart or devour whole loaves warm from the oven with their unwashed hands, but when Miss Emily made bread for them, they were invited to eat it without manners or decorum. These experiences had created a special bond between them and Emily. They felt privileged to be among the select few with which she shared her time and society.

Emily had risen early, fired up the wood burning stove, and spent her glorious summer morning baking whole wheat bread for the neighborhood kids. She was an excellent cook, enjoying the time honored tradition of kneading the dough with rhythmic aggression, cleansing her soul in the process. She then granted the dough a reprieve and a rest by letting it rise before punching it harshly once more. She tenderly shaped the mass into loaves, dusting them lightly with corn meal, and sliding them into the hot oven. When the bread finally appeared, it was dark brown and perfect, rendering a faint hollow sound when she tapped it with her knuckles.

Emily carefully removed it from the pans, transferring it onto a special board, cautiously lowering it by a pulley from the window to the ground below, where she knew it would be savagely torn apart and greedily consumed by the neighborhood kids. She waved shyly, and then moved quickly back out of the window, disappearing into her room, delighted to see her hospitality so well received. She loved children; in fact, she wished that she could have remained one all of her life.

Emily Dickinson had a reputation for being an eccentric recluse. Her grandfather had been one of the founders of Amherst

College in Massachusetts, and her father, an attorney, was the treasurer at the university and later a member of the U. S. House of Representatives. Even though Emily's father was a very authoritative man with a "pure and terrible" heart, Emily never minded trying to please him. Her mother was distant emotionally, not the type of mother one went to with problems or crushed dreams. Emily claimed that as a child she went to her brother, Austin, for comfort, relating that "He was a terrible mother, but he was better than none at all."

Her father, though an educated man himself, held the views of his day about the needless extravagance of educating women. He was also concerned with modern education and his daughter's accepting ideas that might "joggle" her Calvinistic upbringing, but he needn't have worried, for Emily was hardly a staunch Calvinist to begin with. Because Emily was a very compliant young woman, abiding by her father's rules came easily to her. Although she spent one year at college and made a few trips to Boston and one trip to Philadelphia and Washington when she was young, she lived almost all of her fifty-five years in her father's home, the last twenty years rarely leaving it at all. Her need for privacy and her simplicity enabled her to find her contentment in the ordinary.

Her poetry has become Emily's love letter to the world.

Because Emily scorned fame and ambition, she never intended to publish any of her more than 1700 poems. Her father held the opinion that a woman who published her writing would never have a chance to be accepted in society, or to get married, or become a mother. To Emily, however, her poetry was a private, personal matter. She published ten poems anonymously in her lifetime, but she requested that all of her correspondence be destroyed at her death, a request her sister felt obliged to honor. The box of poetry that her sister Vinnie found after Emily died did not have similar instructions, and her sister, amazed at the volume and quality of the work, began working immediately to publish it.

In a sense, her poetry has become Emily's love letter to the world, because it comes from deep within her spirit, where she chose to live, in touch with nature, God, words, and very few people. She spent her whole life processing the pain of death and doubt and unrequited love, and experiencing an almost child-like joy from interfacing with nature, friendship, and beauty. She recorded her life in the safety of her poetry which was as unique in style as Emily was herself, creating a very contemporary form of writing with loose rhyme and simple words hiding complex meanings.

Her escape came through her poetry and her vivid imagination.

Then she placed all of it - her entire life's work - in a box that would become her unexpected and unauthorized posthumous gift to the world, one the world has cherished tenderly for its insight into humanity and into the hidden chambers of Miss Dickinson's heart. It is a glimpse into the private chambers of a very complicated individual: reflective, dreamy, introspective, analytical, as well as a prudent, obedient, and simple. She is sometimes melancholy, sometimes joyful, at times playful, but always deep and insightful. Her complexity is fascinating, while her simplicity is reassuringly safe and warm, unpretentious and inviting.

This is my letter to the World
That never wrote to Me -
The simple News that Nature told -
With tender Majesty

Her Message is committed
To Hands I cannot see -
For love of Her - Sweet countrymen -
Judge tenderly - of Me

She preferred to remain secluded and anonymous, and yet to read her poems is to be on intimate terms with the author herself who writes at an emotional level with surprising passion and intriguing transparency. To read her poetry without relating to the author will certainly result in a shallow comprehension. How ironic that in life she was private, and now the world is privy to her innermost thoughts and those thoughts have brought us into her company, and in some ways, into God's. They have comforted and amused and given insight to the world. Our favorite recluse has come not just to visit, but to stay.

Emily lived an extraordinarily common life, largely by choice. She was elusive, self-disciplined, moral, and simple in the pleasures she enjoyed. She had a circle of close friends, although through the years it grew smaller and smaller. Still she corresponded with friends and family all of her life, adored her brother's children, pampering and indulging her nieces and nephews, and championing the neighborhood kids.

She was a brilliant gardener who had studied botany at nine years old earning her the role of chief gardener by the time she was twelve. She spent her life designing and tending to her extravagant gardens of the most exquisite flowers, sculpting lilies-of-the-valley, pansies, sweet peas, hyacinths, peonies, daffodils, marigolds, into what her niece called a "butterfly utopia." She loved exotic flowers with strange scents and kept them in hanging baskets in the conservatory, visiting them often, so that the tempting smells of a faraway island could be hers for the taking, in but a few steps. She lived next door to her brother, Austin, and his wife, Susan Gilbert, who was her best friend before she married Austin, and she saw them frequently. One might say that she selected her society carefully.

She was not a religious person, if one tried to define her relationship with God by the forms of the day. Her family's arrival to America dated back to the 1600's and the Puritan migration, and although New England was undergoing a revival during her youth, she never apprehended it as many of her friends did. She could not seem to relate to God except in the most private and personal sense, through nature and her poetry. It troubled her that she could not conform to the theology of the intellect which was prevalent at the time, and she lamented that she was once again walking out of step, "feeling" her way to God, and yet her integrity would not allow her to be hypocritical about the only way she knew to approach her creator. She said that communing with Him and feeling that He heard her prayers was the greatest pleasure she had ever known. Many people have concluded that because she stopped attending church, she was never saved, but her countless poems to and about God would indicate a very real relationship.

I Never saw a Moor -
I never saw the Sea -
Yet know I how the heather looks
And what a Billow be.

I never spoke with God
Nor visited in Heaven -
Yet certain am I of the spot
As if the Checks were given -

Real grief and pain were her companions throughout much of her life. It was not her whimsical imagination that caused her to believe the world had woes and to wish to escape; however, she always regarded escape with a sort of exaggerated longing. In one of her poems she says, "I never hear the word 'escape' without a quicker blood, a sudden expectation, a flying attitude." She might have desired escape, but in truth, she spent all life living in her mother's home; her escape came through her poetry and her vivid imagination.

By the time she was fourteen, she experienced the traumatic death of her second cousin and close friend. The principal at her school, a young man of 25, died when she was fifteen. When she was twenty, her difficult mother became bed ridden. Emily and her sister, Vinnie, cared for her until her death in 1882, just four years before Emily's own death. At last, her mother was vulnerable, and even though the care was long and difficult, something worthwhile came from the battle. Emily said, "We were never intimate…while she was our Mother - but Mines in the same Ground meet by tunneling and when she became our Child, the Affection came." Oddly enough, Emily was in her thirties during the Civil War, but she never mentioned the suffering of that conflict. She seemed far more interested in individual pain.

The Heart asks pleasure first,
And then excuse from pain;
And then, those little anodynes
That deaden suffering;

And then to go to sleep;
And then, if it should be
The will of its Inquisitor,
The liberty to die.

Emily was not so reclusive as to be unaware of what was going on in the world. She read the romantic writers of her day and was a student of Shakespeare and the Bible, as well as the Bronte sisters, the works of George Eliot, and Elizabeth Barrett Browning. She was extremely intelligent, and although her poems appear to be very simple at first glance, they are often complex and sometimes difficult to decipher.

While some of her poems can be appreciated without regarding the author, others are intriguing, precisely because they are written by her. The fact that she is a woman and a particular kind of woman in a particular time period is part of the ongoing fascination with her work. She is both enigma and revelation at once, a deep well of still water from which the reader is aware he is privileged to drink.

Although she failed to address social or political issues of the day, she centered her work on a very inquisitive and introspective study of pain, death, love, nature, eternity and God. As she said in one of her poems, "I dwell in possibility." She never seemed limited by the smallness of her life because of the immensity of her imagination. She saw deprivation of experience as a way of not only intensifying her sense of reaching, but in some way helping her define the experience through the lack thereof. She often referred to being thirsty and starving; those were emotional longings, making "crumbs" and "drops" were all the more precious to her.

Success is counted sweetest
By those who ne'er succeed,
To comprehend a nectar
Requires sorest need.

Not one of all the purple host
Who took the flag to - day
Can tell the definition
So clear, of victory,

As he, defeated, dying,
On whose forbidden ear
The distant strains of triumph
Break, agonized and clear.

Pain seemed to be the emotion with which she was most familiar: the pain of loss, abandonment, unfulfilled hopes, all made her feel like the "distant strains of triumph" were for her only in the distance, agonizingly clear, but forbidden, granting her, nevertheless, a depth of feeling that a life of victories never could have.

> Pain has an element of blank;
> It cannot recollect
> When it began, or if there were
> A day when it was not.
>
> It has no future but itself,
> Its infinite realms contain
> Its past, enlightened to perceive
> New periods of pain.

It is obvious that she did suffer from emotional pain, possibly because she felt so deeply. There is much speculation about a romance that had proved impossible, a fixation of hers for a season, one she processed slowly over time, battling the deep feelings of abandonment and rejection through her poetry that is quite revealing and passionate.

> If you were coming in the fall,
> I'd brush the summer by
> With half a smile and half a spurn,
> As housewives do a fly.
> If I could see you in a year,
> I'd wind the months in balls,

And put them each in separate drawers,
Until their time befalls.

If only centuries delayed,
I'd count them on my hand,
Subtracting till my fingers dropped
Into Van Diemen's land.

If certain, when this life was out,
That yours and mine should be,
I'd toss it yonder like a rind,
And taste eternity.

But now, all ignorant of the length
Of time's uncertain wing,
It goads me, like a goblin bee,
That will not state its sting.

She was able to find irony in the simplest and most common experiences. While she uses robins, flies, worms, flowers, and domestic duties as commonplace objects in her writing, she is able to make them rich in meaning. Her words may be simple, but her insights are not. "Remorse is memory awake," she says, in the next line calling "remorse" both a "window" and a "door." Two very simple words, and yet, to think of remorse as each of those, is a complex concept about the value of pain which allows us "to see in" and "to walk out." She seemed more at home with pain, and puzzled as to what to do with joy.

I can wade grief,
Whole pools of it,
I'm used to that.
But the least push of joy
Breaks up my feet,
And I tip - drunken.

She broke the conventions of her day with her unique poetic style by using dashes, hesitation, random capital letters, and rhymes that bend the rules of rhyming. She experimented with style, changed it to suit the feeling of her poetry, and explored its possibilities with words as she did in thought. "My business is circumference," she said because she liked to ask the questions that complicated simple facts, a process she described this way:

Tell all the Truth but tell it slant-
Success in circuit lies
Too bright for our infirm Delight
The Truth's superb surprise
As Lightening to the Children eased
The Truth must dazzle gradually
Or every man be blind -

It actually enhances her work to read it aloud to hear how the words sound as one observes the dashes and hears the rhymes, not always evident to the eye. In order to appreciate her work, one needs to be actively engaged. She is not always consistent, even in her thoughts, because she is always examining the object, turning it about in her hands, exploring the circumference. Her imagination is vivid and alive; she fantasizes and puzzles over her subjects because of an intense dissatisfaction with the answers. She searches, thinks, explores, and asks the questions that will reveal the truth. To do this she uses imaginative language, irony, and satire. There is a challenge to decipher the deepest meaning from the simplest line, and an ever present sense of the author, a real person who is hidden and very difficult to know, who is expressing her very interesting heart.

She was not a victim of her father's tyranny. She was a deeply private person and a dutiful daughter who expressed her deep emotions through her poetry, which was the safest way she could express her views without fear of rejection or reprisal.

> The soul selects her own society,
> Then shuts the door;
> On her divine majority
> Obtrude no more.
>
> Unmoved, she notes the chariot's pausing
> At her low gate;
> Unmoved, an emperor is kneeling
> Upon her mat.
>
> I've known her from an ample nation
> Choose one;
> Then close the valves of her attention
> Like stone.[1]

The last and most grievous loss that she was to suffer was in 1883 when her favorite nephew, Gilbert, Austin's youngest son died of typhoid fever. After his death she said, "The Dyings have been too deep for me, and before I could raise my Heart from one, another has come." Her own health was failing and although she lived three more years, Bright's Disease was poised to end her life.

She wrote her last correspondence to her cousins saying good-bye in her simple style, "Little Cousins, Called Back, Emily." Emily felt that soon she too would be called back to the Father's house. She was right: she died on May 15, 1886. She was laid in a white coffin that held some of her precious flowers: a vanilla scented heliotrope, a Lady's Slipper orchid, and some violets. Her funeral was held in the library of her home and Emily Bronte's poem, a favorite of Emily's was read. She had discovered her truest friend in Emily Bronte, a kindred spirit; although they had never met, she had read her biography and her poetry and discovered how alike they were. Both were Emily, had been raised as Calvinists, had distant or absent mothers, were elusive, loved to garden, lived common lives, loved domestic chores like baking and gardening, owned large dogs, and hated social encounters. They were both passionate and thoughtful women, separated by an ocean, but kindred spirits. Emily admired Bronte for being the "master of pain." It strengthened her immensely to find her kindred, even if only in the pages of a book. Emily Bronte's poem:

No coward soul is mine,
No trembler in the world's storm-troubled sphere:

I see Heaven's glories shine,
And faith shines equal, arming me from fear.

O God within my breast.
Almighty, ever-present Deity!
Life - that is in me has rest,
As I - undying Life - have Power in Thee!

Vain are the thousand creeds
That move men's hearts: unutterably vain;
Worthless as withered weeds,
Or idlest froth amid the boundless main,

To waken doubt in one
Holding so fast by Thine Infinity;
So surely anchored on
The steadfast Rock of immortality.

With wide - embracing love
Thy Spirit animates eternal years,
Pervades and broods above,
Changes, sustains, dissolves, creates, and rears.

Through earth and man were gone,
And suns and universes ceased to be,
And Thou wert left alone,
Every existence would exist in Thee.
There is not room for Death,
Nor atom that his might could render void:

Thou - Thou art Being and Breath,
And what Thou art may never be destroyed.[2]

The poem undoubtedly brought her courage and reassurance in her life. Pain and death had been her enemies in life, but at last they had been conquered. There was now a permanent place of escape, a place where there was no room for death, and all existence would be in Him, a place where her tender heart would be forever wrapped in perfect peace. Her coffin, at her request, was carried through a field of bright, yellow buttercups to the family plot.

Character	Redemptive Gift
Simon	Prophet
Florence Nightingale	Prophet
Andrew Jackson	Prophet
Joseph	Servant
Kate	Servant
Duncan	Servant
Samuel	Teacher
Dr. Lyles	Teacher
John Calvin	Teacher
Queen of Sheba	Exhorter
William Wilberforce	Exhorter
Huey Long	Exhorter
Job	Giver
Lyman Stewart	Giver
Al Capone	Giver
Nehemiah	Ruler
Dr. Olsen	Ruler
Tom Watson Sr.	Ruler
Tom Watson Jr.	Mercy
Jehoshaphat	Mercy
Emily Dickinson	Mercy
John Lennon	Mercy

Chapter 7

[1]James Andrews and David Zarefsky, American Voices: Significant Speeches in American History 1640-1945 (Longman: White Plains, New York, 1989) 445-446.

[2]Harry T. Williams, Huey Long (New York: Vintage Books, 1981) 3.

[3]Ibid. Pg.181.

[4]Ibid. Pg. 876.

Chapter 13

[1]Imagine Lyrics. John Lennon Lyrics. Copyright 2004-2009 MetroLyrics.com.

Chapter 15

[1]Viggo Olsen with Jeanette Lockerbie, Daktar: Diplomat in Bangladesh (Chicago: Moody Press, 1973) 332.

[2]Ibid. Pg. 327.

[3]Ibid. Pg. 23.

[4]Ibid. Pg. 40.

Chapter 21

[1]Thomas, Johnson, ed. The Complete Poems of Emily Dickinson (Little, Brown, 1960.)

[2]C.W. Hatfield, ed. The Complete Poems of Emily Jane Bronte (New York: Columbia University Press, 1941.)